ALTRUISM AND
CHRISTIAN ETHICS

Separated from its anchorage in religion, ethics has followed the social sciences in seeing human beings as fundamentally characterized by self-interest, so that altruism is either naively idealistic or arrogantly self-sufficient. Colin Grant contends that, as a modern secular concept, altruism is a parody on the self-giving love of Christianity, so that its dismissal represents a social leveling that loses the depths that theology makes intelligible and religion makes possible.

The Christian affirmation is that God is characterized by self-giving love (*agape*), then expected of Christians. Lacking this theological background, the focus on self-interest in sociobiology and economics, and on human realism in the political focus of John Rawls or the feminist sociability of Carol Gilligan, finds altruism naive or a dangerous distraction from real possibilities of mutual support. This book argues that to dispense with altruism is to dispense with God and with the divine transformation of human possibilities.

COLIN GRANT is Professor of Religious Studies at Mount Allison University, Sackville, New Brunswick. Author of *A Salvation Audit* (1994) and *Myths We Live By* (1998), he has also published journal articles in Britain, America, and Canada. He is a member of the American Academy of Religion, the Canadian Society for the Study of Religion, and the Canadian Theological Society.

Christian ethics has increasingly assumed a central place within academic theology. At the same time the growing power and ambiguity of modern science and the rising dissatisfaction within the social sciences about claims to value-neutrality have prompted renewed interest in ethics within the secular academic world. There is, therefore, a need for studies in Christian ethics which, as well as being concerned with the relevance of Christian ethics to the present-day secular debate, are well informed about parallel discussions in recent philosophy, science or social science. New Studies in Christian Ethics aims to provide books that do this at the highest intellectual level and demonstrate that Christian ethics can make a distinctive contribution to this debate – either in moral substance or in terms of underlying moral justifications.

ALTRUISM AND CHRISTIAN ETHICS

COLIN GRANT

Mount Allison University

PUBLISHED BY THE PRESS SYNDICATE OF THE UNIVERSITY OF CAMBRIDGE
The Pitt Building, Trumpington Street, Cambridge, United Kingdom

CAMBRIDGE UNIVERSITY PRESS
The Edinburgh Building, Cambridge CB2 2RU, UK   www.cup.cam.ac.uk
40 West 20th Street, New York, NY 10011–4211, USA   www.cup.org
10 Stamford Road, Oakleigh, Melbourne 3166, Australia
Ruiz de Alarcón 13, 28014 Madrid, Spain

First published 2001

Printed in the United Kingdom at the University Press, Cambridge

Typeface Baskerville 11/12.5 pt   *System* 3b2   [CE]

A catalogue record for this book is available from the British Library

ISBN 0 521 79144 8 hardback

*This book is dedicated to the memory of
recently deceased colleagues and friends
on both side of the Atlantic.*

Canadian philosophers Ross Stanway and Gordon Treash

and

Church of Scotland ministers Robin Hall and George Poustie

.

Contents

General editor's preface

This book is the eighteenth in the series New Studies in Christian Ethics. It shares with an adjacent series title, Stephen Clark's *Biology and Christian Ethics*, a critique of writers such as Richard Dawkins and E. O. Wilson. It also works closely with the central thesis of an earlier book in the series, Garth Hallett's *Priorities and Christian Ethics*, namely that a radical concern for others should be a key feature of morality and that it is Christian, not secular, ethics which is best able to defend this concern. Colin Grant's new book is essentially a book examining modern critics of altruism, which uses historical resources only when relevant. It does not intend to examine in detail the historical sources that may lie behind the essentially modern concept of altruism.

Altruism and Christian Ethics is a scholarly and well-written book which offers an extended analysis of the secular literature on a single concept, followed by an examination of how a specifically theological understanding can make an additional contribution. As result, it reflects well the two key aims of the series – first, to promote monographs in Christian ethics which engage centrally with the present secular moral debate at the highest possible intellectual level and, secondly, to encourage contributors to demonstrate that Christian ethics can make a distinctive contribution to this debate.

What emerges at the end of this study is that altruism is a vital but paradoxical moral concept. Christian ethicists would scarcely be wise to endorse all forms of altruism in secular society. Kamikaze pilots in World War II, or suicide bombers in modern Israel, may well act altruistically, yet Christian ethicists would hesitate to applaud them. In addition, those who explicitly and deliberately seek to act altruistically soon discover that their motives may appear less than altruistic to others. Furthermore, although there does seem to be evidence that the religiously active are more inclined to altruism that other people (as I attempt to show in my own book in the series, *Churchgoing and Christian Ethics*), this evidence is not ubiquitous or irrefutable. Colin Grant is sensitive to these difficulties in his defence of altruism. While remaining critical of much of the actual behavior of Christians, he argues that it is finally theology which makes most sense of altruism.

In presenting such a full defence of altruism against scientific, sociological, philosophical, and even theological critics, Colin Grant's *Altruism and Christian Ethics* is a very welcome addition to the series.

ROBIN GILL

Preface

Few themes enjoy such prominence in so many varied areas of contemporary life and thought as the subject of altruism. To popular perception, the ills of contemporary life are largely traceable to a deficiency of altruism. The greed and self-seeking of consumer culture are seen to be indicative of the erosion of social bonds that kept life more humane in earlier ages. This prominent view is directly contradicted by much contemporary scholarship, which sees altruism, and the assumptions that underlie it, as detractions from our most positive possibilities. Altruism is seen to represent an ideal of self-sacrifice that really reflects a domineering and condescending attitude on the part of the altruist, in contrast to the possibilities for mutual growth that a more egalitarian social vision would encourage. This critique of altruism extends to the religious domain, as traditional notions of divine grace, represented in the understanding of God in terms of *agape*, for instance, are challenged in the name of a life-seeking *eros* and the humane mutuality of *philia*.

The thesis defended here is that altruism is a modern secular concept that betrays theological overtones, and that dismissal of the notion endangers the lingering theological sensibility it echoes. The origin of the concept is generally attributed to the pioneer of sociology, Auguste Comte. For him, it designated the prospects for socially enlightened humanity, now that the restrictions of theology were being outgrown. Although theology was consigned to the past, religion enjoyed a much more positive status with Comte. This was not religion in any conventional sense, but the new positive religion of humanity, as was befitting the positive age that was dawning through the incomparable mastery of science. Altruism emerges as one of the central doctrines of this new religion of humanity. It is a confession of belief in the social prospects for humanity, once the shackles and distortions of conventional religion are abandoned. In this way, altruism represents a naively humanistic concept, but it also reflects lingering influences of theological sensibility in its vision of prospects for human greatness. Theological unease with this idealistic secular concept are understandable; however, when this unease results in dismissal of the whole notion, this may entail not only an accompanying dismissal of that lingering theological sensibility, but in fact one that succumbs to the social horizon in the secular form promoted by Comte.

John Rawls' program for allowing people to cooperate politically, in spite of holding diverse metaphysical and religious visions, for example, assumes an inherent cooperativeness on the part of humanity, not unlike the religion of humanity envisioned by Comte, along with a marginalization of fundamental visions that renders them irrelevant to requirements of political consensus. Ethicists who extol mutuality, and renounce hierarchy in such totalitarian terms that any sense of transcendent reality is displaced by a humanistic leveling, can be seen to reflect the social horizon pioneered by Comte. Transcendent theological claims recede before an acquiescence in a religion of humanity shorn of Comte's hope for altruistic achievement.

Suspicion of altruism is not without foundation, precisely because it has emerged in, and become identified with, a secular humanistic horizon, a religion of humanity in Comte's sense. Sociobiologists, who regard altruism as unnatural, and communitarian ethicists of various stripes who regard it as a distraction from the real possibilities of mutual assistance, are right to see altruism as radically idealistic. It does not belong in a world where we are programmed genetically to look out for ourselves, or at most for those who share our genes, and preoccupation with it can be an excuse for offering the real assistance that is possible in our own situation. The question is whether this is our real situation. One prominent, long-standing reading of the Christian gospel would proffer a very different assessment. On this view, the despair over altruism, in terms of both the high odds against it and the distortions that it can entail, are fully justified, but these are not the last word on the human situation. They represent a depiction of humanity considered on its own; in other words, humanity in a state of sin. Redeemed humanity, on the other hand, recognizes that it lives by divine grace, and in that recognition a possibility for living opens up that encompasses even the extreme of altruism. This theological vision is implicit in the extreme other-regard of altruism. Separated from the theological background, as altruism was from its inception, it is bound to founder. Sociobiological and social critics of it are right. In itself, it is wildly idealistic, and perhaps also domineering and condescending. But this may be more a comment on the superficiality of modern secularity, and a reflection of the reality of sin, than exposure of inherent inadequacy in the direction identified by altruism.

Dismissal of altruism, and substitution of more circumscribed visions, represents an impoverishment of human vision, and one that is likely to promote further long-term erosion of human community, rather than facilitating its development, as its advocates hold. It is especially disturbing to see this direction embraced in the name of theology. Thus, Stephen J. Pope basically accepts sociobiology's "naturalization" of altruism, finding there an adequate base on which to graft a Thomistic extension of the order of love. Stephen G. Post proposes a similar extension of sympathy from the immediate relations in which we find ourselves to the stranger. Such treatments assume a natural order, intelligible in itself, and perhaps even essentially as portrayed in sociobiology, from which anything approaching altruism can only emerge from a base of caring for ourselves and those closest to us. Such a depiction fits our experience of life generally. However, as Garth Hallett has argued, in this present series, it does not fit the gospel. Far from advocating an expansion of a native self-concern, the whole thrust of the gospel is toward extravagance of caring that is identified in the modern notion of altruism. Of course, this is not practical. It is not sensible. It is not reasonable. But it is what Jesus is reported to have taught, and it is indicative of the radical way in which he lived and died. Practical sociability seems much more accessible, but this direction courts Comte's new horizon, without the theological legacy he retained, and it places in jeopardy the most distinctive direction of the gospel.

Radical acknowledgment of the direction of altruism, as proposed here, is impractical and dangerous. It encourages lofty visions, invites fanaticism, and promotes neglect of practical realities. Thus it is by no means the last word for Christian practice. In *Priorities and Christian Ethics*, Garth Hallett wrestles with the ethical dilemma of a father who must decide whether to finance his son's university education or contribute to famine relief. Common sense, and considerable current opinion, would hardly hesitate in affirming the father's responsibility to his son. However, Hallett recognizes that the gospel is pulling in the opposite direction. This is the dilemma of ethics, not how to choose between good and evil, but how to identify and decide between better and best. The gospel presents us with a radical claim that is not easily reconciled with the ordinary circumstances of life. Other volumes in this series also wrestle with this challenge. Lisa Cahill examines the complexities of contemporary gender issues in the light of the directives of the gospel in *Sex, Gender, and Christian Ethics*, for example, and Jean Porter develops an approach to ethics in terms of a Thomistic version of moral agency in *Moral Action and Christian Ethics*. The present volume does not deal with specifics of ethics, Christian or otherwise, but rather with the context of ethics, especially any ethics that would claim Christian sponsorship. Its claim is that it is difficult to see how an ethics that does not have a place for something like what we have come to think of as altruism could or would want to claim the label Christian.

In addition to not dealing with the nitty gritty of ethics, this volume does not attempt to trace any intricate link between the modern concept of altruism and the Christian tradition. It focuses on altruism as a modern concept, and sees it reflecting a prominent direction of the gospel represented in the unique New Testament notion of love as *agape*. Even here, however, the focus is on recent treatments of *agape*, and particularly on challenges to it in the name of the other forms of love, *eros* and *philia*. Reflection is restricted to the central thesis that this modern notion of altruism represents a crypto-Christian concept that invites criticism because of its untenability apart from the gospel that gives it meaning and motivation, but that criticism that dispenses with the concept also risks domesticating the radical gospel of extravagant care.

The book begins by examining the concerted effort of sociobiology to explain away every semblance of altruism in favor of its own self-interest vision, and the contrasting recent rediscovery of altruism in the social sciences. Already at this level, basic ambiguities that cling to considerations of altruism begin to appear. These become even more evident at the level where altruism could be expected to be embraced more directly, namely in ethics. The prominent rational approach of Kantian duty ethics treats altruism as the rational requirement of impartiality, that I treat myself as an other, so that any inclination to self-indulgence is submitted to the moral law. The sympathy ethics, sketched by Hume, and developed recently in feminist ethics, sees altruism as much more "natural" because ethics is seen in terms of our relations with those closest to us, and human life is seen to be characterized essentially by relation. Although modern ethics finds a place for altruism, it is a chastened and restricted altruism that is acknowledged in either rational duty ethics or relational sympathy ethics.

Altruism is a modern concept, but its roots lie in the Christian understanding of love as *agape*, the self-giving love that is seen to be characteristic of God and in which human beings are called to participate. The suspicion that academics direct to altruism is directed to *agape* by some contemporary theologians, and while their critique of the neglect of *eros*, needy acquisitive love, and *philia*, the love of mutuality, is germane, it is not clear why an appreciation for *eros* and *philia* would have to displace *agape*. There may even be point to the claim of recent theologians that God must be seen to be qualified by *eros*, if the world is to have the alterity that would make divine altruism possible. This does not have to be seen to demean God because the dynamic reality of God encompasses and transcends the distinctions between *agape* and *eros*, just as altruism encompasses and transcends the distinctions between self and other. Indeed, the transcendent dimensions of both *agape* and altruism point to the fact that the significance of altruism is finally religious.

Altruism displays ambiguities that conceal three fundamental paradoxes. Seeing life in terms of self-interest provides the contrast that allows altruism to be identified in the first place; however, it also entails the corollary that any putative instances of altruism are inherently suspect. This poses the psychological paradox that since any pleasure, including pleasure in the welfare of others, is our own pleasure, there is a sense in which altruism can never escape the suspicion of really being a variation on self-interest. Altruism comes into its own on the moral level, but that exposes the moral paradox, namely, that the more altruism is seen as an ideal, the less basis it is seen to have in reality, whereas the more it is seen to be real, the less urgency and scope it has as an ideal. Most devastating of all is the third paradox, the religious one, involved in the realization that self-conscious, deliberate altruism is a contradiction in terms. This carries the implication that genuine altruism is intrinsically impossible.

The solution to the paradoxes of altruism proposed here builds on the recognition that genuine altruism is possible only by indirection. Deliberateness undermines the genuineness of altruism. From its recognition against the background of the self-interest perspective, through its pursuit in some form in moral terms, to its explicit promotion in religion, altruism becomes increasingly problematic. This is what renders it paradoxical to the point of appearing impossible. Altruism that is explicit and deliberate raises suspicions of self-interest and ultimately of self-righteousness. The answer to this dilemma, however, lies not in abandoning interest in altruism, but in recognizing a deeper dimension in life to which it is pointing. The implication of the elusiveness of altruism is that at its fullest life is lived in terms of indirection. Thus altruism is most genuine when it is "natural," rather than deliberate. Ironically, this also applies to the interests of the self. The biggest barrier to self-fulfilment is its deliberate pursuit. Just as happiness happens when we are involved in something, rather than seeking to be happy as such, so self-fulfilment happens when we are engaged from beyond ourselves. Self-fulfilment ultimately depends on self-transcendence. This is essentially the claim that is made by religion, that the meaning of our lives is to be found beyond ourselves. Thus the indirectness required by genuine altruism finally points to the reality of religion. Altruism at its richest may be seen as the formal principle of religion; religion, then, is the material principle of altruism. Contemporary suspicion of altruism reflects our secular inability to live from beyond ourselves.

Some portions of this book have appeared in journal articles. The substance of chapter 1 appeared as "The Odds Against Altruism: The Sociobiology Agenda," *Perspectives on Science and Christian Faith* 45/2 (1993): 96–110, and of chapter 2 as "Altruism: A Social Science Chameleon," *Zygon* 32/3 (1997): 321–40. The first half of chapter 3 draws on material from "The Gregarious Metaphor of the Selfish Gene," *Religious Studies* 27/4 (1991): 431–50, and portions of chapter 6 appeared in "Why Care? The Basis and Implications of Care Morality," *Studies in Religion/Sciences Religieuses* 24/3 (1995): 331–49. Chapter 7 is a variation on "For the Love of God: Agape," *Journal of Religious Ethics* 24/1 (1996): 3–21.

Sabbatical leaves and research grants from Mount Allison University, for which I express gratitude, made this book possible. Within the university, I am grateful to Anne Ward of the Ralph Pickard Bell Library for her efficient acquiring of books and photocopies of articles through Inter-library Loan, and to Robin Hamilton and Marilyn Settle for technical assistance with the manuscript. I am also indebted to Robin Gill, general editor for the New Studies in Christian Ethics series, and to staff at Cambridge University Press; those known to me are Kevin Taylor, publishing director, Kay McKechnie, copy-editor, and Karl Howe, production controller. My greatest debt remains to my alter-ego, my wife, Sheina.

PART ONE

Alien altruism

CHAPTER I

Explanations for altruism

There is no shortage of evidence to suggest that we are fundamentally, and all but irreparably, characterized by selfishness. If reports of consumptive greed and callous disregard for the obvious distress of others do not clinch the point, the representations of science, particularly the portrayals of sociobiology, confirm that impression beyond any reasonable doubt. This emerging discipline shows how altruism is fundamentally unnatural, an aberration that runs directly counter to the natural flow of life.

THE IMPOSSIBILITY OF NATURAL ALTRUISM

Sociobiologists contend that the altruism that concerns them is not the everyday variety of one agent assisting another agent, perhaps at significant cost to the assisting agent. At its most basic, the biological point of life is more life, reproduction. Consequently, from this perspective, altruism refers to one organism enhancing the reproductive advantage of another, especially at cost to itself. Yet this biological restriction has a way of encompassing broader, more conventional senses of the term that far exceed issues of reproductive advantage and disadvantage.

From a biological point of view, altruism should not exist. The Darwinian theory of natural selection holds that those organisms survive and reproduce which are best adapted to their environment. They are "selected" by the natural processes of geography, climate, food supplies, predation, etc. Any organism that devotes itself to the welfare of other organisms, to that

3

extent jeopardizes its own prospects for reproduction and
enhances those of the recipient of the assistance. As that trend
continues, it would seem that the altruist strain would be bound
to be selected out of existence.

The dilemma is given vivid expression through the more
precise genetic focus of sociobiology. Through the application
of game theory, sociobiologists work out projections for what
would happen as more and fewer altruists emerge in a given
population. A prominent interpreter of the mysteries of sociobiology to the uninitiated, Richard Dawkins, sketches a widely
endorsed reading of the situation through the identification of
three behavioral types, tellingly labeled suckers, cheats, and
grudgers.[1] How the presence of each would affect a given
population, and how each of these types would fare, is projected
in terms of an imaginary situation involving a species of bird
that is parasited by an injurious and potentially lethal kind of
tick. Each bird can rid itself of these parasites on most of its
body, but it cannot reach the top of its own head, and so the
only solution is for each bird to have its head ticks removed by
another bird. And, of course, this is where the different strategies emerge. "Suckers" refers to those birds that will groom
other birds indiscriminately. They are complete altruists.
"Cheats" are those birds that accept this grooming, but never
perform this service themselves. Now the projections indicate
that in a population of suckers, everyone will have their head
ticks removed, but as soon as a cheat emerges, the situation
changes. Cheat genes will begin to spread through the population and the sucker genes will be driven to extinction. For the
more cheats there are, the more suckers will go ungroomed,
dying from the parasitic infection, and thus having their genes
removed from the collective gene pool. The cheats, for their
part, thrive as long as there are enough suckers to help keep
them tick-free. Of course, as the sucker population declines, the
cheats will be affected, but never to the extent of the suckers
themselves. "Therefore, as long as we consider only these two

[1] Richard Dawkins, *The Selfish Gene* (London: Granada, 1978), pp. 197ff.

strategies, nothing can stop the extinction of the suckers, and very probably, the extinction of the whole population too."[2]

The third option, represented by the "grudger," involves grooming those who have groomed them. They never groom a cheat a second time. In a cheat population, grudgers would be almost as vulnerable as suckers. They would spend most of their time practising unrequited grooming, and paying for this with their lives, to the detriment of their own genetic legacy. But when a significant number of grudgers emerges, they will groom each other to the detriment of the cheats, who will be driven to the brink of extinction, but not over, because the lower the population of cheats, the more chance each of these individuals will have of being groomed by grudgers they have not encountered before.

Common sense, and perhaps the lingering legacy of Christian sentiment, might suggest that the ideal evolutionarily stable strategy would be represented by a population consisting exclusively of suckers. This would assure that each bird would be groomed simply because they were in need of grooming. And this might well be the ideal situation. But it is ideal. In the real world, allowance must be made for grudgers and even cheats. But once this is done, as we have seen, the way of the sucker ceases to represent an evolutionarily stable strategy. On the contrary, the way of the grudger holds the most promise for maintaining itself against the interruption of cheats or suckers. The way of the cheat is also equally effective in achieving an evolutionarily stable strategy against grudgers and suckers, but the way of the cheat achieves this at the high price of courting extinction because cheats cannot groom each other. The conclusion to which we are led, then, is that neither pure altruism, nor pure selfishness, offer long-term prospects on their own. The most promising course is the calculative reciprocity of the grudger. This strategy is effective against both cheats and suckers. But as long as there are cheats and suckers as well as grudgers, the cheats are next in order of stability, with suckers

[2] Ibid., p. 199.

coming in a distant third. Their strategy invites exploitation by cheats and receives only marginal support from grudgers.

Thus from the biological point of view, especially as this is sharpened through the genetic focus of sociobiology, the prospects for serious altruism are particularly bleak. The situation cannot be described more succinctly than it is by Dawkins himself.

Even in the group of altruists, there will almost certainly be a dissenting minority who refuse to make any sacrifice. If there is just one selfish rebel, prepared to exploit the altruism of the rest, then he, by definition, is more likely than they are to survive and have children. Each of these children will tend to inherit his selfish traits. After several generations of natural selection, "the altruistic group" will be overrun by selfish individuals, and will be indistinguishable from the selfish group. Even if we grant the improbable chance existence initially of pure altruistic groups without any rebels, it is very difficult to see what is to stop selfish individuals migrating in from neighbouring selfish groups, and, by intermarriage, contaminating the purity of the altruistic group.[3]

This biological account of altruism accords with the contemporary experience. It is no wonder that self-interest should be the prevailing strategy. We have inherited a genetic bias in this direction. Any inclination to concern for others that might have been present has been diminished by the genetic triumph of the drive to self-preservation and self-enhancement. And yet altruism continues to exist. There are individuals who apparently sacrifice themselves, and *a fortiori* the transmission of their genes, for the sake of others. Why is it that altruism has not been eliminated entirely? This represents what the leading pioneer of sociobiology, E. O. Wilson, calls "the central theoretical problem of sociobiology: how can altruism, which by definition reduces personal fitness, possibly evolve by natural selection?"[4] Indeed, the problem is even more acute than this. For the reality is almost contrary to the picture we have considered in abstract terms. The truth is that in the broad scope of nature, far from altruism having been diminished, the

---

[3] Ibid., p. 8.
[4] Edward O. Wilson, *Sociobiology: The New Synthesis* (Cambridge, Mass.: Harvard University Press, 1975), p. 3.

reverse would seem to be the case. It is in the most developed species, namely ourselves, that altruism has attained its most striking expression, evoking what Wilson has called the "culminating mystery of all biology."[5] On the premise of modern biology, especially as this is sharpened by sociobiology, altruism should not exist at all, much less have evolved through the process.

The biological problem of altruism is at least as old as Darwin's theory of natural selection. Indeed, even for Darwin himself it constituted the "one special difficulty, which at first appeared to me insuperable, and actually fatal to the whole theory."[6] The altruism that Darwin found so threatening was that of social insects. In bees and ants, for example, worker castes devote their lives to work to the total exclusion of reproduction, and yet these sterile castes reemerge generation after generation. How? Why does such apparent total altruism not result in its own destruction through the lack of offspring? A possible answer is in terms of group selection. Then workers continue to be reproduced because, in these instances, selection takes place at the level of the colony. Workers are an integral part of the colony, and thus contribute to the fitness of the whole group, so that their own lack of reproductive ability is compensated for at the group level. They do not have to reproduce themselves because their lineage is provided for in the reproductive mechanisms of the group.

This identification of a group level as the focus of the selection process represents something of a minority report in modern biology. V. C. Wynne-Edwards contends that its day has come,[7] but even to allow for group selection as a counterpart to the dominant assumptions of individual selection is a concession that does not appear to be forthcoming in any significant measure. To the novice, Wynne-Edwards' claim for group selection can appear to offer a credible way of accounting for the continued appearance of non-reproductive worker

[5] Ibid., p. 362.
[6] Charles Darwin, *The Origin of Species*, 6th edition (London: John Murray, 1888), p. 228.
[7] V. C. Wynne-Edwards, *Evolution through Group Selection* (Oxford: Blackwell Scientific Publications, 1986), p. 357.

castes. "In group selection theory there is no problem about sacrificing the fitness of some individuals if it benefits the fitness of a group as a whole to do so; and this applies not only to vertebrates in changeable habitats but to the special-duty sterile castes of insects as well."[8] Sensible though this might appear to sociobiologically untutored common sense, it does not find favor with sociobiologists. They maintain their focus on individual selection through the concept of kin selection, which might sound like a variation on group selection, but is intended precisely to avoid any compromise of the individual focus.

In a series of articles in the 1960s and early 70s, W. D. Hamilton worked out a theory of kin selection in precise mathematical terms.[9] Because each parent contributes half the genes that make up their offspring, there is a 50% chance that a parent and his or her offspring will share any particular gene. Thus the ratio in the genetic relationship between parent and child is half. Roughly the same ratio holds between siblings, because they share the same parents. For more distant relations, the calculation is more complicated, but the results, genetically speaking, are that there is half of ourselves in our parents, our offspring, and our siblings; a quarter in our uncles, aunts, nephews and nieces, and in our grandparents and grandchildren; one-eighth in our first cousins, our great-grandparents and great-grandchildren.

The significance of these degrees of relatedness for sociobiology is that they provide a basis for explaining altruism that is directed to an individual's immediate kin. Thus if a bird risks attracting a predator to ensure the safety of a flock or of her own brood, as birds often do, sometimes feigning a broken wing to lead a fox away from a nest, and leaping into the air at the last possible moment to escape the fox's jaws,[10] or warning a whole flock with an alarm call when a flying predator such as a hawk is spotted,[11] this has all the appearance of dangerous, sacrificial, altruistic behavior. From the genetic point of view,

---

[8] Ibid., p. 345.
[9] W. D. Hamilton, "The Genetical Theory of Social Behavior," *The Journal of Theoretical Biology* 7 (1964): Part I, 1–16, Part II, 17–32.
[10] Dawkins, *The Selfish Gene*, p. 7.   [11] Ibid., p. 6.

however, it is entirely explicable in terms of gene ratios. A mother bird is not risking anything if her diversionary behavior saves two of her chicks because together they are likely to possess 100% of her genes. Similarly, the bird raising the alarm call is also protecting its own genes if it has a couple of siblings in the flock, or four nieces or nephews or eight first cousins. It is not that a bird calculates these odds, or even deliberately acts in this seemingly altruistic fashion. The level of agency is not the bird but the genes that constitute it, and every other living being, including ourselves. Genes are the ultimate subjects. "They are in you and me; they created us, body and mind; and their preservation is the ultimate rationale for our existence."[12] All plants and animals exist as vehicles for the replication of genes. "We are survival machines – robot vehicles blindly programmed to preserve the selfish molecules known as genes."[13] It is not a group or an individual that is finally at stake in the biological process, but genes. Instances of apparent altruistic behavior in groups or on the part of individuals are really gene strategies. The individuals that are at risk, or appear to put themselves at risk, are probably acting to preserve genes they share with kin. It is kin altruism that is at stake, rather than any pure, self-sacrificing variety.

Kin altruism, by its very nature, only accounts for altruism among close relatives. It is not clear that this covers all apparently altruistic behavior among animals, and it is especially precarious in light of the more wide ranging altruistic behavior that can sometimes characterize human actions in particular. The difficulty that is especially evident with human altruism is that there may be no apparent relationship between the altruist and his or her beneficiary and so no apparent rationale for the action other than the altruistic one of actually benefiting the other person. Saving a drowning person, who is unknown and unrelated to me, can hardly be attributed to an ulterior strategy promoted by the genetic drive for replication. However, this unlikely situation is also encompassed by the sociobiological explanation of altruism. The mechanism that accounts for this

---

[12] Ibid., p. 21.   [13] Ibid., "Preface," p. x.

is known as "reciprocal altruism." Although the immediate act may appear purely altruistic, in a larger perspective, it can be seen to represent a relatively minor risk to the benefactor, with the prospect that should he find himself in any similar life-threatening situation, he will be more likely to receive the aid he requires. Thus ironically, Wilson suggests that reciprocal altruism "is less purely altruistic than acts evolving out of interdemic and kin selection."[14] Note that the pioneer socio-biologist is pronouncing on "pure altruism," and not the biological, reproductively focused variety.

Thus sociobiology accounts for apparent altruistic behavior with an arsenal of three primary weapons, the two versions of altruism we have sketched and the underlying assumption that the fundamental behavioral orientation is one of self-interest. On the most primary level, behavior generally is self-interested, especially in the form of genetic self-interest. Beyond this, most altruistic behavior among insects, birds, and animals can be explained by the mechanism of kin selection. Finally, wider versions of apparently altruistic behavior, most evident among humans, can be more accurately understood as reciprocal altruism, engaged in with the expectation, at least genetically speaking, of receiving a return in the future, should occasion require it. Thus sociobiology demonstrates the totally illusory nature of the whole notion of altruism. What appears to be altruism is really genetically sophisticated selfishness.

The very thoroughness of this account of altruism might really be indicative of its inadequacy. Perhaps the explanations are simply too good. This is the charge of the Sociobiology Study Group. "There exists no imaginable situation that cannot be explained; it is necessarily confirmed by every observation."[15] Any putative case of altruistic behavior that is not susceptible to the calculations of kin selection is bound to succumb to the unlimited scope of reciprocal altruism.

Even such a comprehensive program as the sociobiological

---

[14] Wilson, *Sociobiology*, p. 120.

[15] Sociobiology Study Group, "Sociobiology – A New Biological Determinism," in *Biology as a Social Weapon*, ed. Ann Arbor Science for the People Editorial Collective (Minneapolis: Burgers Publishing Co., 1977), p. 145.

explanation of altruism does have awkward instances to
contend with, though, as its more forthright exponents admit.
Dawkins points to the phenomenon of female herd animals
adopting orphaned offspring that bear no particular relation to
them, thus investing their care in individuals that hold no
prospect of perpetuating their own genetic legacy. The only
explanation he can provide for this is that it represents a
mistake of nature. "It is presumably a mistake which happens
too seldom for natural selection to have 'bothered' to change
the rule by making the maternal instinct more selective."[16] A
more difficult example, and one which Dawkins concedes might
well be taken as evidence against this whole genetic explanation
of altruism, is the practice of bereaved monkey mothers who
steal a baby from another female, and look after it. This is really
a double mistake, from the perspective of the genetic account,
because, as Dawkins observes, the adopting mother not only
invests her time and care in someone else's child rather than
getting on with producing further offspring of her own, but she
also thereby frees the stolen child's mother to do precisely that
herself, to the benefit of that mother's genes and the detriment
of those of the adoptive mother. This behavior, then, constitutes
a direct contradiction to what the sociobiological account
should lead us to expect.

Yet even these obvious exceptions to sociobiology's central
thesis are accommodated by its more imaginative proponents.
So D. D. Barash explains the apparent altruism of adoption of
non-relatives on the human level as a hangover from the past
when humanity lived in small groups, so that there was likely to
be a significant genetic relationship between adopter and
adoptee.[17] If this extreme explanation does not represent the
snapping of this highly elastic theory, other more empirical
difficulties almost certainly do. We saw how Darwin was particularly troubled by the apparent altruism of social insects. He
wondered how workers which did not reproduce themselves
had ever evolved. We also noted the consideration that the
answer in this case might lie at the group level. Their altruism is

[16] Dawkins, *The Selfish Gene*, p. 109.
[17] D. D. Barash, *Sociobiology and Behaviour* (Amsterdam: Elsevier, 1977), pp. 312f.

in the interest of the group, and so they are reproduced by the reproductive members. We also saw that this deviation from the individual version of natural selection was not favored by socio-biologists. In fact, the explanation sociobiology has developed for this apparent altruism of the worker castes of social insects not only reaffirms individual selection but is regarded by Dawkins as "one of the most spectacular triumphs of the selfish gene theory."[18] The triumphal account focuses on the means of reproduction in these insects, which leads to the recognition of a closer relation between the reproductive queen and her sterile sister workers than the normal one-half genetic relationship that generally prevails between siblings. A queen bee, for example, makes one mating flight, storing up the sperm for rationing out during the rest of her reproductive life. The sperm is released as required to fertilize the eggs that will develop into females. Males develop from eggs that are not fertilized at all. Whether a female develops into a worker or a queen is due to environment, rather than to genetic make-up, the principal factor being the food she receives. Thus queen and worker are full sisters. But because males develop from unfertilized eggs, they contain only their mother's genes, a single set rather than the double set that generally characterizes a species propagated by sexual reproduction. This means that the male will pass on the same genes to all offspring. Thus any two females will receive half of their mother's genes and all of their father's genes, with the result that the degree of relatedness between full sisters will not be half but three-quarters, because each will receive the same genes from their common father.

This increase in relatedness goes a long way toward explaining the apparently altruistic behavior of worker castes among social insects. For in relinquishing their reproductive capacity to the queen, the worker bees, for example, are actually ensuring the replication of approximately 75% of their own genes in each of her offspring, whereas direct reproduction would pass on only 50% of their own genes. This is the major triumph achieved by sociobiological theory in this area that

---

[18] Dawkins, *The Selfish Gene*, p. 187.

presented particular problems for Darwin. Unfortunately, there is a major impediment to this explanation, which arises from the fact that on her mating flight the queen must copulate with several males, a honey bee queen up to twelve times, in order to store enough sperm for the rest of her life. "Hence workers very often rear *half* sisters with whom they share only 25% of their genes – whereas they would pass on 50% of their genes through their own daughters."[19] Dawkins acknowledges this difficulty at the conclusion of his explanation of the spectacular triumph of sociobiology, but the best response he can offer is: "My head is now spinning, and it is high time to bring this topic to a close."[20] This closure might well be fatal to the sociobiological explanation of altruism, if it depends on our not recognizing that in the final paragraph of this triumphal explanation for altruism in social insects, Dawkins glosses over a crucial fact which runs directly counter to what sociobiological theory should expect.

THE RATIONALE FOR THE IMPOSSIBILITY OF
NATURAL ALTRUISM

In this analysis of the treatment of altruism and selfishness in sociobiology, it is possible that we have forgotten one crucial fact, namely that the altruism and selfishness under consideration are biological. It is a matter of genes rather than of intentions. "None of the definitions of altruism in biology refers to the altruistic animal's motives, and it is in this way that they differ from the concept of altruism in human behavior."[21] It is a mistake to read into these terms the usual moral connotations they have in their everyday usage. The biological meaning is measured by a scale of prospects for reproduction rather than by any kinds of value judgments about the quality of particular modes of behavior. As E. O. Wilson puts it: "Altruism is the

[19] Georg Breuer, *Sociobiology and the Human Dimension* (Cambridge: Cambridge University Press, 1982), p. 59.

[20] Dawkins, *The Selfish Gene*, p. 194.

[21] Brian C. R. Bertram, "Problems with Altruism," in *Current Problems in Sociobiology*, ed. King's College Sociobiology Group, Cambridge (Cambridge: Cambridge University Press, 1982), p. 256.

surrender of personal genetic fitness for the enhancement of personal genetic fitness in others."[22] To say that an animal acts altruistically is not to imply that it cares about other animals, but rather to affirm that it is endangering the replication of its own genes in a form of behavior that enhances the reproductive success of other individuals.

The restricted scope of this biological sense of "altruism" suggests a much more modest agenda than we have been attributing to sociobiology. If we were to go back over the evidence we have considered with this chastened reminder of the true biological meaning of the term, things might appear quite different. The issue is not whether the worker caste in social insects, the sentry bird or the stotting gazelle, leaping for the apparent purpose of warning the herd of a predator, are intentionally sacrificing themselves for the sake of others, in the ordinary sense of "altruism." The point is that these forms of behavior do appear to entail genetic sacrifice. The worker caste foregoes reproduction completely, while the sentry bird with its alarm call and the stotting gazelle with its exaggerated leaps not only appear to risk their lives by issuing their warnings, but in so doing would foreclose all prospects for ensuring the reproduction of their own genes. This is the altruism that sociobiology seeks to explain, and indeed must explain to salvage its own theory. And explain it it does. The principal explanation is that these forms of behavior do not entail genetic sacrifice at all, but, on the contrary, are genetically calculated to ensure the safety of these identical genetic strains in the close kin who are served or warned. The explanation then amounts to explaining away altruism, even at this minimal biological level. "In short, when one speaks of 'animal altruism' one is simply speaking of instinctive behaviors, selected because their possessors thereby maximize their gene-transmission capacities."[23] It is the genes, and not the insect or animal, that are the fundamental agent. Individuals do not sacrifice themselves. They may be sacrificed by their genes, but this is only because those genes are present in other individuals and their perpetuation through those indi-

---

[22] Wilson, *Sociobiology*, p. 106.
[23] Michael Ruse, "The Morality of the Gene," *The Monist* 67 (1984): 170.

viduals will be enhanced by the sacrifice. Thus from the genetic perspective, altruism is impossible, rather than being voluntary, much less being morally laudable, and is ultimately an expression of the opposite of altruism, the pure self-interest of genetic manipulation.

In genetic terms, there is no such thing as altruism. That selfishness is an adequate way of characterizing this most basic biological level might be questioned, but, even if this is granted, it is clear that the meaning of selfishness, and the exposure of altruism, is by no means confined to that level. For it is not adequate to explain the risks of apparent genetic altruism by theories such as kin selection which assures the perpetuation of the same genes. Sociobiologists also feel constrained to extend this elimination of altruism from the level of genetic explanation to that of the phenotype. So the actual behavior of individual animals is not only not altruistic in the genetic sense, that is, in not actually endangering the genes that they share with close kin who are saved by their apparent altruism, but there is a compulsion to explain away any connotation of altruism attaching to the behavior itself. Thus sentry birds are not only assuring the preservation of their genetic strains in their close kin; they are actually ensuring their own individual safety by silencing the flock or summoning them to fly up into the trees in the safety of numbers. Stotting gazelles are not only serving the interests of the genes they share with other members of the herd, because their exaggerated leaps that seem to be warnings to the herd of the presence of a predator are actually advertisements of the health and vitality of the stotting individual, intended to divert the predator to more vulnerable members of the herd,[24] regardless of how closely they may be related.

This compulsion to explain away every semblance of altruistic behavior suggests that the restrictions of the biological sense of altruism are not determinative. The point is not only the preservation of genetic strains, or even the reproductive prospects of the apparently altruistic individual, but the nature of the behavior itself. The behavior that appears altruistic is

---

[24] Dawkins, *The Selfish Gene*, pp. 182ff.

really fundamentally an expression of self-interest. The explanation for genetic altruism expands to take in the more conventional sense of the term. The point is made succinctly by
Wilson. "The theory of kin selection has taken most of the good
will out of altruism. When altruism is conceived of as the
mechanism by which DNA multiplies itself through a network
of relatives, spirituality becomes just one more Darwinian
enabling device."[25] The pursuit of this sociobiological explanation of altruism thus involves what Philip Hefner calls "reverse
reductionism."[26] Rather than a direct equation of altruism with
the biological version of genetic processes, the explanation at
that level, which rules out altruism by definition,[27] expands to
absorb the usual sense of the term; or, perhaps, more realistically, the ordinary sense of the term has been present all along.
The scheme which attempts to explain away all altruism
through the devices of kin selection and reciprocal altruism is
the logical result.

The repeated warnings that talk of altruism is metaphorical[28]
may begin to sound hollow in light of this crusade against all
forms of altruism, but this ploy is even less credible when
applied to the other side of the picture, the ascription of
selfishness. There can be no question that far from representing
a metaphoric shorthand for alluding to impersonal genetic
processes, the processes themselves are understood under these
essentially selfish terms. If selfishness was a metaphor for an
impersonal genetic process, there would be no reason to attribute that same orientation to the level of the phenotype. In fact,
the reverse would seem to be implied. If organisms are essentially vehicles for the propagation of "selfish" genes, then the
organisms themselves are, almost by definition, unselfish, if not
actually altruistic. One would expect to find a treatment at the
level of the phenotype along the lines suggested by Michael
Ruse. "To talk of selfish genes is to talk metaphorically, and the
whole point is that the phenotypes they promote are anything

---

25 Wilson, *Sociobiology*, p. 120.
26 Philip Hefner, "Sociobiology, Ethics and Theology," *Zygon* 19/2 (1984): 194.
27 Dawkins, *The Selfish Gene*, p. 38.
28 Ruse, "The Morality of the Gene," p. 170.

but selfish."[29] But this is not what happens. As we have seen, the supposedly metaphorical talk of selfishness at the gene level continues to apply at the level of the phenotype. Apart from the particular examples considered, this is also evident in the insistence on the individual, as opposed to the group, version of natural selection. Granted that genetic variations occur at the individual level, it is the species, and not the individual, that is ultimately modified. Why then should the focus fall so exclusively on the individual? The obvious answer is that the assumption of the pivotal significance of selfishness that is taken to characterize the gene level continues to be affirmed on up the scale. "Opposing individual selection to group selection as egoism is different from altruism, biologists represent the scientific content of the first opposition as the folk concept of the second."[30] The contrast between egoism and altruism provides the horizon within which biological processes themselves are understood. Thus it is perhaps not extravagant of Mary Midgley to suggest that sociobiologists are fixated on selfishness.[31] Far from being merely a metaphor to facilitate communication about the intricate and impersonal ramifications of genetic structures, we must wonder whether it can even be seen as a generalization drawn from observations of biological phenomena. The tenacity with which it is held and the comprehensive scope of its influence suggest that what is involved is something much broader than sociobiology or even than modern biology as a whole.

The precariousness of claims to be operating with a peculiar biological and genetic sense of altruism is betrayed by the enthusiastic vendetta against any and every semblance of altruism. M. T. Ghiselin is under no illusions that the explanation is confined to the genetic level.

Where it is in his own interest, every organism may reasonably be expected to aid his fellows. Where he has no alternative, he submits to the yoke of servitude. Yet, given a full chance to act in his own interest,

---

[29] Michael Ruse, *Sociobiology: Sense or Nonsense?* (Dordrecht: D. Reidel, 1979), p. 198.

[30] Marshall Sahlins, *The Use and Abuse of Biology: An Anthropological Critique of Sociobiology* (Ann Arbor: University of Michigan Press, 1976), p. 20.

[31] Mary Midgley, "Gene-Juggling," *Philosophy* 54 (1979): 444.

nothing but expediency will restrain him from brutalizing, from maiming, from murdering – his brother, his mate, his parent, or his child. Scratch an "altruist" and watch a "hypocrite" bleed.[32]

D. D. Barash attempts to explain the apparent altruism of Kamikaze pilots by contending that their families would enjoy enhanced social status, an explanation that hardly seems to eliminate altruism. It might be a sense of the inadequacy of this explanation that leads him to the further desperate expedient of suggesting that these pilots might have received "sexual privileges" as inducements for their sacrifices.[33] E. O. Wilson himself even goes to the extent of impugning the integrity of Mother Teresa. "Mother Teresa is an extraordinary person but it should not be forgotten that she is secure in the service of Christ and the knowledge of her Church's immortality."[34] The comprehensive scope of the attack on altruism not only far exceeds the level of genetic explanation, through this wholesale attack on any semblance of altruistic behavior, but as Mary Midgley suggests, it even results in blatant self-contradiction. The indiscriminate and total attack on altruism described by Barash has parents attacking their own genetic legacy represented by their children. Midgley points out that genetic selfishness, which is supposedly the focus for sociobiology, appears in parental behavior in the form of care for offspring. To describe parents as inherently selfishly disposed against their children is a direct contradiction of this genetic version.[35] When everyday selfishness is promoted to the direct detriment of the supposedly pristine sociobiological version of selfishness, we have a very clear indication that something much more fundamental than biological theory is at stake.

The tenacious dedication to the principle of self-interest, and corresponding opposition to all appearances that suggest any tinge of altruism, despite the apparent contradiction of this in

[32] M. T. Ghiselin, *The Economy of Nature and the Evolution of Sex* (Berkeley: University of California Press, 1974), p. 247.

[33] D. D. Barash, *The Whispering Within* (Harmondsworth: Penguin, 1979), pp. 167f.

[34] Edward O. Wilson, *On Human Nature* (Cambridge, Mass.: Harvard University Press, 1978), p. 165.

[35] Mary Midgley, *Evolution as a Religion* (London and New York: Methuen, 1985), pp. 126f.

significant aspects of animal behavior, is indicative of a prior foundational vision. The most obvious candidate for the source of that vision is the pervasive culture that shapes the wider background against which sociobiology has developed. "What is inscribed in the theory of sociobiology is the entrenched ideology of western society: the assurance of its naturalness, and the claim of its inevitability."[36] That ideology centers particularly on this assumption of the primacy of self-interest, whether in the intellectual vision since Descartes, in the political theory of democratic individualism, or in the economic version of *laissez-faire*, free-market capitalism. This latter form seems to be particularly influential for sociobiology.

There is probably more truth than public relations in Michael Ghiselin's description of his *The Economy of Nature and the Evolution of Sex* as a "cross between the *Kama Sutra* and the *Wealth of Nations*."[37] E. O. Wilson clearly reflects what is generally taken to be the guiding sentiment of the *Wealth of Nations* when he suggests: "True selfishness, if obedient to the other constraints of mammalian biology, is the key to a more nearly perfect social contract."[38] Once again, however, the presentation is made most vividly by Richard Dawkins. Thus he applies the calculations for kin selection, which represent a sophisticated exercise in economic theory in their own right, to the situation of a mother bird attempting to determine her optimum clutch size.[39] The strategy proposed is for her to lay one more egg than she "thinks" likely to be the true optimum. If there is sufficient food supply, she can raise all the children. "If not, she can cut her losses." She would do this by feeding the runt of the litter last, making sure that it got less than it required so it would die off, leaving enough food for the others. Then she is only out her "initial investment of egg yolk or equivalent." Sahlins, the Chicago anthropologist who is one of the most prominent advocates of this cultural critique of socio-

---

[36] Sahlins, *The Use and Abuse of Biology*, p. 101.
[37] David L. Hull, "Sociobiology: Another New Synthesis," in *Sociobiology: Beyond Nature/Nurture?*, ed. George W. Barlow and James Silverberg (Boulder, Col.: Westview Press, 1980), p. 82.
[38] Wilson, *On Human Nature*, p. 156.
[39] Dawkins, *The Selfish Gene*, p. 140.

biology, points out that this focus on optimization or maximization stands in direct contrast to the fundamental opportunism
of classical natural selection theory,[40] and suggests that the
likely source of this shift is the marketplace ideology that gives
such prominence to this notion of optimization, the most for the
least.

In fact, a great deal of the genetic strategy outlined by
Dawkins can be read as straightforward cost-benefit analysis.
The bird seeking to "optimize" her clutch size might also face
the challenge of assuring that her mate accepts his share of
responsibility in the raising of the young when they do arrive.
One possible strategy would be to spurn the male's amorous
advances until the nest is built, on the theory that having
invested in the nest building, the male will have too much at
stake to abandon his family for new prospects. Although this
line of reasoning appealed to fellow sociobiologist, Robert
Trivers, Dawkins challenges it. The challenge, however, is based
on economics, not on biology. "This is fallacious economics,"[41]
Dawkins charges. The prudent business person "should always
ask whether it would pay him *in the future*, to cut his losses, and
abandon the project now, even though he has already invested
heavily in it."[42] It is no wonder that we have to remind
ourselves sometimes that it is biology, and not economics, that
we are reading. "After listening to the discussions of the Dahlem
workshop on Animal and Human Mind for a couple of days the
American sociologist Henry Gleitman asked whether all biologists were economists."[43] It is certainly impossible to imagine
sociobiology shorn of the outlook and apparatus of economics.

So integral to the central theses of sociobiology is this
perspective of economics that it is difficult to refute the charges
of people like Sahlins and the Sociobiology Study Group when
they contend that economics contributes to the substance, and
not simply to the articulation, of sociobiology. So the Study
Group contends that sociobiologists like Wilson impose human
institutions, especially those of the free-market economic

---

[40] Sahlins, *The Use and Abuse of Biology*, p. 78.
[41] Dawkins, *The Selfish Gene*, p. 162.   [42] Ibid.
[43] Breuer, *Sociobiology and the Human Dimension*, p. 257.

system, on animals. "Then, having imposed human traits upon animals by metaphor, he rederives the human institution as a special case of the more general phenomenon 'discovered' in nature."[44] This is how radical selfishness is "discovered" in nature. The discovery is actually imposed from the assumptions of the prevailing economic culture. Or, as Sahlins puts it: where Hobbes reduced human beings to an animal level and helped provide the rationale for the modern free-for-all view of economics whereby "man was seen as a wolf to man," sociobiology extends this assumption to the whole animal kingdom, rendering animals as conniving and calculating as robber barons or single-minded executives (remember Dawkins' "calculating" birds) so that "the wolf is a man to other wolves."[45] Then, contrary to the usual understanding that sees the pure economic ideal of modern business as a reflection of the "law of the jungle," the "law of the jungle" might well be more a reflection of modern business ideals. J. L. Mackie has pointed out how the intent of that phrase in Kipling's original usage was to refer precisely to the cooperation among wolves.[46] This is certainly much closer to what wolf cub leaders intend to encourage among their young charges in the scouting movement than the connotation that has been invested in that term, apparently largely through the impact of this understanding of economic reality. To recognize this "contribution" of economics to sociobiology is not to deny that nature includes viciousness and selfish behavior. There is always a danger of romanticizing natural processes. Yet the uncompromising insistence that nature represents nothing but this, so that every hint of altruism must be explained away, must be challenged. We are bound to ask how much that picture truly reflects what goes on in the natural order, and how much it reflects the imposition on that order of this particular reading of life developed in modern economics.

The explicit cost-benefit calculations of animal behavior

---

[44] Sociobiology Study Group, "Sociobiology – A New Biological Determination," p. 141.
[45] Sahlins, *The Use and Abuse of Biology*, p. 99.
[46] J. L Mackie, "The Law of the Jungle," *Philosophy* 53 (1978): 455ff.

presented by sociobiologists are only a more detailed version of the fundamental orientation of modern biology generally. "Evolution is basically a selfish doctrine, preaching that the individual that maximizes its own welfare and reproduction relative to others will gain the selective edge – by leaving more descendants who, themselves, carry the same behavioral traits."[47] The parallel with the modern economic vision is unmistakable, but the dynamics of the parallel are even more revealing. We have noticed the suggestion that this modern economic reading crept in through the influence of social Darwinism. Thus Sahlins concludes that "Darwinism, at first appropriated to society as 'social Darwinism,' has returned to biology as a genetic capitalism."[48] On this reading, Darwin's biological vision was applied to human society through "social Darwinism" and then, in turn, this free enterprise social vision was read back into nature with the result that, as Sahlins suggests, the wolf comes to be seen in light of the acquisitive behavior associated with the aggressive human entrepreneur. It may be, however, that in spite of the sharpness of Sahlins' attack on the genetic capitalism developed by sociobiology, his historical reading of Darwinism itself is really too conservative.

At the very least, there is a reciprocal relationship between natural and social Darwinism in their origins, and not simply in their long-term development. "The social Darwinian description of nature, with its emphasis on the survival of the fittest and a claw-and-fang mode of natural selection, precisely reflected the relations that prevailed in the 19th century marketplace. The fit is almost perfect, and it is hard to say whether natural Darwinism produced social Darwinism or the very reverse."[49] Thus it is not the case that natural Darwinism developed as a biological theory in pristine isolation, and then received social application. The theory itself reflects the outlook of the age in which it developed. Ashley Montagu points out that though

---

[47] Stephen T. Emlen, "Ecological Determinism and Sociobiology," in *Sociobiology: Beyond Nature/Nurture?*, ed. Barlow and Silverberg, p. 125.

[48] Sahlins, *The Use and Abuse of Biology*, p. 72.

[49] Murray Bookchin, "Ecology, Society and the Myth of Biological Determinism," in *Biology as a Social Weapon*, ed. Ann Arbor Science for the People Editorial Collective, p. 124.

Darwin himself was by nature a gentle person, he grew up in a world torn by repeated warfare and with the industrial revolution at its height in England and well under way elsewhere.[50] The result is that this climate provided the perspective from which Darwin viewed nature. "It was not that the human struggle was seen as a part of the struggle of nature, but rather that nature was interpreted in terms of the struggle for existence of men living and attempting to live in a ruthless industrial society in which the fittest alone survive."[51] Thus the origins and development of Darwinism are the reverse of what they are generally taken to be. Rather than representing a natural biological theory applied to human society, the theory itself, in its natural as well as its social versions, reflects the way human life appeared in the first half of the nineteenth century.[52]

Evidence of the origin of Darwin's theory in human circumstances is found in his starting point in Malthusian speculations about the fate of human populations occupying an industrial society.[53] This assumed background becomes even more specified, however, when account is taken of the significance of Adam Smith, the patriarch of modern free-market economics, for Darwin. Smith's notion of individuals pursuing their own interests somehow contributing to overall prosperity and harmony through an invisible hand becomes in Darwin individual random mutations resulting in new species through the invisible agency of natural selection.[54] But more important than this theoretical parallel is the parallel in fundamental vision. Darwin accepts the common reading of Smith, which affirms the primacy of the individual and its corollary, that the whole is simply the sum of the parts. Life builds up from individual units to form aggregates. There is no wider unity beyond this aggregation itself. That not only a biologist, but one who developed what is almost certainly the most influential organic vision of life ever known, could disown this requisite recognition

---

50 Ashley Montagu, *Darwin: Competition and Cooperation* (Westport, Conn.: Greenwood Press, 1973 (1952)), pp. 18f.

51 Ibid., p. 28.   52 Ibid., p. 32.   53 Ibid., p. 47.

54 Silvan S. Schweber, "The Origin of the *Origin* Revisited," *Journal of the History of Biology* 10/2 (1977): 280.

of the intimate interrelatedness of life in preference for a mechanistic individualism demands explanation. None is more obvious than the direct acceptance of the *laissez-faire* economic vision that was moulding the fabric of his own society. It is hardly an exaggeration then, when Stephen J. Gould suggests that "Darwin grafted Adam Smith upon nature to establish his theory of natural selection."[55] It is not surprising either that sociobiology should corroborate this origin by refining the Darwinian direction in explicit economic cost-benefit calculations. Whether this reflects an adequate understanding of either the natural or the human order, however, is another matter.

THE IMPLAUSIBILITY OF NON-NATURAL ALTRUISM

Even though it is altruism itself that is the target of sociobiology, and not simply the biological anomaly of reproductive altruism, according to some critics, this extravagance could be alleviated if only sociobiologists would recognize the uniquely human quality of altruism. "The uneasiness with the 'atmosphere' of sociobiology can, in my view, be reduced to one central question: sociobiology does not take notice of the fact that man – and only man – can identify with any conspecific and feel sympathy with him; and that this can be a source of emotions that cannot be explained or even dealt with within a system of genetic cost-benefit relations."[56] If sociobiologists would only recognize the distinctiveness of altruism as a capacity peculiar to human beings, so this response suggests, the assault on natural altruism would not be particularly significant, because genuine altruism is really cultural, and not biological. "The conclusion seems to me inevitable that man can have achieved his social-insect-like degree of complex social interactions only through his social and cultural evolution, through the historical selection and cumulation of educational systems, intragroup sanctions, supernatural (superpersonal, superfamilial) purposes, etc."[57] On the surface, social insects and human beings both

---

[55] Stephen Jay Gould, *Ever Since Darwin* (New York: Norton, 1977), p. 100.
[56] Breuer, *Sociobiology and the Human Dimension*, p. 259.
[57] Donald T. Campbell, "On the Genetics of Altruism and the Counterhedonic

seem to act with a significant degree of altruism. Beneath the surface, however, it becomes evident that the apparent altruism of insects is genetically programmed. Human beings are unique in having developed altruism as a cultural phenomenon.

An immediate difficulty with this neat division between humans and other animals is that the more the distinctiveness of the human is emphasized, the more the organic unity of the evolutionary process appears threatened. The nature of biological science itself is at stake in this type of contrast. This helps to account for the ambiguity among sociobiologists over this matter of human distinctiveness. Even within the writings of a single sociobiologist, the ambiguity is apparent. In what has become the Bible of sociobiology, Wilson's *Sociobiology*, the author contends that sharing is rare among non-human primates, with rudimentary forms occurring in chimpanzees and perhaps in a few Old World monkeys and apes. "But in man it is one of the strongest social traits, reaching levels that match the intense trophallactic exchanges of termites and ants. As a result only man has an economy."[58] But elsewhere, Wilson explicitly denies that economics is peculiarly human. "The point is that human economics is not really general economics, but rather the description of economic behavior in one mammalian species with a limited range of the biological state variables."[59] Such explicit self-contradiction, added to the basic ambiguity over biological and everyday meanings of altruism, makes the sociobiological position on the naturalness of altruism even more difficult to pin down. Are human beings peculiar in their capacity for sharing, and so able to enter into the exchanges that constitute economics in a way that other species cannot approximate, or is human economics only one version of a more general phenomenon? The salient issue, of course, is the distinctiveness or commonality of human altruism.

Even if this ambivalence can be overcome, it is not clear which direction would constitute the preferred resolution.

Components in Human Culture," in *Altruism, Sympathy and Helping*, ed. Lauren Wispé (New York: Academic Press, 1978), p. 51.

[58] Wilson, *Sociobiology*, p. 551.

[59] Edward O. Wilson, "Biology and the Social Sciences," *Daedalus* 106 (1977): 127–40.

Recognition of the distinctiveness of the human might well silence those critics of sociobiology who perceive its threat to consist in subjecting the human to biological reductionism. However, it will hardly answer the concerns of those who contend that the fundamental direction of sociobiology, and indeed of modern biology generally, is determined by a particular vision derived from the modern understanding of the human fabricated under the influence of *laissez-faire* economic culture. Indeed, from the perspective of this concern, any emphasis on the distinctiveness of the human, far from representing a concession on the part of the reductionistic tendencies of sociobiology, may really only represent a further expression of the self-assertion taken over from the modern economic managerial mandate. Thus when at the end of a book dedicated to extolling the absolute primacy and authority of selfish genes, we are confronted with a concept of the "meme"[60] (an abbreviation of the Greek *mimeme*, "imitation," to achieve a parallel to "gene"), as a term for units of cultural evolution, this can appear as an abrupt modification of the thesis affirming the determinative significance of genes. However, when we are told that even these memes are at our disposal, we seem to have arrived at a complete repudiation of the solemn assurance of the preface: "we are survival machines – robot vehicles blindly programmed to preserve the selfish molecules known as genes."[61] Now we are assured that we can leave all this evolutionary legacy behind. "We have the power to defy the selfish genes of our birth and, if necessary, the selfish memes of our indoctrination. We can even discuss ways of deliberately cultivating and nurturing a pure, disinterested altruism – something that has no place in nature, something that has never existed before in the whole history of the world."[62] The prospects for such an unprecedented phenomenon do not appear great, but of more immediate consequence for this whole position is the high cost at which even this prospect is achieved, the apparent repudiation of the central conviction of the position itself, that genes are the determinative agents of life.

[60] Dawkins, *The Selfish Gene*, p. 206.
[61] Ibid., "Preface," p. x.   [62] Ibid., p. 215.

In spite of the apparently total about-face represented by this assurance that "we are built as gene machines and nurtured as meme machines, but we have the power to turn against our creators,"[63] this does not necessarily mean a complete repudiation of the detailed delineation of genetic strategies. It can rather entail drawing on the knowledge of these strategies as the means for the rebellion against them. So, as Peter Singer observes, "the better we understand evolution, the better we can outfox it."[64] Then rather than a direct repudiation of the selfish gene reading of life, the promotion of an unprecedented altruism requires precisely this knowledge of the endemic selfishness at the heart of nature as a measure of the odds against which any prospect for genuine altruism must contend.

As a revolt, the suggestion of an unprecedented altruism is more credible than it would be as a direct repudiation of the genetic theory that led up to the reversal. The odds may still be very high against genuine altruism, but at least these odds are recognized. It is not as if sociobiologists like Dawkins are saying "forget the genetic base, and act altruistically." The point is rather that if there is going to be genuine altruistic behavior, it is going to have to be in defiance of the predilection for selfishness characteristic of the genetic base. Whether this actually harmonizes the major premise that we are born survival machines for selfishly replicating genes and the conclusion that we have the power to rebel against these same genes, however, is another matter. The crucial question is: is this reversal itself independent of any genetic base? "What could it mean to transcend our genes, turn against them, or be freed from slavery to them – particularly since the organism that turns against is thoroughly dependent on genetic evolution?"[65] Conversely, if the fundamental thrust of life is as uncompromisingly selfish as Dawkins claims, how does the vision of altruism ever arise? "For what reason does Dawkins *wish* 'to build a society in which individuals co-operate generously and unselfishly towards a common good', if it is true that such a desire is

63 Ibid.
64 Peter Singer, "Ethics and Sociobiology," *Zygon* 19/2 (1984): 155.
65 Hefner, "Sociobiology, Ethics and Theology," 198.

in contradiction to his inborn human nature?"[66] The chasm remains between a supposedly inescapable genetic endowment and an equally independent human initiative, lending credence to R.W. Burhoe's characterization of Dawkins' conclusion as offering "an admittedly lame hope for any explanation of human altruism."[67] The unrelenting insistence on the utterly selfish orientation of the most formative life forces is bound to render any account of altruism from within this kind of socio-biological perspective arbitrary.

The only plausible source of Dawkins' abrupt interest in altruism in the final chapter of a book dedicated to its extermination is the same cultural milieu that nurtured that very drive to extinguish every spark of altruism from the natural order. Paradoxical though this may appear at first sight, on reflection it can be seen to be so perfectly consistent that we might wonder why the apparent reversal of the final chapter seemed so surprising. The appeal to a heroic, unnatural altruism is completely consistent with modern western self-centeredness, and can very readily accompany a reading of the natural order as genetically programmed for selfishness. The only device that is needed to effect this otherwise unlikely amalgam is one that has developed and flourished in the self-centered managerial mentality of the modern west, the fact/value dichotomy. The genetic explanations then represent a factual account of the order of nature, in contrast to which the call to altruism represents a volitional value judgment that we are free to make, and can only make, independently of the factual situation. Indeed, this promotion of non-natural altruism illustrates not only the perspective of the fact/value dichotomy, but also a very prominent reading of that dichotomy, focusing on what has become known as "the naturalistic fallacy." The essence of this fallacy is the attempt to derive what ought to be from an examination of what is the case. To avoid the naturalistic fallacy, then, in this context, we must recognize that "socio-biology can *not* be used to make value judgments on what an

[66] Breuer, *Sociobiology and the Human Dimension*, p. 263.
[67] Ralph Wendell Burhoe, "Religion's Role in Human Evolution: The Missing Link Between Ape-Man's Selfish Genes and Civilized Altruism," *Zygon* 14/2 (1979): 141.

organism 'should' do."[68] This provides the leeway for saying that just because the genetic predisposition favors the un-flinching pursuit of self-interest, this does not mean that the pursuit of self-interest is right. The value of that direction is a further question, beyond establishing that that is the factual situation.

We have seen that this supposedly factual account of the natural order really reflects the "values" of modern economic self-interest applied to nature. The total selfishness of natural processes is read into at least as much as it is read out of the biological evidence, as the extreme contortions required to abolish every hint of altruism demonstrate. But if the suppo-sedly factual descriptions of nature involve valuational perspec-tives, as the recognition of the determinative significance of the economic outlook for sociobiology suggests, should we not expect that the reverse will also hold, that is, that valuation will have some reference to the way things are seen to be? We might formulate this expectation as a counter fallacy. Just as it is fallacious to seek to derive any kind of moral prescription from a purely factual description, so too it must surely be tenuous to the point of absurdity to think that we can affirm values in complete disregard of the way things are. We might call this "the valuational fallacy." But absurd though it may be, this fallacy represents a bed-rock assumption in the modern western mentality. The natural order awaits our manipulation, pure raw material for the imposition of our designs. Thus the plea for a totally unnatural altruism in defiance of the totally selfish determinations of the natural order is not finally a repudiation of the modern self-centered perspective, but a further instance of it. It is our prerogative to assert whatever values we choose over this alien realm of nature.

Flattering though the confinement of altruism to our species might be, it is ultimately self-defeating because it requires a fundamental gulf between biological and cultural evolution. The idea that something could emerge at the cultural level that not only does not draw on the biological base, but actually

[68] Emlen, "Ecological Determinism and Sociobiology," p. 127.

stands in fundamental contradiction to it, is an incredible doctrine from the point of view of biology itself. It is even tenuous from a humanistic perspective, precisely because it is so unequivocally anthropocentric. No doubt, there is a uniqueness to human altruism. It is entirely plausible that it involves a capacity for identifying with the plight of others that is not matched in other species.[69] But to regard this as totally discontinuous with the behavior of animals and birds is much more readily attributable to the anthropocentric perspective of modernity than to generalization from observations of nature. Parental care, alarm calls, and adoption of orphaned animals all suggest approximations to what we know as altruism in the human sphere. The rejection of this link is indicative of theoretical requirements of a vision that cannot countenance this possibility. The vision of cardinal self-interest has no place for what Laurence Thomas calls "transparent" love.[70] In contrast to opaque love, which depends on the object which elicits it, transparent love, in Thomas' usage, is a love which is independent of the qualities of the object of the love. In contrast to the sociobiological construal of parenthood as a matter of genetic calculation, Thomas sees it more generally as an instance of transparent love, and, as such, representing a dominant element of biological reality. "Now, may we not suppose that the (much of the) continuum comes in the wake of the capacity for parental love and, therefore, that if human beings (or, for that matter, any creatures) are biologically endowed with the former capacity, then they are biologically endowed with the latter, unless the latter is specifically selected against?"[71] This entirely plausible reading represents the only basis for any serious prospect for genuine altruism. Far from an anomaly invented by humans, human altruism rather represents a refinement of a tendency evident to some extent in the wider natural order.

The arbitrariness of the attempt to salvage altruism as an

---

[69] Breuer, *Sociobiology and the Human Dimension*, pp. 137f.

[70] Laurence Thomas, "Love and Morality: The Possibility of Altruism," in *Sociobiology and Epistemology*, ed. James H. Fetzer (Dordrecht: D. Reidel, 1985), pp. 120f.

[71] Ibid., pp. 121f.

invention of human culture is not relieved by attributing a special role in this cultural evolution to religious sensibility. No doubt, just as the human capacity for imaginative identification gives human altruism a scope that distinguishes it from approximations in animal behavior, it is also true that, as R. W. Burhoe notes, religion has played a particular role in providing motivation and rationale for serious altruism.[72] To attribute altruism to religion as a cultural phenomenon, however, would only magnify the inadequacy of the cultural explanation as such. For not only is this still subject to the suspect anthropocentrism of the modern outlook, but it also implies a theological perspective that amounts to what might be called an inverse deism. Where deism located God back at the beginning as a designer who set the universe in motion and sent it on its largely independent way, the confinement of altruism to our own species, and the particular identification of it with religious sensibility, has the effect of implying that God, understood along altruistic lines as in Christian theology, is located almost exclusively on this end of the process. The difficulty with this is that from within the religious perspective itself, God must be seen to encompass the whole process, past, present, and future. If God is characterized by something like what Thomas designates as transparent love, the overflowing love of pure altruism that the Christian gospel refers to as *agape*, then that reality must be expected to permeate life, rather than being confined to a latter-day development peculiar to our own species. And the evidence for this would seem to be at least as compelling as the evidence for unmitigated selfishness apart from the supposed altruistic breakthrough of our own species. Further, in both cases what is involved is not simply a matter of evidence but of a formative vision of life through which the evidence is read, and, as we have seen, in the interests of which the evidence may well be contorted or ignored. It would represent a considerable advance, if even this were to be recognized, so that the aura of pure scientific factuality might be dispelled and the importance of fundamental visions appreciated. Then

---

[72] Burhoe, "Religion's Role in Human Evolution," pp. 149ff.

rather than assuming that the depiction of endemic selfishness is pure scientific description and that any hint of authentic altruism is simply religious romanticism, there might be some hope of recognizing the comprehensive visions of life that are at stake, and perhaps even opening up the contrary possibility that it is this so-called scientific account of altruism that is romantic in expecting altruism to materialize out of thin air in utter defiance of a diametrically opposed selfish genetic base.

The prospects for such recognition, however, are not good. The assumption of selfishness is so pervasive and pivotal in the modern outlook that it represents a serious breach of conventional wisdom to contend that there might be something natural about altruism. Sociobiology itself deserves some of the credit for confirming and refining this perspective. In spite of its own indebtedness to this cardinal modern direction in general, and to its economic instantiation in particular, it has, in turn, provided an aura of scientific respectability to this vision of life. Thus not only does it reflect this wider cultural influence, rather than simply constituting a direct factual reading of natural phenomena, but it also contributes to the promotion of this vision with its requisite anticipation of selfishness and corresponding dismissal of any serious expectation of altruism in others or motivation for it in ourselves. The result can only serve to discourage any prospects for altruism that people might entertain. "It can only mean that their feeble efforts to behave more decently are futile, that their condition will amount to the same whatever they do, that their own and other people's apparently more decent feelings are false and hypocritical."[73] Thus far from the neutral air that sociobiology professes to represent, the reality is that not only does it draw on a particular cultural era for its primary inspiration, but it further enforces that vision through this very aura of neutrality that it enjoys as science.

The point of this conclusion is not to reject the scientific ideal of factuality. Indeed this critique of sociobiology presupposes that ideal. The problem is precisely that it does not recognize

---

[73] Midgley, "Gene-Juggling," pp. 455f.

the apparent altruism that exists in the natural order. How different modern life, and not simply biological science, might be, if Darwin had not been consumed by the vision of competition, and had been able to acknowledge the cooperation that is also evident in the natural order![74] How different our present prospects might be, if sociobiologists were to relinquish their obsession with selfishness and give sufficient scope to the cooperation and apparent altruism that they themselves are constrained to mention! A more balanced agenda in sociobiology might even penetrate the omnipresent contemporary commercial culture, whence it derives its present perspective, and at least prompt some questioning of this incessantly insistent endorsement of the self-centered vision of life.

[74] Montagu, *Darwin: Competition and Cooperation*, p. 100.

CHAPTER 2

Evidence of altruism

The self-interest perspective reflected in sociobiology is one that has come to be taken for granted as conventional wisdom that is too obvious to be noticed, much less questioned. At least, this has been the case until relatively recently. Over the past couple of decades the obviousness of the self-interest dogma has been questioned from several quarters where it had tended to be all but totally presupposed. In each of the social sciences, rebels have emerged, suggesting that humanity may not be as uniformly and thoroughly characterized by self-interest as had been assumed. In addition to self-interest, there would seem to be indications of genuine altruism that resist transposition into selfishness, except through machinations prompted by the self-interest dogma itself. In fact, in light of this recent simultaneous questioning from several quarters, it is difficult to determine which is the more surprising phenomenon, the tenacity and thoroughness of the grip that this perspective has held on modern consciousness or the variety and extent of the questioning to which it has rather suddenly become subjected. Consideration of one of the most impressive exhibits of the recent interest in altruism, C. Daniel Batson's experiments purporting to provide empirical evidence of the existence of altruism, provides a striking contrast to the treatment of altruism by sociobiology.

THE SOCIAL SCIENCE BIAS AGAINST ALTRUISM

The ubiquity of the self-interest assumption in social science makes it difficult to document. Perhaps the most direct documentation of this predominance is to be found in summations offered in surveys, such as the conclusion that "the dominant modern psychological theories of motivation are fundamentally egoistic and hedonistic."[1] Or, more broadly stated: "Whether one spoke to a biologist, a psychologist, a psychiatrist, a sociologist, an economist, or a political scientist the answer was the same: Anything that *appears* to be motivated by a concern for someone else's needs will, under closer scrutiny, prove to have ulterior motives."[2] The prevailing assumption in social science has been the one represented by sociobiology, that anything that looks like altruistic behavior has to be a cloak for more primitive and determinative selfish motivation.

The predominance of the egoistic perspective in psychology is evident in the basic orientations that have characterized that discipline from its inception. The recently favored behaviorist approach sees human beings as stimulus-response mechanisms, open to the egoistic appeals of social engineers. The result is a division of humanity into manipulators and manipulated, and while the manipulators will probably cloak themselves in the kinds of goals that are reflective of noble aspirations, the manipulative nature of their methods implies an even more egoistic characterization of them than of their unwitting sub-jects. The more humanistic approach associated with Freud's clinically oriented psychoanalysis is still more blatant in its egoistic orientation than its behavioral successor. The vision and goal behind the psychoanalytic perspective is that of freeing the Ego from undue restrictions imposed by the biological promptings of the Id and the social constraints of the Superego. The assumption is that humanity is essentially composed of egocentric individuals whose ego development is distorted by their hereditary legacies and environmental impositions.

Common sense might suggest that while such an individual-

---

[1] David O. Sears and Carolyn L. Funk, "Self-Interest in Americans' Political Options," in *Beyond Self-Interest*, ed. Jane J. Mansbridge (Chicago: University of Chicago Press, 1990), p. 148.

[2] J. A. Piliavin and H. W. Charng, "Altruism: A Review of Recent Theory and Research," *Annual Review of Sociology* 16 (1990): 28; see also M. L. Hoffman, "Is Altruism Part of Human Nature?" *Journal of Personality and Social Psychology* 40 (1981): 124f.

istic outlook is understandable in psychology, it will not find accommodation in sociology. Consideration of dominant trends in sociology, however, suggests otherwise. Prominent approaches like the conflict theory identified most readily with Karl Marx and the exchange theory promoted by Homans and Blau[3] reflect direct assumptions of an egocentric view of humanity. Here sociology represents an expanded version of this vision in terms of the collective interests of classes and other kinds of interest groups. Not only individuals, but their associations as well, are characterized by a fundamentally acquisitive drive to possess and control. Organization theory, pioneered by Weber and developed by people like Taylor and Simon, clearly reflects this same vision of human nature. "Frederick W. Taylor, the founder of 'scientific management,' accepts the set of psychological requirements of the market system as tantamount to human nature," suggests A. G. Ramos,[4] as part of his much wider thesis that "modern social science was constructed for the purpose of liberating the market from the fetters which throughout mankind's history up until the rise of the commercial and industrial revolution, kept it within definite confines."[5] The image of humanity that is assumed in this social science liberation is that of the rational calculator, approaching life from the vantage point of cost-benefit analysis. That outlook even impinges on the more holistic approaches to sociology, such as Mead's symbolic interactionism. Reference to "the other" in Mead's notion of "the generalized other" turns out to involve capacities of the self to incorporate others, individually and collectively,[6] and so once again raises the specter of a fundamentally egocentric outlook.

As pervasive as the self-interest assumption is in psychology and sociology, it is totally pivotal in political science and economics. The long-standing equation of politics with self-

[3] Leon H. Warshay, *The Current State of Sociological Theory: A Critical Interpretation* (New York: David McKay Co., 1975), pp. 21ff.

[4] Alberto Guerreiro Ramos, *The New Science of Organizations: A Reconceptualization of the Wealth of Nations* (Toronto: University of Toronto Press, 1981), p. 81.

[5] Ibid., pp. 21f.

[6] Richard E. Sykes, "Toward a Sociology of Religion Based on the Philosophy of George Herbert Mead," in *Sociology and Human Destiny: Essays on Sociology, Religion and Society*, ed. Gregory Baum (New York: Seabury Press, 1980), pp. 171f.

interest became explicit in the attempt to be truly scientific about politics around the middle of the twentieth century. "Rational choice" or "public choice" modeling of political positions gave clear expression to the self-interest assumption by the 1970s.[7] So deeply does this assumption run that political scientists are even prepared to sacrifice rationality to preserve the egoistic characterization of humanity. Behavior that does not fit the self-interest model is dismissed as irrational. Thus Dennis Mueller proposes that "we retain the egoistic portion of rational egoism, and drop, or better modify the rational assumption, at least in the strong form in which this assumption is usually employed."[8] The significance of self-interest for economics is too obvious to require comment, since it is there that the equation of self-interest with rationality was originally effected on a broad scale.

The triumph of self-interest is often attributed to Adam Smith and what turned out to be his program for free-market economics. "Prior to Smith, self-interest was often identified with vice, and benevolence with virtue."[9] Although Smith did not effect a straightforward reversal of these, the net result was not far from this. Where self-interest was highly suspect in previous eras, especially throughout Christendom, it acquired an air of neutrality as descriptive of the fundamental state of human nature, if not an actually positive connotation as indicative of seriousness, industry and reliability. The full development of this reversal was left to Smith's successors, although the role of Smith and his contemporaries was crucial in the transition. From the other side, Smith's approach was not entirely without precedent. Smith's free-market economics had its antecedents in the political vision of Thomas Hobbes, whereby life is naturally "solitary, poor, nasty, brutish, and short"[10] because

---

[7] Jane J. Mansbridge, "The Rise and Fall of Self-Interest in the Explanation of Political Life," in *Beyond Self-Interest*, ed. Jane J. Mansbridge, p. 10.

[8] Dennis Mueller, "Rational Egoism vs. Adaptive Egoism," *Public Choice* 5 (1986): 2–23.

[9] Thomas Donaldson, *Corporations and Morality* (Englewood Cliffs, NJ: Prentice-Hall, 1982), p. 62.

[10] Thomas Hobbes, *Leviathan*, in *The English Philosophers from Bacon to Mill*, ed. Edwin A. Burtt (New York: The Modern Library, 1939), p. 161.

everyone is instinctively out for themselves. This instinctive aggression and acquisitiveness is only checked by a social contract whereby we relinquish some of our natural independence to a sovereign in exchange for the protection of that great Leviathan, the state. John Locke's democratization of the social contract provided an inspiration for the American constitution, with the result that it is difficult to know which is the more significant factor in the shaping of America and the world it has pioneered, the economic version of self-interest articulated by Adam Smith or the political version drafted by Locke. Together they provided a formidable framework for fashioning the modern era.

The foundational role that the self-interest assumption has played in the formation of our world obscures the radical nature of the transition involved in its triumph. From an indicator of vice – the seven deadly sins being variations on selfishness – self-interest takes on this neutral, and even positive, connotation. Such a dramatic reversal demands explanation. It is hardly credible that people like Hobbes and Locke and Smith suddenly decided that bad was good. If that is the import of the shift that they signal, there must have been reasons for reconsidering what makes for good and bad.

One crucial factor that separates the modern era from previous periods is precisely the fact of self-consciousness. Where even the more reflective segments of humanity tended to go about their business with little sense of self-awareness prior to the modern era, the Cartesian ego signaled the setting of the self on center stage with a profile that could not be ignored. When to this we add the consideration of the impetus toward individualism instigated by the Renaissance and Reformation and consolidated by the Enlightenment, there can be no doubt that the challenge of self-awareness was in the air in the early stages of the modern era. It is perhaps not a huge leap from incipient self-awareness to the assumption that self is the center of life, whether life is approached in economic or political terms, or indeed in terms of political economy, which was the original organic form that gave rise to the later separate disciplines of political science and economics, or still later in more explicitly self-conscious social terms with the emergence of sociology and psychology.

Self-consciousness thus constitutes a necessary condition for the emergence of the self-interest assumption as the defining characteristic of humanity, but it is hardly a sufficient one. Some more definite motivation is demanded to account for the depth of this reversal. Albert Hirshman finds this more precise motivation in what he characterizes as a reaction of interests against the passions, particularly the passions for glory and honor.[11] Although self-interest was fundamentally suspect prior to the modern period, and in retrospect we might be surprised at the favor it found from the early stages of the modern era, at that time itself it may well have appeared as a promising alternative to the enthusiasms of political, military, and ecclesiastical establishments. The pursuit of glory and vindication of honor through endless bloody battles represented the reality of the supposedly virtuous civil and ecclesiastical aristocracy. Richard Hooker's *Of the Laws of Ecclesiastical Polity*[12] depicted the official thinking at the end of the sixteenth century, representing the common people as motivated by self-interest, while civil and ecclesiastical leaders were presented as devoted to the common good and motivated by love of virtue. Hirshman sees the elevation of self-interest toward the status of virtue as a reaction against the hypocrisy of this aristocratic vision. Demeaning though it might be, self-interest held the promise of a less vicious and violent means of arbitrating differences than the clashes and wars launched in the name of virtue. The result, as Hirshman sees it,[13] was that self-interest became established as the human paradigm through the seventeenth and eighteenth centuries, through a curious process of expansion and contraction in meaning. The originally broad sense whereby self-interest was equated with rational behavior as such gave way to an identification with commercial interests in

---

[11] Albert O. Hirschman, *The Passions and the Interests: Political Arguments for Capitalism before Its Triumph* (Princeton: Princeton University Press, 1977).
[12] Richard Hooker, *Of the Laws of Ecclesiastical Polity*, in Stephen Holmes, "The Secret History of Self-Interest," in *Beyond Self-Interest*, ed. Mansbridge, p. 284.
[13] Albert O. Hirschman, "The Concept of Interest: From Euphemism to Tautology," in *Rival Views of Market Society* (New York: Viking, 1986).

particular, but at the same time the notion of self-interest was taken to typify human motivation as such. In this way, commercial ambition was legitimized as a variation of the general basic direction of motivation, and at the same time this was reinforced by contrasting the innocuousness of self-interest with the more obviously destructive passions. That this ambiguity between self-interest as one of several possible motivations and as the essence of human motivation itself was not only tolerated, but generally unnoticed, testifies to the endorsement that the self-interest assumption received, and also helps explain how it could come to exercise such influence.

In addition to the reaction against the dangerous aristocratic passions, the legitimization of self-interest received institutional support from the blossoming of democracy and the development of the market economy. Jane Mansbridge points out[14] that the endorsement of self-interest coincided with the acceptance of conflict in political life as evidenced by the shift in the British Parliament from decision by consensus to the expedient of the majority vote. The mutual reinforcement of theory and practice is perhaps even stronger in the economic realm, where the success of the market system rendered the self-interest rationale all but impregnable. Thus egalitarian developments in politics and economics represent the positive institutionalization of the revolutionary motivations identified by Hirshman.

One other factor neglected by Hirshman, and most other "social" historians, is the significance of the religious context.[15] The transformation of a concept that epitomized vice into the pivotal characterization of humanity and its prospects has vast moral, if not theological, implications. At the very least, it would seem to reflect a massive shift from a theological to a secular perspective. Any sense of ultimate allegiance is disowned in the name of the rights of individuals to determine their own lives. It can certainly be argued that this was the net result of this inversion, but that rationale can hardly be attributed to most of the major players at the time when the

---

[14] Mansbridge, "The Rise and Fall of Self-Interest in the Explanation of Political Life," p. 6.

[15] Holmes, "The Secret History of Self-Interest," p. 276.

basic transition was effected. Smith himself was a moral philosopher, and Hobbes and Locke are by no means lacking in
theological profession, unorthodox though it may be. In
general, the initial endorsement of self-interest in the early
modern era, far from representing a rejection of morality, is
probably much more accurately understood as itself constituting a moral project. It is not accidental that people like
Smith and David Hume are involved at the heart of the
transition. One possible explanation for their recourse to self-
interest is that they had accepted the somber picture of the
human condition that had been promoted particularly through
the Protestant emphasis on the sinfulness of humanity in such
concepts as total depravity and original sin, but where theologians took this as indicative of the need for divine grace to
deliver sinful humanity from its fallen condition, the moralist
champions of self-interest saw this reading of the situation as a
challenge to individuals to take responsibility for their own
lives. For contrary to the assumptions congenial to the contemporary secular horizon, the religious context represented a
significant dimension for seventeenth- and eighteenth-century
thinkers, even if they were reacting against it. Self-interest
offered a calculative way of dealing with sinners realistically
and constructively. Whatever the direct significance of this
factor may be, in conjunction with the others mentioned, it is
surely striking that through this self-interest assumption, the
one Christian doctrine that has been endorsed by modern
secular culture in general, and by the social sciences in particular, is the doctrine of original sin.

Other factors no doubt play a part in the enthronement of
self-interest as the virtually unquestioned dogma of modernity,
but pursuit of these diminishes in importance in light of the
questioning to which the dogma itself has been subjected of
late. "In the last ten years, at the same time that economists
were advancing rational choice models based on self-interest to
explain phenomena as varied as industry regulation, marital
stability, and suicide, social science disciplines other than political science were preparing the theoretical and empirical
ground for a massive revision both of the larger adversary

paradigm and of the rational choice standard within it."[16] And while psychologists study "pro-social behavior" and sociologists turn their attention to "helping behavior" such as blood and organ donation and aid to those in distress, economists and political scientists have also begun to question the adequacy of the rational choice standard and its basis in the self-interest assumption. In 1978, David Collard published *Altruism and the Economy*, suggesting that self-interest is not a sufficient basis for accounting for human motivation even in the economic sphere. A decade later, Roger Friedland and Alexander Robertson present a further example of a challenge to the self-interest assumption from within economics itself in their *Beyond the Marketplace: Rethinking Economy and Society*.[17] Examples could be multiplied, but in the interests of economy, it should suffice to cite the conclusion of a 1990 survey of the social sciences by two social scientists themselves. "In all these areas we are now seeing a 'paradigm shift'."[18] The direction of the shift is indicated by their title: "Altruism: A Review of Recent Theory and Research." In all of the social sciences, even in the fields of economics and politics where it received its initial endorsement and instantiation, the self-interest assumption has been called into question, and the need to consider that people are also to some extent motivated by something approaching genuine altruism has come to be entertained and explored with increasing seriousness.

THE SOCIAL SCIENCE DISCOVERY OF ALTRUISM

Without detracting from the basic direction of this summation of the situation, it must be acknowledged that the hegemony of the self-interest assumption was neither as total, nor the emergence of interest in altruism as completely novel, as this depiction would suggest. Although the self-interest assumption

---

[16] Mansbridge, "The Rise and Fall of Self-Interest in the Explanation of Political Life," p. 16.

[17] Roger Friedland and Alexander Robertson, *Beyond the Marketplace: Rethinking Economy and Society* (New York: Aldine and de Gruyter, 1989).

[18] Piliavin and Charng, "Altruism: A Review of Recent Theory and Research," p. 28.

figured prominently in the development of modern self-understanding, popularly and academically, "there was never any blanket endorsement of the idea."[19] The original exponents of self-interest were not inclined to give it the absolute endorsement accorded by some of the later more ardent rational choice social scientists, with Adam Smith, for instance, subordinating the pursuit of self-interest to the requirements of justice; and even amid the most enthusiastic acceptance of the assumption, there were moments and individuals that foreshadowed the more extensive challenges that have developed of late. In his 1956 survey of what he called "a forgotten aspect of social thought" in his article "Altruism Arrives in America," Louis J. Budd noted a particular burst of interest in this subject in the 1890s, and a further eclipse of interest until the decade in which he was writing, when it began to receive scientific attention as a dimension of human behavior that merited study.

The extent of that attention is indicated by the fact that between 1962 and 1982 more than one thousand empirical studies of altruism were reported.[20] However, these studies tended to focus on the social contexts in which helping behavior occurs more than on the reality of altruism itself, so that in 1970 Dennis Krebs was complaining that, in spite of the research on altruism, "the concept . . . is still unclear and no way has been found to measure its motivational base."[21] By the middle of the decade, he was still lamenting: "psychologists have manipulated antecedents of helping behavior and studied their effects, and they have measured a number of correlates of pro-social events; however, they have done little to examine the extent to which the acts that they investigated were oriented to the welfare of either the person who was helped or the helper."[22] This pivotal failure to focus on the distinguishing characteristic of altruism,

---

[19] Holmes, "The Secret History of Self-Interest," p. 285.
[20] John F. Dovido, "Helping Behaviour and Altruism: An Empirical and Conceptual Overview," in *Advances in Experimental Social Psychology*, ed. L. Berkowitz (New York: Academic Press, 1984).
[21] D. L. Krebs, "Altruism: An Examination of the Concept and Review of the Literature," *Psychological Bulletin* 73 (1970): 297.
[22] D. L. Krebs, "Empathy and Altruism," *Journal of Personality and Social Psychology* 32 (1975): 1134.

its orientation in terms of the welfare of the other, was addressed throughout the 1980s in a series of experiments headed up by C. Daniel Batson.[23]

Batson and his colleagues were determined to establish whether or not there was such a thing as altruism, concern for the other prompted by the perceived needs of the other, which was not reducible to any ulterior motive attributable to the self-interest of the putative altruist. Not only did their experiments appear to provide empirical evidence of a genuine altruistic focus; this result was confirmed in further experiments designed to meet counter-explanations proposed by self-interest-oriented skeptics. In fact, this experimental pursuit of altruism could be thought of as the ABCs of altruism, since Batson's experiments respond to challenges from advocates of the established self-interest perspective, Archer and Cialdini, and, as we shall see, we even move into the Ds with an interesting mediating role being played by J. F. Dovido.

The central experiment is one reported by Batson and his colleagues in 1981.[24] The obvious way to seek to determine

---

[23] Although the Batson experiments are particularly striking, they are by no means isolated. Another reconsideration of the self-interest assumption, from a different angle, consideration of the importance of community and communication for decisions about contributions to group interests, is represented by Linda R.Caporael, Robyn M. Dawes, John M. Orbell, and Alphons J. C. van de Kragt, "Selfishness Examined: Cooperation in the Absence of Egoistic Incentives," in *Behavioral and Brain Sciences* 12 (1989): 683–739 and includes an extensive reaction in the form of an "Open Peer Commentary." Alfie Kohn, *The Brighter Side of Human Nature: Altruism and Empathy in Everyday Life* (New York: Basic Books, 1990), offers a very readable, but extensively documented, survey of social science reconsideration of the self-interest assumption.

[24] The central Batson experiments are: C. D. Batson, B. D. Duncan, P. Ackerman, T. Buckley, and K. Birch, "Is Empathic Emotion a Source of Altruistic Motivation?" *Journal of Personality and Social Psychology* 40 (1981): 290–302; C. D. Batson, J. S. Coke, and Virginia Pych, "Limits on the Two Stage Model of Empathic Mediation of Helping: A Reply to Archer, Diaz-Loving, Gollwitzer, Davis and Foushee," *Journal of Personality and Social Psychology* 45 (1983): 895–8; J. Fultz, C. D. Batson, V. A. Fortenbach, P. M. McCarthy, and L. L. Varney, "Social Evaluation and the Empathy-Altruism Hypothesis," *Journal of Personality and Social Psychology* 50 (1986): 761–9; C. D. Batson, J. Dyck, J. R. Brandt, J. G. Batson, A. L. Powell, M. R. McMaster, and C. Griffitt, "Five Studies Testing Two New Egoistic Alternatives to the Empathy-Altruism Hypothesis," *Journal of Personality and Social Psychology* 55 (1988): 52–77; and C. D. Batson, J. G. Batson, C. A. Griffitt, S. Barrientos, J. R. Brandt, P. Sprengelmeyer, and M. Bayly, "Negative-State Relief and the Empathy-Altruism Hypothesis," *Journal of Personality and Social Psychology* 56 (1989): 922–33.

whether someone is acting out of concern for others or is simply pursuing his own self-interest is to put him in a situation where he has an opportunity to help someone else. If the situation is set up so that it is easy for some to escape without helping, and more difficult for others to get away, this will indicate how far helping is simply the easiest way for someone to get out of a situation. If those who can escape easily without helping tend to do so, and more of those in the more difficult escape condition actually offer help, this is an indication that helping can be regarded as an act of least resistance.

This result would tend to confirm pessimistic expectations regarding altruism, but this is an indirect inference. The difficulty is that motivation defies direct detection. How can one determine whether a person is acting out of altruistic or self-interest motivation? The experimental evidence of altruism that the Batson researchers were able to establish was made possible by finding a way to identify altruism at the level of behavior, where it can be detected, in contrast to its elusiveness at the level of motivation. The basis for this behavioral test was the hypothesis that altruism is a reflection of empathy. People can be expected to act altruistically, Batson hypothesized, to the extent to which they feel empathy for another or others. The testing of this hypothesis constituted the more elaborate element of the experiment. The ease and difficulty of escape were supplemented by a means of dividing subjects into high and low empathy categories. This involved giving the subjects a placebo and telling half of them, those in the high empathy condition, that it had the side-effect of producing a feeling of uneasiness and distress, and the other half, those in the low empathy condition, that it had the side-effect of producing a feeling of warmth and sensitivity. The assumption, which in fact was borne out by the results of the experiment, was that those

Batson sums up these experiments, with convenient tables outlining the methods and results of each, in C. D. Batson, "How Social an Animal? The Human Capacity for Caring," *American Psychologist* 20 (1990): 336–46. A fuller exposition, supplemented by consideration of the historical and philosophical background as well as speculation about the present implications and future prospects for altruism, is provided in C. D. Batson, *The Altruism Question: Toward a Social-Psychological Answer* (Hillsdale, NJ: Lawrence Erlbaum Associates, 1991).

who expected to feel distress due to the placebo would perceive their response to the person requiring help to be primarily one of empathy, and those who expected the placebo to produce empathic feelings would perceive their response to be primarily one of personal distress.

Dividing subjects in these two ways results in four different groups: easy escape/low empathy, difficult escape/low empathy, easy escape/high empathy, and difficult escape/high empathy. This is what is called a 2 × 2 design, since the two divisions in terms of escape and empathy combine to produce these four states among the subjects. If the self-interest hypothesis is right, we should expect only those in the high empathy/ difficult escape condition to demonstrate any significant indication of altruistic behavior. However, the empathy-altruism hypothesis that Batson wishes to test would predict that there should be significant evidence of altruistic behavior in all but the low empathy/easy escape condition.

The experiment itself involved having subjects watch a young woman, Elaine, receive electric shocks, and being given the opportunity to take the remaining shocks in her place. Ease or difficulty of escape from this potentially altruistic situation was effected by varying the number of shocks subjects were told Elaine was to receive, with those in the easy escape condition being told the series was short and those in the difficult escape condition being told there were several more to come. The division in terms of empathy was made by the deception of the placebo. Those told that the placebo induced contentment were expected to attribute any empathy to the placebo and to focus on their own feelings of distress at seeing Elaine receive the shocks, whereas those told that the placebo induced uneasiness were expected to attribute feelings of distress at Elaine's plight to the placebo and to focus on Elaine's plight itself.

The results confirmed the one-versus-three interaction pattern predicted by the empathy-altruism hypothesis. Of the four sections, the only one where helping was low was in the easy escape/low empathy group. The high rate in the other three is what is expected from the perspective of the empathy-altruism hypothesis. The salient implication is drawn by the

researchers themselves. "In the distress conditions, where motivation was assumed to be egoistic, the rate of helping was
significantly lower under easy than under difficult escape. In the
empathy conditions, where motivation was assumed to be at
least in part altruistic, the rate of helping remained high, even
when escape was easy."[25]

This evidence not only confirms the empathy-altruism hypothesis, that there is such a thing as altruism, willingness to
assist others motivated by empathy for them, but also contradicts the egoism thesis that such behavior is simply the less
costly way for egoists to deal with distressing situations. In that
case, helping should not have remained high when escape was
easy for those in the empathy condition. However, Batson and
his colleagues are characteristically cautious about proclaiming
the demise of such a deep-rooted assumption as the egoistic
one. "For now, the research to date convinces us of the
legitimacy of *suggesting* [their italics] that empathic motivation
for helping may be truly altruistic." The most they are willing
to infer from their results in regard to the egoistic perspective is:
"we are left far less confident than we were of reinterpretations
of apparently altruistically motivated helping in terms of instrumental egoism."[26]

The A was added to Batson's B of altruism research when
R. L. Archer challenged the empathy-altruism hypothesis with
the contention that the explanation for the apparently high
incidence of altruism among the Batson subjects is that they
were really responding to wider social evaluation. They did not
want to let their self-interest show, and so acted with the
altruistic response that would win the approval of others. The
source of this social pressure might have been as innocent and
indirect as the fact that a researcher gave the subjects instructions. The specific instructions themselves might have been
quite neutral, favoring neither self-interest nor altruism, but the
fact that the researcher is in charge gives the subjects a sense of
being watched.

The Batson researchers addressed this challenge with two

[25] Batson et al., "Is Empathic Emotion a Source of Altruistic Motivation?" p. 301.
[26] Ibid., p. 302.

further experiments, one in which the element of social evaluation was explicitly excluded for the subjects and another with
the 2 × 2 design, where high and low empathy conditions were
combined with high and low exposure to social evaluation. The
results indicated that high empathy led to more helping under
both high and low social evaluation. With characteristic
caution, the Batson team propose that "it does seem appropriate to conclude that the present research casts serious doubt
on the suggestion that empathy leads to increased helping
because more empathically aroused individuals are more concerned about negative social evaluation for declining to
help."[27]

The C of altruism research is represented by R. B. Cialdini
and his associates who suggested that the apparent altruistic
behavior is to be accounted for by what they term a "negative
state relief explanation."[28] Supposed altruists are really motivated by concern to relieve their own sad or depressed mood,
rather than by empathic identification with the victim.[29] In
stating their conclusions, they offer a somewhat back-handed
compliment to the Batson work, summarizing the significance
of their own experiments as "providing a plausible egoistic
explanation for the first powerful experimental evidence for
pure altruism [i.e., Batson et al.]."[30]

The Batson researchers countered with a report of no less
than five experiments designed to test the empathy-specific
thesis advanced by Cialdini.[31] The most dramatic of these
involved the 2 × 2 design, this time combining a distinction
between whether or not the person in need of help received
help with a distinction between allowing half the subjects to be
the source of that help and half not to be. The assumption was

[27] Fultz et al., "Social Evaluation and the Empathy-Altruism Hypothesis," p. 769.

[28] D. J. Baumann, R. B. Cialdini, and D. T. Kenrick, "Altruism as Hedonism: Helping
and Self-Gratification as Equivalent Responses," *Journal of Personality and Social
Psychology* 40 (1981): 1039–46.

[29] R. B. Cialdini, M. Schaller, D. Houlihan, K. Arps, J. Fultz, and A. L. Beamann,
"Empathy-Based Helping: Is It Selflessly or Selfishly Motivated?" *Journal of Personality
and Social Psychology* 52 (1987): 749–58.

[30] Ibid., p. 757.

[31] Batson et al., "Five Studies Testing Two New Egoistic Alternatives to the Empathy-
Altruism Hypothesis," pp. 52–77.

that if subjects are offering assistance out of concern with their own feelings of distress, rather than out of genuine concern for the person in need of assistance, then those who have no opportunity to provide relief will show less elation over the fact that relief has been provided than those who have the opportunity to be the source of that relief themselves. However, the mood improvement for high empathy subjects was high when relief was assured, whether they were able to be the source of that relief or not, confirming the empathy-altruism hypothesis that the real focus is the need of the victim and not the need for negative-state mood relief on the part of the subject. Batson and his colleagues are somewhat more daring in their summation of the results of these five studies, taken in conjunction with the results of the earlier studies:

the claim that the motivation to help evoked by empathy is directed toward the egoistic goal of avoiding empathy-specific punishments seems very doubtful. As with a claim for the existence of unicorns, we cannot categorically say that it is wrong, but we have looked hard in a number of likely places to find supporting evidence and have found none.[32]

Yet, in spite of consigning counterevidence to the status of unicorn hunts, the Batson team continue to qualify their claims. "Still, at this point the possibility that a negative-state relief version of the empathy-specific reward hypothesis can account for the empathy-helping relation cannot be entirely ruled out."[33]

Three further studies, aimed directly at Cialdini's negative-state relief hypothesis, further confirmed that high empathy subjects score high rates of helping even when anticipated mood enhancement offered relief without helping.[34] But still, they do not take this as disposing of the negative-state relief hypothesis or as complete vindication of the empathy-altruism hypothesis. Batson and his colleagues acknowledge the presence of negative-state relief among high empathy subjects. Their

[32] Ibid., p. 75.   [33] Ibid.
[34] Batson et al., "Negative-State Relief and the Empathy-Altruism Hypothesis," pp. 922–33.

own studies, as well as those of Cialdini et al., and others, confirm this. Their quarrel with Cialdini is over the contention that this egocentric motivation dispenses with any real altruistic motivation. Their own studies strongly suggest otherwise.

Apparently, the empathy-helping relation is not simply the product of an egoistic desire for negative-state relief. There is more to it than that. Whether this "more" is the product of an altruistic desire to relieve the victim's distress, as the empathy-altruism hypothesis claims, remains to be seen. Certainly, our results are entirely consistent with that hypothesis. Moreover, plausible alternative explanations for the growing support for the empathy-altruism hypothesis are increasingly hard to find.[35]

Thus Batson and his various colleagues have addressed the challenges to their empirical identification of altruistic motivation with experiments that have consistently supported the empathy-altruism hypothesis and rendered the alternatives problematic. They can even claim converts from the other side. "Our work, from an independent laboratory and conducted by researchers who have typically adopted the egoistic perspective,[36] replicated the findings of the critical tests used by Batson and his colleagues (see Batson and Coke, 1981)."[37] In a book summing up his own experiments, and exploring the historical and philosophical background, as well as speculating about the overall significance of the altruism question, Batson concludes that, contrary to the sense of altruism as an unnatural chore, typified by Kantian morally autonomous individuals facing a constraining duty, the truth may be almost the exact opposite, that we are characterized by a natural inclination to care about other people. Still this conclusion is proposed with characteristic caution. "Admittedly, this answer is still tentative, but the evidence does seem strong enough that we should start looking for the party hats."[38]

[35] Ibid., p. 932.
[36] Dovido, "Helping Behaviour and Altruism."
[37] D. A. Schroeder, J. F. Dovido, M. E. Sibicky, L. L. Matthews, and J. L. Allen, "Empathic Concern and Helping Behaviour: Egoism or Altruism?" *Journal of Experimental Social Psychology* 24 (1988): 352.
[38] Batson, *The Altruism Question*, p. 230.

THE SOCIAL SCIENCE PROBLEMATIC OF ALTRUISM

Our inclination to look for the party hats will depend on how impressive we take the evidence to be. Even Batson's critics recognize that his discovery could have dramatic repercussions. "The implications for fundamental characterizations of human nature are considerable."[39] In a culture based on the self-interest assumption, empirical evidence of the presence of an altruistic strain is no small matter. Some see this evidence not only as potentially revolutionary, but also as incontrovertible. "This is publicly verifiable; the conditions of falsifiability are explicit. No one can wriggle off the hook."[40] But there are elements that suggest that the hook is not as firmly imbedded as such enthusiasm would suggest. For one thing, there is an element of artificiality about these kinds of laboratory experiments with people. The technique for classifying empathy, for instance, through administering a placebo and planting suggestions designed to divert people so that they focus on the opposite dimension to that which the placebo supposedly promotes, although apparently effective, does not deal with the reality of first-hand empathy in the subjects themselves, as critics of Batson have pointed out. Beyond these kinds of reservations about elements in the experiments, however, there is a more pervasive source of concern, namely that the difficulty is perhaps not so much a matter of the quality of the evidence as such, but with the evidence criterion itself.

Evidence of an altruistic strain in humanity is not just another piece of scientific information, if there is such a thing, not least because it is information about ourselves and our relations with others. If it is true, it can be expected to have significance for our living. In fact, if it is believed to be true, it can be expected to have such significance. This is Batson's view. "If it turns out that we are capable of altruism," he suggests, "then our moral horizon – and our potential for moral respon-

---

[39] Cialdini et al., "Empathy-Based Helping: Is it Selflessly or Selfishly Motivated?" p. 749.

[40] Paul Rigby and Paul O'Grady, "Agape and Altruism: Debates in Theology and Social Psychology," *Journal of the American Academy of Religion* 57 (1989): 733.

sibility – broadens considerably."[41] But this means that far from being a matter of empirical revision of our understanding of human nature, what is involved is a vision of human potential. Not only what we are, but what we might become, as individuals and as a society, is at stake. "If our belief in universal egoism is wrong and we are actually capable of altruism, then possibilities arise for the development of more caring individuals, and a more compassionate, humane society."[42] Here we are dealing not only with empirical information, but also with moral transformation. How this transformation is to be achieved is the decisive question.

Batson does not naively anticipate any direct transformation. He recognizes two crucial limitations on altruism in the evidence he and his colleagues have uncovered. The support for the empathy-altruism hypothesis suggests that altruism tends to be commensurate with the range of empathy, and, in practice, that range may be quite restricted. The other crucial factor is the competing concerns that emerge as the cost of helping increases. The higher the cost, the more considerations of self-interest are likely to arise.[43] These limitations might suggest that the evidence for altruism is not so significant after all. But this is where the question about the nature of evidence arises. For these limitations themselves might be due to some extent to the acceptance of the self-interest paradigm. If that paradigm was displaced to some extent by the recognition and expectation of altruism, those limitations might change. Erosion of the self-interest paradigm might have the effect of encouraging altruism. As Jane Mansbridge puts it, from the opposite direction: "because thinking that another has acted unselfishly often leads people to behave unselfishly themselves, underestimating the frequency of altruism can itself undermine unselfish behavior."[44] Thus if we were to come to expect altruistic concern more than we are encouraged to under the self-interest paradigm, the range of our empathy might be increased and the

---

[41] Batson, *The Altruism Question*, p. 4.   [42] Ibid.

[43] Batson, "How Social an Animal? The Human Capacity for Caring," pp. 344f.

[44] Jane J. Mansbridge, "On the Relation of Altruism and Self-Interest," in *Beyond Self-Interest*, ed. Jane J. Mansbridge, p. 141.

point at which we begin to calculate our own interests might be deferred somewhat.

Clearly, what is at stake is something different from the conventional understanding of empirical evidence. Revision to the understanding of human nature turns out to be a challenge as much as a description. However, if this seems disappointing from the perspective of scientific expectation, we must realize that it places the prevailing self-interest reading of human nature in the same position. That reading is not simply a description of the way human beings are, but also functions somewhat as a self-fulfilling prophecy. This is presumably why Batson sees the recognition of the reality of altruism challenging not only our basic view of human nature, but the fundamental approaches of social science as well. "If we are capable of altruism, then virtually all of our current ideas about individual psychology, social relations, economics and politics are in an important respect wrong."[45] The reality of altruism challenges the factuality of the self-interest paradigm in two senses, in terms of its accuracy and of its adequacy. One claim is that it is simply inaccurate. Human beings are characterized by altruism as well as by self-interest. But what we have been considering is a wider sense in which this whole way of representing human beings is basically inadequate. Human beings react to descriptions, so that there is no such thing as a neutral description of human nature. Putative descriptions are at the same time invitations for individuals to confirm these descriptions by their actions. Consequently the accuracy of any proposed description depends on how far human beings do adopt it as well as on how far it reflects any present reality. Any depiction of human beings that does not take this into account is inadequate. What we are now beginning to see is the possibility that implicit in the inadequacy of the self-interest paradigm to depict human beings is the question of the adequacy of this ideal of depiction itself, at least as far as human beings are concerned. This is tantamount to questioning the adequacy of the social sciences themselves as they have been fashioned in terms of the self-

---

[45] Batson, *The Altruism Question*, p. 3.

interest paradigm. Not only is it not just facts about human nature that are questionable; the fundamental fact/value dichotomy itself is at stake.

In one sense, social science can deal with altruism very easily. What could be more natural for any social perspective than a view of social relatedness? From this point of view, it should not come as any surprise that this is precisely the background against which the concept of altruism originated. The notion is generally traced to the widely acknowledged founder of sociology, Auguste Comte, who is credited with coining the term for his depiction of the cohesion of humanity that he expected to emerge in the positive era, now that the distractions and deflections of theology and militarism were left behind. "In a word, Biocracy and Sociocracy will be alike pervaded by Altruism; whereas during the long period of theology and military training egoism predominated."[46] Indeed, for Comte, "the greatest problem of life [was achieving] the ascendancy of altruism over egoism."[47] It is at least ironic that a discipline founded to champion altruism should have come to be so dominated by the self-interest paradigm. It is apt to appear totally contradictory, until we notice that the background against which the notion of altruism is advanced is one of self-interest and egoism. Nor is this simply the egoism attributed to ecclesiastical and military ambition. The point is that in seeking to displace these egoisms, Comte invoked an even more ambitious one through his own positivistic prescriptions. The ideal of total control that distinguished the positivism Comte advocated is precisely the corollary of the self-interested understanding of human beings. The ideal of the self-interested individual is to be in complete control. Thus in devising the notion of altruism in the context of his advocacy of positivism, Comte was subordinating altruism to self-interest right from the start. There is no particular irony, then, in the loss of interest in altruism in social science. It would be ironic, however, and also dangerous, if the self-interest basis of this origin of the concept were neglected in the renewed interest in altruism today.

[46] Auguste Comte, *System of Positive Polity*, vol. 1 (New York: Burt Kranklin, 1875), p. 500.
[47] Ibid., p. 146.

The danger lies in the very concentration on altruism itself, as can be seen in Batson. Batson's discovery of altruism was effected by strict concentration on the focus on the other as its distinguishing characteristic. He is totally uncompromising in this insistence. "As soon as benefit to the other becomes an instrumental rather than an ultimate goal, the altruistic motivation evaporates. Only egoistic motivation remains."[48] There can be no question that this is a courageous stand in the present climate, even allowing for the growing dissatisfaction with the self-interest paradigm. Whether it constitutes an adequate basis for portraying what altruism involves, however, is another matter. The dominant impression conveyed by conspicuous instances of altruism is of spontaneity and naturalness. Not only did rescuers of Jews in Nazi Germany not set out to be heroes; they were not inclined to see their activities in terms of explicit goals at all, instrumental or ultimate. They tend to see themselves as ordinary people doing what the situation demanded.[49] In such a serious matter as kidney donation, even though the recipient was a close relative, it is surely significant that "a majority of kidney donors decided instantaneously to give this gift."[50] This lack of deliberateness and calculation suggests that understanding altruism in terms of a direct focus on the other may be as unsatisfactory as the self-referential concern this is taken to preclude, and may even be a subtle version of the latter.

Genuine altruism seems to be characterized by paradox of the kind intimated in the famous remark of Henry David Thoreau: "If I knew for a certainty that a man was coming to my house with the conscious design of doing me good, I should run for my life."[51] Thoreau feared being the object of a meddling do-gooder precisely because of the "conscious design" that would render him an object for this person's

---

[48] Batson, *The Altruism Question*, p. 224.

[49] Samuel P. Oliner and Pearl M. Oliner, *The Altruistic Personality: Rescuers of Jews in Nazi Europe* (New York: Free Press, 1988).

[50] Roberta G. Simmons, "Presidential Address on Altruism and Sociology," *The Sociological Quarterly* 32 (1991): 15.

[51] Henry David Thoreau, *Walden and Other Writings* (New York: Bantam Books, 1962), p. 160.

purposes. Thoreau's lesson may be that the direct focus on the other, that Batson takes to be the distinguishing feature of altruism, renders altruism instrumental just as surely as any assistance afforded to another with ulterior, self-interested motive. The implication is that the focus on the other that is the literal meaning of altruism only makes sense in connection with the self-focus from which it derives. Serious altruism seems to be characterized by an involvement that is as oblivious to the otherness of the other as to the interests of the self. This does not mean that the direct evidence of altruism that Batson provides is not important. It could be a significant factor influencing the climate of expectation, so that the obviousness of self-interest is challenged and more scope is given for altruistic directions. That altruism can be encouraged and practiced in this deliberate manner, however, is not so obvious.

Evidence of altruism in a culture dominated by the promotion of self-interest provides reason to look for party hats. It is heartening to find assurance that we are not as selfish, or even as self-interested, as we have been led to believe. However, before the music gets too loud for us to hear one another, we would do well to reflect on just how adequate a deliberate focus on altruism really is. Thus, while we can take heart that social scientists are questioning the sole-sufficiency of the self-interest paradigm, and even finding evidence of the presence of altruism, perhaps there will be real cause for celebration only when we appreciate the sentiment of Dietrich Bonhoeffer, "too much altruism is a bore."[52]

[52] Dietrich Bonhoeffer, *Letters and Papers from Prison* (London: Collins, 1953), p. 96.

CHAPTER 3

The elusiveness of altruism

Empirical evidence of altruism discovered by the Batson researchers will not convince sociobiologists. Their initial reaction is apt to be that it is not altruism in the ordinary sense that they are concerned with, but altruism in the biological sense. It is not a matter of actions that reflect concern for others, but of actions that threaten the reproductive prospects of the actor, while enhancing the reproductive prospects of others. However, we have seen this concern escalate into a vendetta against all semblance of altruism. Clearly the ordinary sense is at stake. Part of what is involved is the nature of understanding itself. The biological is supposed to provide a factual description of the way life actually is. References to selfishness, or to selfish genes for that matter, are only metaphors drawn from the ordinary meaning of selfishness and altruism. They are not to be taken literally. What the literal reality is, or whether it makes sense even to think in such terms, is an issue that is not normally considered. However, this issue of the nature and role of metaphor is crucial for unraveling what is at stake in treatments of altruism.

THE METAPHORIC NATURE OF THE SELFISH GENE

The power of Dawkins' portrayal of the selfish gene is due in large measure to the skill with which he develops this metaphor. His "biography of the selfish gene"[1] represents a highly literate and imaginative account of reality. It is important to see that

---

[1] Richard Dawkins, *The Selfish Gene* (London: Granada, 1978).

this account owes as much to the force of the metaphor as to empirical evidence. Dawkins' claim is that in his portrayal of the selfish gene using the organisms it produces to replicate itself, he is speaking metaphorically. He does not mean to personify genes, or to attribute to them anything like deliberate agency. His subject is the biological mechanism which makes life possible. The portrayal of that mechanism in terms of genes operating like computer programmers is simply a vivid way of presenting this mechanism, employed purely for didactic purposes. Indeed, *The Selfish Gene* repeats the caution that it must be borne in mind that we are dealing with metaphors, and that if we want to be accurate we would have to transpose these metaphors into the impersonal scientific descriptions for which they are the shorthand expressions.[2]

The immediate difficulty with Dawkins' pledge that "we shall always keep a sceptical eye on our metaphors, to make sure they can be translated back into gene language if necessary,"[3] is that it is difficult to know what that literal gene language is. Critics complain that "sociobiologists' talk about single genes as controlling behavior, or about the effects of selection upon a single genetic variant in a population [is unwarranted because these] situations . . . simply do not square with biological reality."[4] Dawkins himself recognizes that "it is almost impossible to disentangle the contribution of one gene from that of another."[5] The legitimacy of this "almost" is even called in question by his own earlier admission: "It is not easy, indeed it may not even be meaningful, to decide where one gene ends and the next one begins."[6] In fact, it turns out that this bedrock reality behind the metaphor is really a definitional construct. "What I have done [Dawkins admits] is to define a gene as a unit which, to a high degree, *approaches* [his italics] the ideal of indivisible particulateness."[7] Dawkins suggests that "gene" might be equated with "cistron" as the minute component of

[2] Ibid., p. 48.   [3] Ibid.

[4] Arthur L. Caplan, "A Critical Examination of Current Sociobiological Theory: Adequacy and Implications," in *Sociobiology: Beyond Nature/Nurture?*, eds. George W. Barlow and James Silverberg (Boulder, Col.: Westview Press, 1980), p. 102.

[5] Dawkins, *The Selfish Gene*, p. 25.

[6] Ibid., p. 23.   [7] Ibid., p. 35.

chromosomes, but hesitates because even cistrons can be divided.[8] In the end, the best definition he can come up with is to equate the term "gene" with the most enduring segment of chromosomes, and this, he suggests, is the reality behind the metaphoric title. "To be strict, this book should be called not *The Selfish Cistron* nor *The Selfish Chromosome*, but *The Slightly Selfish Bit of Chromosome and the Even More Selfish Little Bit of Chromosome*."[9] Where that title might have been appropriate in the eighteenth century when books were given elaborate titles commensurate with the scope of their cosmological speculations, in this more parsimonious age a more compact designation is required. "To say the least this is not a catchy title so, defining a gene as a little bit of chromosome which potentially lasts for many generations, I call the book *The Selfish Gene*."[10] At any time this metaphor can be cashed in to yield this more prosaic, but more accurate, scientific description. The gene is that portion of chromosome which endures over generations, and the smaller the portion the more likely it is to endure,[11] so that the most successfully selfish genes would also be the most difficult to detect in themselves.

If we accept Dawkins' definition of the gene, and allow his claim that the way he talks about genes pursuing their own replication is but a shorthand way of articulating this more subtle reality, we still face a fundamental difficulty in his account. For even if the idea of distinct genes is intelligible, the emphasis on the selfishness of these genes, however metaphoric this may be, is at odds with genetic theory as described by Dawkins himself. For he recognizes that genes do not function in splendid isolation. "They cooperate and interact in inextricably complex ways, both with each other, and with the external environment."[12] This would seem to imply that the genes most likely to endure are not those that are characterized by ruthless selfishness, metaphorically speaking of course, but those that are able to cooperate with other genes. Yet although Dawkins recognizes this necessity for cooperation among genes, this fact receives only grudging recognition in his schemata. Rather than representing a characteristic of genes in any way compar-

[8] Ibid.   [9] Ibid.   [10] Ibid.   [11] Ibid., p. 30.   [12] Ibid., p. 39.

able to their selfishness, cooperation is, at most, a tactical requirement imposed by the circumstances in which the inherently selfish gene finds itself.

Our fundamental assumption must be that genes are "selfish" entities, working for their own propagation in the gene pool of the species. But because the environment of a gene consists, to such a salient degree, of other genes also being selected in the same gene pool, genes will be favored if they are good at cooperating with other genes in the same pool.[13]

In fact, as Dawkins goes on to explain, this is why bodies exist. Genes have found it advantageous to cooperate in the formation of bodies as vehicles for their own preservation. Obviously, we are still very much in the realm of metaphor. It is not that genes decided to cooperate to build bodies, but rather that those genes that have functioned in this way are the ones that have survived. But while the notion of cooperation is metaphoric, it is quite clear that the notion of selfishness is not. "Our fundamental assumption must be that genes *are* 'selfish'"[14] (emphasis added). Why? It is hardly intelligible to speak of distinct genes. Genes only function in conjunction with other genes. Why is selfishness the fundamental characteristic of genes, rather than cooperation? This insistence not only on the distinctiveness, but on the selfishness, of genes is not obvious even from the account of genetics supplied by Dawkins himself. The apparent lack of cash value for this side of the metaphor suggests that there is more at stake here than a popularization of the insights of genetic research.

The dual difficulty with Dawkins' metaphor of the selfish gene has been characterized bluntly by G. S. Stent in his contention that the selfish gene "is neither selfish in the context of morality, nor is it a gene in the context of genetics."[15] The ascription of selfishness entails applying this moral category where it is not really appropriate, in the sphere of genetics; but even in terms of that sphere, this isolationist approach to genes

---

[13] Richard Dawkins, *The Blind Watchmaker* (Harlow: Longman Scientific and Technical, 1986), p. 193.
[14] Ibid.
[15] G. Stent, "Preface," in *Morality as a Biological Phenomenon*, ed. G. S. Stent (Berkeley: University of California Press, 1981).

is contrary to the prevailing understanding of how genes operate. The definition of the gene itself comes perilously close to being "tautological and meaningless."[16] In fairness to sociobiologists, it must be recalled that the selfishness and altruism that is at stake is of the biological variety. It is not a matter of individual insects or animals deliberately shunning or assisting other individuals, much less of genes acting with deliberation and consciousness. The criterion is the biological one of reproduction, and so anything that enhances another's reproductive prospects to the detriment of one's own is not only the definition of altruism, but also entails the corollary that by definition altruism is bad. As Dawkins says: "At the gene level, altruism must be bad and selfishness good. This follows inexorably from our definitions of altruism and selfishness."[17] This biological version of altruism and selfishness makes sense in its own terms. If the point is to ensure replication, then what assures that is good and what detracts from it is bad, by definition. But this does not apply to the more conventional senses of those terms. We have seen that Dawkins acknowledges that even at the genetic level, genes must cooperate to achieve their purposes; and so in the conventional sense, the biologically selfish gene may actually act altruistically. This is even more evident at the level of the phenotype. Social insects, birds, wild animals, and human beings may all act altruistically, in the ordinary sense of the term, but this would only be altruism from the sociobiological point of view if it involved an enhancement of other genes than those possessed by the perpetrator of the purportedly altruistic action, and even then, this would only qualify as reciprocal altruism, altruism that anticipated a return payoff in the future. In other words, any form of altruism that is recognized at all must be identifiable in terms of the basic level of selfishness. If selfishness is a metaphor, it is clearly a very powerful one.

Selfishness is taken to characterize life at its deepest level. What is involved at this deepest level is everyday "selfishness," and not an impersonal biological mechanism. Mary Midgley

16 Mary Midgley, "Gene-Juggling," *Philosophy* 54 (1979): 451.
17 Dawkins, *The Selfish Gene*, p. 38.

points out how David Barash betrays this through his promise
to show how even parental behavior is selfish; for since the
sociobiological meaning of furthering our own genes is implicit
in all parental care, the negative connotation implied by Barash
indicates how it is the ordinary sense of "selfishness" that is
really at stake in sociobiology.[18] This involves special difficulties
for Dawkins' contention that his depiction of the "selfish gene"
is merely a metaphoric device, as Midgley notes elsewhere,
where she contends that far from representing a mere metaphoric expression to facilitate communication, the concept of
the selfish gene is of the essence of his position. His warnings
that this language is not to be taken seriously, she regards as
vacuous, if not ingenuous. "These disavowals do occur now and
then, but, like the *paternoster* of Mafia agents, they have no force
against his practice of habitually relying on the literal sense."[19]
This contention that the metaphor is the substance of the selfish
gene version would account for the tenacity with which
Dawkins clings to the concept of the selfish gene, despite his
own recognition of the difficulty in talking meaningfully about
single genes, much less selfish ones.

   The apparent lack of sensitivity to their reliance on metaphor, on the part of sociobiologists generally, might seem to
stand in stark contrast to the way in which Richard Dawkins
explicitly employs metaphor in his portrayal of the sociobiological agenda. Any consideration that this might undermine the
charge of metaphoric neglect will be quickly dispelled, however,
as soon as we recall that he employs metaphor as a didactic
device. The metaphor he is interested in is in speaking of genes
as though they were active agents, and conscious ones at that.
There is no suggestion that the use he makes of the economic
calculus, so central to his position, is at all a metaphoric
adaptation, or that information technology provides the voca-
bulary for his equally central understanding of the genetic code.
For Dawkins, metaphor is decidedly peripheral. It is a literary
device which makes it easier to communicate a message that is

---

[18] Mary Midgley, *Evolution as a Religion* (London and New York: Methuen, 1985),
   pp. 126f.
[19] Midgley, "Gene-Juggling," p. 447.

known independently of the metaphors employed, and which might more accurately, though less compellingly, be articulated in its own more prosaic form.

The irony of this understanding of metaphor is indicated in the treatment it receives from Kai Nielsen. While acknowledging that metaphor must not be treated in a cavalier fashion, Nielsen yet warns that "we must also not forget that genuine metaphor can – to use a metaphor myself – be cashed in; that is, to use another, they can in principle be redeemed in the sound currency of straightforward assertion."[20] As with Dawkins' "selfish gene," Nielsen's "cashing in" and "redeeming" are merely literary devices, as of course, is also the "sound currency" of assertion, which invites skepticism about whether such assertion is as straightforward as Nielsen suggests. The view of metaphor held by Nielsen and Dawkins presupposes a literal level of factual truth in relation to which metaphor represents a picturesque elaboration. When truth is at stake, these additional embellishments, otherwise useful for simplifying and enlivening communication, can be cut through to expose the literal substance that is at stake.

The implications of this understanding of metaphor can be seen most clearly when it is set beside the contrasting view which sees metaphor playing a much more foundational role. Quotations from the frontispiece of Warren A. Shibles' *Metaphor: An Annotated Bibliography and History*, regarded as the most comprehensive bibliography of metaphor available, not only illustrate the intrinsic importance that metaphor is seen to have by many people, but also the diverse perspectives from which that respect for metaphor comes.

"Both philosophers and poets live by metaphor," S. Pepper; "All thinking is metaphorical," R. Frost; "The history of philosophy should be written as that of seven or eight metaphors," T. Hulme; "The most profound social creativity consists in the invention and imposition of new, radical metaphors," R. Kaufman; "Something like a paradigm is prerequisite to perception itself. . . . paradigms prove to be constitutive of the research activity," T. Kuhn; "All our truth, or all

---

[20] Kai Nielsen, *God, Scepticism and Modernity* (Ottawa: University of Ottawa Press, 1989), p. 75.

but a few fragments, is won by metaphor," C. S. Lewis; "To know is merely to work with one's favorite metaphors," F. Nietzsche; "The conduct of even the plainest, most 'direct" untechnical prose is a ceaseless exercise in metaphor," I. A. Richards.[21]

The fundamental difference between this substantive view of metaphor and the ancillary view espoused by Dawkins and Nielsen is that on this view, metaphor has epistemological, and not simply linguistic, significance. Or more radically, the inadequacy of the Dawkins–Nielsen view could be seen to involve a faulty sense of the nature and significance of language itself. It is not just that metaphor is not merely a decorative or didactic device, available to enliven the articulation of more directly known truths, but that truth itself, its apprehension as well as its articulation, is inextricably linguistic.

These different views of metaphor thus fan out to disclose different underlying understandings of language in general, of the processes of human knowledge and understanding, and, by implication, of ourselves. The Dawkins–Nielsen optional indulgence in metaphor entails a sense of ourselves as commanding subjects presiding over a world of disposable objects. The depth of that self-understanding for Dawkins is indicated by the fact that in the end it even displaces the otherwise omnipotent power of the selfish gene. "We have the power to defy the selfish genes of our birth,"[22] he assures us. For some, this final-chapter reversal renders Dawkins' sociobiological agenda palatable. It does not include us after all. The distinctiveness of the human is recognized, and we are spared the ignominy of having to understand ourselves as simply a further link in the ongoing chain of genetic determinism. On reflection, however, we might conclude that this rescue of the human is achieved at a very high price, since for Dawkins himself, it seems to constitute a repudiation of his fundamental position. His opening paean to Darwin credited him with discovering "the ultimate rationale for our existence."[23] In claiming the power to defy our selfish

[21] Warren A. Shibles, *Metaphor: An Annotated Bibliography and History* (Whitewater, Wis.: Language Press, 1971), cited in Sallie McFague, *Metaphorical Theology: Models of God in Religious Language* (London: SCM Press, 1983), p. 201, n. 2.
[22] Dawkins, *The Selfish Gene*, p. 215.   [23] Ibid., p. 21.

genes, Dawkins is thus defying "the ultimate rationale for our existence." The abrupt and defiant summons to willful action is so astounding in light of the uncompromising insistence that we are totally at the mercy of formative biological genes, and now suddenly also of cultural memes, that we are apt not to notice how this apparently arbitrary about-face is not as radical as it is bound to appear. For the call to defiance and self-assertion is an expression of the same vision that underlies the saga of the selfish gene. The guiding vision is the metaphor of self-interest that has informed and formed our modern mentality and institutions.

The wider consistency in Dawkins' position, despite the appearance of outright contradiction in his closing summons to defy the selfish genes that supposedly have us at their disposal, is indicative finally of the range of the metaphor with which he operates. Far from being a dispensable device to aid communication, it represents a formative vision that shapes his fundamental understanding of life. The root metaphor is not the selfish gene, but selfishness as such. The call to defy our selfish genes is a call for us to assert ourselves, and as such, remains completely within the self-centered perspective that has characterized modern thought since Descartes and modern institutions since the emergence of free-for-all economics. In the articulation of this living metaphor, Dawkins is entirely consistent.

Recognition of the depth and influence of this formative perspective has implications for our understanding of metaphor. It suggests that not only is metaphor not simply a didactic device that can be picked up to facilitate communication, neither is it adequately understood as an intellectual category that can aid in comprehension. As the determinative horizon that shapes our understanding and communication, metaphor is ultimately a living reality rather than an academic one. The academic treatment of metaphor inevitably leaves us confronting a cold laboratory specimen. Metaphor will appear as the juxtaposing of otherwise disparate elements; we think of a gene as though it were a person; we look at biological phenomena through categories drawn from the sphere of economics. But the self-consciousness of this academic perspective is not present in the direct employment of metaphor. When it is actually in use, metaphor itself is not noticed. It is in this direct employment that metaphor functions as the vehicle of perception and understanding. As a result, it either recedes behind its own familiarity, in which case it functions as the dead metaphor of cliché, or else it becomes transparent, opening up aspects of reality that would otherwise remain inaccessible. This is ultimately what is at stake in the metaphor of the selfish gene. This literary metaphor that Dawkins finds so convenient as a communications tool really reflects the much more pervasive vision of living metaphor which is not at his disposal, one crucial feature of which is the pervasive assumption that selfishness is the cardinal fact of life.

The formative influence of this vision of endemic selfishness has been articulated forcefully by Mary Midgley in her charge that sociobiologists generally, and Dawkins in particular, are obsessed with selfishness.[24] Her remedy for this obsession, however, seems to belie recognition of the depth and influence of this most pervasive sense of metaphor. Her solution amounts to the proposal that the metaphor be pruned down to the level of a scientific model. She sees this as having happened with natural selection itself, where the suggestion of an agent of selection has been eradicated in the interests of recognizing a purely natural process. The parallel with the selfish gene would involve the elimination of the notion of active agency and the more careful depiction of the process in terms of genetic mutations and their survival in relation to the processes of nature that are designated as natural selection. Whether scientific models can be so completely extracted from this comprehensive type of metaphor, however, is open to question. The concept of natural selection plagued Darwin throughout his career,[25] and the connotation of agency continues to cling to the term itself. What is selection without a selector? What is natural selection, if not the personification of nature as a surrogate God? The reference to nature might suggest a more

---

[24] Midgley, "Gene-Juggling," p. 444.
[25] Robert A. Young, "Darwin's Metaphor: Does Nature Select?" *The Monist* 55 (1971): 461–6, 471–3, 481, 484.

immediate, and less transcendent form of agency, but is it not agency nevertheless? "Society and science have been so steeped in the ideas of mechanism, utilitarianism, and the economic concept of free competition, that instead of God, selection was enthroned as ultimate reality."[26] Darwin himself wished that he had spoken of natural preservation, rather than natural selection,[27] but while this might have been more accurate scientifically, it almost certainly would have deprived his theory of the comprehensive sense that caught the popular imagination. To say that those mutations that are best adapted to natural conditions are the ones that tend to be preserved would seem to be little more than the truism that evolutionary theory is sometimes accused of being, and to lack any kind of significant explanatory power.

The resistance of Dawkins' metaphor of endemic selfishness to reduction to an inoffensive scientific model is illustrated in his treatment of DNA. "If we wish to speak teleologically, all adaptations are for the preservation of DNA; DNA itself just *is*."[28] This foundational function of DNA is even presented in opposition to the claims that have been made by theology. "To explain the origin of the DNA/protein machine by invoking the supernatural Designer is to explain precisely nothing, for it leaves unexplained the origin of the designer."[29] It would be understandable if Dawkins said that to explain the origin of DNA by referring to God is useless as a scientific explanation, since such an explanation would not tell us anything about how DNA came to be. But to object to using God as an ultimate explanation on the grounds that God still requires explanation is poor theology. It makes sense to reject the concept of God as unintelligible or to say that, though intelligible, the evidence for belief in God is inadequate or that the counterevidence is overwhelming, but to expect an explanation for God is to

---

[26] L. von Bertalanffy, "Chance or Law," in *Beyond Reduction*, ed. A. Koestler (London: Hutchinson, 1969), p. 11.

[27] Young, "Darwin's Metaphor," p. 465.

[28] Richard Dawkins, "Replicators and Vehicles," in *Current Problems in Sociobiology*, ed. King's College Sociobiology Group, Cambridge (Cambridge: Cambridge University Press, 1982), p. 45.

[29] Dawkins, *The Blind Watchmaker*, p. 141.

betray a lack of awareness of what "God" means. However, if Dawkins is not as sophisticated as he might be about the logic of theology, he is by no means devoid of theological affirmation, or at least of affirmations of theological proportion. For while he would require an explanation for God, no such justification is demanded of DNA. "DNA itself just *is*."

In spite of this absolute faith in DNA as the bedrock of reality, Dawkins recognizes that it really does not have the ultimacy that believers affirm of God. It is not finally self-explanatory. In a curious sense, DNA almost seems to presuppose itself, giving rise to the question of how it could ever have originated in the first place. "Cumulative selection cannot work unless there is some minimal machinery of replication and replicatory power, and the only machinery of replication that we know seems too complicated to have come into existence by means of anything less than many generations of cumulative selection."[30] To invoke God as explanation would not be particularly helpful, from a scientific point of view. But Dawkins' alternative is hardly any better. "At some point a particularly remarkable molecule was formed by accident. We call it the replicator."[31] Nor is this recourse to sheer accident made any more credible by his appeal to the scientific apparatus of statistical probability. His own description of this betrays the note of desperation. "A miracle is translated into practical politics by a multiplication sum."[32]

The miracle of the emergence of life is rendered probable by expanding the range of time and space in which life has emerged to a point where it is seen to be statistically feasible. Fossil records suggest that organic life has existed on earth from within a billion years of its origin 4.5 billion years ago, and so the self-replicating molecule has to have emerged within that billion-year period. Dawkins concedes that chemists cannot say how long it would take for a self-replicating molecule to appear. Yet even if chemists said it would take a billion billion years, so that this would seem to rule out the possibility of life emerging on this planet, we can get around this difficulty if we assume

---

[30] Ibid.   [31] Dawkins, *The Selfish Gene*, p. 16.
[32] Dawkins, *The Blind Watchmaker*, p. 145.

that earth is the only planet on which life has emerged and that there are enough planets in the universe to match the odds required for the billion-billion-year period. This is Dawkins' "scientific" alternative to theological explanation: accident, portrayed as probability, underwritten by postulating the number of planets required to meet what are purely speculative odds to begin with.

Indulgence in such desperate circularity is indicative of the depth and tenacity of the vision out of which Dawkins is operating. Even the arbitrariness of calculating the size of the universe to match the totally arbitrary postulation of the length of time required for the emergence of a self-replicating molecule is preferable to the consideration of the possibility that life might finally be due to a super-human intelligence. Such an acknowledgment would not explain how self-replicating molecules emerged. That remains for science to determine. But to insist that it happened by accident is not a scientific position. It is an articulation of a controlling vision of life, of a living metaphor which is so fixated on self that it cannot acknowledge any more comprehensive reality than ourselves. This is why it is entirely consistent for Dawkins to begin *The Selfish Gene* by insisting that genes are God, that they constitute the foundational and determinative reality for which we serve merely as replicating vehicles, and to conclude the same book by assuring us that we are really in control, and can defy these selfish genes. The whole procedure is grounded in the anthropocentric vision of the modern west.

So profound and pervasive is that vision that it can only be recognized from the vantage point of some other pervasive perspective. Such a vantage point is provided by the sensitivity of classical philosophy and of major religious traditions. Those of us who remain captivated by something of these more venerable visions find ourselves torn between their elevated expanse and the self-conscious anthropocentrism of our own age. There is no question of renouncing this modern view and returning to more direct cosmological perspectives. But neither can we acquiesce in the simplistic assumption of our own centrality. The future of the earth itself might well depend upon our resolution of this ambivalence, and particularly upon our escape from the total domination of the scientifically endorsed and commercially disseminated dogma of the ultimacy of self. There is no shortage of evidence that our literal fate hangs on the future of this reigning metaphor. But then this forecast itself is finally metaphoric, a confession from within the midst of life that lacks the precision and self-assurance demanded by those who seek to live entirely out of that metaphor.

THE METAPHORIC NATURE OF ALTRUISM

As the depiction of biological processes in selfish terms is a metaphoric activity, so too is the depiction of altruism. As the metaphoric depiction of selfishness in sociobiology involves a very definite understanding of reality, so too do metaphoric depictions of altruism. Our conclusion and working assumption is that metaphor and reality are by no means contrasts. Far from metaphor representing a playful or didactic way of dealing with a reality known in more direct and precise ways, metaphor reflects our basic sense of reality. If we depict basic biological processes in terms of selfishness, this is because we believe that reality is basically selfish. If altruism is to have any place in such a perspective, it will only be against this very formidable natural bias against it. Recognition of the metaphoric nature of the selfishness reading does not automatically pave the way for an alternative altruistic reading. Appreciation of the possibility and prospects for altruism faces formidable obstacles of its own. However, loosening the grip of total reverence for the selfishness metaphor at least opens the way for the exploration of these obstacles.

That our grip on reality is finally metaphoric, reflecting the possibilities of language and the peculiarities of vision that defy direct, confirmable, contact with reality, does not mean that the way that metaphors represent reality cannot be explored. In essence, such exploration is what we have attempted in terms of the metaphor of selfishness favored by sociobiology. A similar exploration is possible in terms of the metaphor of altruism. We have seen that the metaphor of selfishness allows grudging scope, at best, for serious altruism. When we approach the issue from the other side, from the perspective of altruism, this assumption of the ubiquity of selfishness appears as but one of several basic options in understanding how self-interest and altruism may be seen to relate.

The self-interest metaphor, favored by sociobiology and assumed in the social sciences generally, sees altruism and self-interest relating in terms of contrast. Altruism is a fringe phenomenon, qualifying a way of life that is characterized essentially by selfishness. The more neutral designation would be self-interest. It may be that Dawkins chose the term self-ishness because of its retail value. A book portraying *The Self-Interested Gene* could hardly be expected to catch the imagination like one depicting *The Selfish Gene.* The metaphoric reference carries overtones of moral evaluation that invite interest in these nasty bits of biological matter that might not be evoked by the self-interest designation. Although this represents a further illustration of the intrinsic connotations of selected metaphors, let us concede that what is at stake is not so much selfishness as self-interest. Even if reference to selfishness is taken to reflect moralistic hyperbole, we have seen that self-interest has the appearance of being a neutral description of the basic human condition only because of the dominance of that vision effected by the hegemony of modern economic priorities. That self-interest, much less selfishness, represents an accurate depiction of "the state of nature" is becoming increasingly questionable: "there is now very strong evidence that Darwin's account of the mechanics of evolution in terms of the struggle for 'survival of the fittest' is profoundly mistaken – *cooperation* between proto-plasm (cells) plant life and animals, is the means of survival in nature."[33]

Although the reality of cooperation is acknowledged even by people like Dawkins, it cannot be taken seriously, so long as the self-interest vision remains the normative default perspective. On this approach, altruism can only stand in contrast to self-

---

[33] Ninian Smart and Steven Konstantine, *Christian Systematic Theology in a World Context* (Minneapolis: Fortress, 1991), p. 313.

interest. It can at best represent a concession to the foundational and pervasive reality of self-interest at all levels of life.
The more likely result, however, is to regard altruism as
Dawkins depicts it, as a strategy for suckers. This result is
confirmed by the proposal of social scientist Herbert A. Simon,
that activities that aid others are so foreign to the foundational
predilection to self-interest that they can only be attributed to
docility and stupidity.[34] Further evidence of the seriousness of
metaphoric designations! In the spirit, if not of the school, of
Nietzsche, any action that could be construed as altruistic in
any form can only be a reflection of lack of initiative on the part
of that individual or of failure to appreciate the biological
mandate to look out for number one. Still, the biological
mandate does not depend on our awareness of it. It is innate.
Simon acknowledges this with the consideration that the docile
serve the evolutionary process, and that is why they continue to
reemerge in a population where the general rule is that the
fittest survive and the weak disappear.

If biological evidence is seen to challenge this dominant
biological ideology, there may be some hope for relief from the
hegemony of the self-interest assumption. Such evidence has
been marginalized in sociobiology, however, because the commitment to self-interest extends beyond evidence to basic
vision. That this is the case is indicated not only by the
persistent attachment to self-interest in practice, but also in the
failure to consider the untenability of absolute self-interest from
a rational point of view. The point is made by Jane Mansbridge,
in reference to the rational choice version of this assumption in
economics and politics: "the claim that self-interest alone
motivates political behavior must be either vacuous, if self-
interest can encompass any motive, or false, as self-interest
means behavior that consciously intends only self as the benefactor."[35] Such a totally one-sided stance is illogical, as well as
conflicting with the more complex and ambiguous empirical

[34] John Horgan, "In the Beginning. . .," *Scientific American* 264 (March 1991): 20.
[35] Jane J. Mansbridge, "The Rise and Fall of Self-Interest in the Explanation of Political
    Life," in *Beyond Self-Interest*, ed. Jane J. Mansbridge (Chicago: University of Chicago
    Press, 1990), p. 20.

evidence of a mix of self-interest and altruism in human motivation and in the operations of biological processes generally.

If self-interest is not as pervasive and unavoidable as academic portrayals of humanity have been inclined to suggest, why is it, we might be inclined to ask, that evidence of altruistic-type behavior is not more apparent? Daily events and our own inclinations tend to confirm the self-interest hypothesis. Even the evidence of altruistic behavior detected in the Batson experiments was subject to definite limitations. Two replies may be made to this consideration. One is that to call for recognition of altruism does not have to be taken to mean that the goal is to displace the self-interest assumption with an altruistic one. Recognition of altruism does not require abandoning the legitimacy and truth of the self-interest perspective. Human history and our own experience will almost certainly incline us to find such a move romantic and naive. Self-interest represents an accurate depiction of human beings in particular. The point is that this depiction has been accorded such veneration that it has distorted our understanding of ourselves, and of our own possibilities, by precluding any significant recognition of contrary dimensions, such as the presence of altruism, which is also attested in human behavior, and indeed among other life forms as well. Mention of the obscuring of our possibilities leads to the other reply to this concern with lack of evidence of altruism. As Jerome Wakefield suggests, altruism may be natural without being inevitable. "Altruistic motivation is easily overridden, is in keen competition with other goals, is extremely fragile, and has not of late been socially nurtured."[36] Rather than being struck by the lack of evidence of altruism today, we might be amazed that there is so much altruistic behavior still evident in a commercial culture that systematically promotes self-interest, with the reinforcement of an academic culture that assumes and proclaims this vision as scientific fact.

If the hegemony of the self-interest vision is penetrated, and a place is found for altruism along with self-interest, this will require a corresponding understanding of how the two are seen

[36] Jerome C. Wakefield, "Is Altruism Part of Human Nature?" *Social Service Review* 67/3 (Sept. 1993): 454.

to relate. If the relation is not one of all or nothing contrast, how is it to be conceived? A second way of thinking of self-interest and altruism relating, beyond sheer contrast, is as complementary. Self-interest and altruism, then, represent two mutually supportive approaches to life. The balance between the two does not have to be at all equal. It may well be that life is characterized far more by self-interest than it is by altruism, but the altruism is there. In fact, on reflection, we might ask if we could characterize life in terms of self-interest, without assuming something like altruism, against which it is understood. "It has been suggested to me by R. P. Foot that only those of one's acts which are somehow related to the wants or interests of others can correctly be called either selfish or unselfish,"[37] Michael Slote informs us. Self-interest might be possible if we were all isolated selves, but even then, it would be difficult to imagine how it could be characterized as such. The basic meaning of self depends on the presence of another, if not others. The characterization of selfishness only makes sense when the wants and interests of others are at stake as well as one's own.

A similar analysis could be made of altruism. We have seen that, historically, the word was coined by Auguste Comte, against the background of the identification of interests that had marked the transition to the modern outlook. Comte hoped to temper the worst excesses of this direction by the promotion of common interests and goals, achieving a state of social harmony, in contrast to the ecclesiastical and military conflict that had characterized the past. Altruism might appear to have more credibility on its own than naked self-interest. The reality of other selves is implicit in its terms of reference. However, this collective credibility of the notion of altruism depends on the contrasting presence of precisely these other selves. Thus altruism is no more intelligible, apart from the assumption of individuals with their own interests and wants, than self-interest or selfishness is apart from the assumption of the reality and claim of other selves with their own interests and wants. Self-

---

[37] Michael A. Slote, "An Empirical Basis for Psychological Egoism," *The Journal of Philosophy* 61/18 (1964): 531, n. 2.

interest and altruism, then, can be seen to represent a complementary relationship, in which each needs the other in order to
be intelligible and credible.

Complementarity offers an inviting way to think of the
relation between self-interest and altruism. They are two sides
of a more comprehensive reality that characterizes human life,
and probably all life. Behavior at all levels of complexity may be
identifiable, at least in principle, somewhere on the spectrum
between self-interest and altruism. Rather than being contrasting and mutually exclusive possibilities, altruism and self-
interest represent extremes on a continuum, along which all
meaningful activity finds its place, however difficult it may be to
specify that place in any particular instance. This solution of
complementarity is particularly attractive at the academic
distance from which issues of self-interest and altruism are
usually considered. In the activities of living, however, the
neatness of this solution might be its biggest liability. Self-
interest and altruism may be most significant not as designations of a connecting spectrum, but as competing and mutually
challenging possibilities. The relation of self-interest and altruism, then, would be one not of contrast or of complementarity,
but of conflict.

The hegemony of the self-interest assumption means that
advocates of the importance of altruism face a struggle to get
their position recognized. Although it is not likely, it is concei-
vable that they might be too successful, so that a case would
then have to be made for the importance of recognizing the
legitimacy of self-interest. Although humanity, and nature in
general, have been seen to be characterized by a primary self-
interest, there is an equally strong bias in the other direction,
when it comes to ideals about how life should be. Recall that
even Dawkins, who sees life to be characterized by selfishness at
its most fundamental level, also calls for a revolution against
our selfish genes, and for the promotion of life characterized by
altruism. The assumption that life is inherently selfish is
matched by the equally entrenched assumption that life at its
best would be altruistic. Here again, however, reflection suggests that selfishness and altruism cannot be related as real and

ideal ends of a common spectrum. Just as self-interest and
altruism feed off each other on the rational level, in order to be
intelligible concepts, so too the contrast they represent continues across the barrier between the real and the ideal. Just as
life is not characterized by unmitigated selfishness, with no
trace of genuine altruism, so too the prospect of a life characterized by total altruism is not necessarily the most ideal conceiv-
able state. Neil Cooper illustrates the dilemma of the altruistic
extreme with the story of the two altruists in the desert who pass
a cup of water back and forth between them, each insisting that
the other drink, until the water evaporates, and both die of
thirst.[38] Not only can altruism be boring, as Bonhoeffer reminded us; it can be deadly. Realism demands some scope for
self-interest in life at its best, as well as for altruism in life as we
normally live it out of our very real proclivity for looking out for
ourselves.

The reality behind the metaphor of altruism is clearly a
complex one. It is not an alternative to self-interest, to be
promoted in its own right in reaction against its exclusion
through the hegemony of the self-interest assumption. Altruism
and self-interest do not relate by direct contrast. The attraction
of a relation of complementarity, in recognizing a role for each
on a common spectrum, is suspect precisely because of its
neatness. The clash and commonality of altruism and self-
interest suggest that the most productive way of envisioning the
ongoing relation between them is in terms of conflict. However,
the realism of that approach also involves recognizing that
altruism and self-interest meet and clash in complex ways,
crossing over prominent barriers such as those between the way
things are and the way things should be. The implication of this
may be that the very notion of altruism, the metaphor itself,
may be characterized by intrinsic paradoxes.

The inherent paradoxes of altruism are hinted at by pioneer
sociobiologist, Edward O. Wilson. "We sanctify true altruism in
order to reward it – and thus make it less true – and by that
means to promote its recurrence in others. Human altruism, in

---

[38] Neil Cooper, *The Diversity of Moral Thinking* (Oxford: Clarendon Press, 1981), p. 274.

short, is riddled to its foundations with mammalian ambivalence."[39] If anything, Wilson's identification may not be strong enough. There are reasons to think that the ambiguity is intrinsic and inescapable. This is seen most clearly by considering three basic paradoxes that appear to be inherent in the fundamental notion of altruism.

At its most basic level, altruism involves the hedonic paradox. In this instance, the reference is not to the usual designation of this phrase. Hedonic paradox generally refers to the resistance of happiness to our direct attempts to grasp it, but what is intended by the present use of this hedonic paradox designation is more direct and virtually tautological. In this usage, hedonic paradox refers to the truism that any pleasure we experience is our own pleasure. Thus no matter how much our focus may be on the other, on their welfare or pleasure, that focus itself will bring satisfaction to us.

This version of the hedonic paradox guarantees that there cannot be such a thing as pure altruism. The most intense concern for another is our concern, and thus compromises total alterity with a reminder of our own interests and concerns. Yet this recognition by no means dispenses with altruism. This result could only be accepted by a thorough embracing of the stance of psychological hedonism. This would amount to the claim that there can be nothing but our own pleasure. But, as Ronald Milo points out: "If this is one's ground for asserting that all actions are egoistic, self-interested, or motivated by self-love [i.e. 'that the pleasure arising from the motivation of any particular desire is always *one's own pleasure*'], then one has purchased evidence for one's thesis at the cost of trivializing it."[40] To make one's own pleasure absolute is to define altruism out of existence. However, as we saw, self-interest is unintelligible apart from the contrast represented by altruism.

The unavoidability of the reference to self indicated by the hedonic paradox and real scope for genuine altruism can both be acknowledged by making a distinction between motivation

---

[39] Edward O. Wilson, "Altruism," *Harvard Magazine* (Nov.–Dec. 1978): 23.
[40] Ronald D. Milo, *Egoism and Altruism* (Belmont, Cal.: Wadsworth, 1973), "Introduction," p. 13.

and object. What I want must be taken into account, as well as
the fact that it is I who is wanting. I can want something for
someone else as well as myself. The fact that I take satisfaction
from someone else having their wants realized is different from
simply taking satisfaction in my own wants. "To take satisfaction from helping someone is hardly acting selfishly,"[41] as
Rodger Beehler points out. Altruism has to do with the object of
my motivation, beyond the psychological truism that it is my
motivation. Thus, as a total position, psychological egoism must
absolutize the subjective side of the psychology of motivation,
as well as defying the requisite contrast with altruism in taking
self-interest to be tautologically true.

Although the challenge of the hedonic paradox by no means
dispenses with altruism, it does constitute a reminder of the
realities of self-interest amid which altruism must take place.
Furthermore, it also has a negative variation. We recall that the
claim of the Batson team to have discovered evidence of
altruistic behavior evoked the "empathetic distress hypothesis."
It was not really altruism that was discovered, critics charged,
but attempts on the part of the putative altruists to avoid the
distress evoked by watching the subject of the experiments
suffer. Jerome C. Wakefield presents this as a further paradox,
the "empathy paradox."[42] However, in light of wider paradoxes
we have yet to identify, it is more suitable for us to classify it as a
reverse version of the hedonic paradox. Rather than taking
pleasure in our own altruism, our altruism may be a way of
avoiding displeasure. The parallel with the hedonic paradox is
further maintained in terms of resolution. Here too the answer
lies in a distinction between object and motivation. For genuine
altruism, the basic concern is for the other, and this is the
source of the distress. Any feeling of discomfort is prompted by
this concern, rather than being the source of it. Such is the
defence that could be made of the independence and integrity
of altruism.

The hedonic paradox is not fatal for altruism, but it is
persistent. While the reality of altruism can be defended against

---

[41] Rodger Beehler, *Moral Life* (Oxford: Basil Blackwell, 1978), p. 134.
[42] Wakefield, "Is Altruism Part of Human Nature?" p. 438.

any totalitarian dismissal that a consistent psychological egoism might involve, the specter of the hedonic paradox ever looms on the horizon. Any act or person that clearly appears to represent altruism can be seen to reflect self-serving interests. As we have seen, even Mother Teresa has not escaped this strategy: "it is surely possible (indeed, *likely*) that Mother Teresa is so constituted that she knows she will get pleasure from helping other people; she knows that she will suffer psychologically from ignoring the plight of others; and she believes that she will experience all the rewards of an afterlife, a belief that itself, no doubt, produces still more pleasure."[43] Richard Fumerton also acknowledges that defenders of the genuineness of altruism can make a similar case from the other side. We have seen reasons to conclude that such a total exclusion of altruism is not only ideologically suspect, but rationally unintelligible.

Beyond the hedonic paradox, in its various ramifications, altruism must also contend with what might be called the moral paradox. Insofar as altruism is a reality, it cannot constitute an ideal to be realized; conversely, insofar as altruism represents an ideal to be realized, it cannot be a present reality. Some of the confusion over altruism is due simply to failure to distinguish between the issue of how far altruism is a reality and how far it might be a reality. The Batson researchers claimed to be showing that there is empirical evidence of altruism. Under laboratory conditions, it is shown that people do act out of concern for another person. Further experiments attempted to eliminate other possible explanations for the behavior. Such evidence addresses what purports to be an empirical generalization in sociobiology, claiming that nature is driven by self-interest, and that what appears to be altruism is subject to more correct interpretation in terms of self-interest. The Batson evidence is not likely to convince someone coming from the sociobiology stance for two reasons. Their first response is apt to be that they are not concerned with altruism in the ordinary sense of doing something to help someone else; their concern is altruism in the biological sense of risking one's reproductive

---

[43] Richard A. Fumerton, *Reason and Morality: A Defense of the Egocentric Perspective* (Ithaca and London: Cornell University Press, 1990), p. 160.

prospects to the enhancement of the reproductive advantage of someone else. This is the issue of the metaphoric nature of the reference to altruism. We have seen that the division is not sustainable both because sociobiologists attack altruism in the ordinary sense, and by no means confine themselves to a biological reproductive focus, and because metaphor, far from being a decorative addition or didactic device, is our avenue to reality. No amount of empirical evidence would convince the hardline sociobiologist of the reality of altruism, because their position is not an empirical one. The self-interest vision, with its allowance only for kin and reciprocal altruism, is a comprehensive paradigm that processes all empirical evidence in its own terms. In dealing with putatively empirical treatments of altruism, it is important to make the distinction between altruism as fact and as possibility because it is often the case that what purports to be a factual position is really ruling out altruism *a priori* as intrinsically impossible.

Sociobiologists tend to be committed to the anti-altruistic vision as an account of the way life is. They divide, however, on the prospects and value of altruism as a way that life might be. Some follow Herbert Spencer in the direct derivation of social Darwinism from the supposedly empirical Darwinian picture. The struggle for survival is not only the way life is, but the only way it can be. The rational approach is to accept that and to allow the dominant to have their way. Others, like Dawkins, operating from the same supposedly empirical base, call for rebellion against this direction. Humanity has been programmed genetically, like the rest of nature, to seek dominance at the expense of others; however, now that we recognize that, we can change this direction. We can, for the first time in history, Dawkins suggests, promote altruism as a genuine possibility. We can rebel against our selfish genes, and construct a society of compassion and caring.

Here again the distinction between altruism as fact and as possibility is crucial. One view equates the two, concluding that because life is supposedly inherently selfish by nature, this is the only possibility, while the other implies a fundamental separation, finding possibilities that are directly contrary to the way we are supposedly constituted by nature. What is at stake here is not simply the importance of the distinction between what is the case and what may be possible, but the question of how the two are to be related. Is possibility directly dependent on actuality, or is there such a gap between the two so that total novelty is possible? Sociobiology offers both extremes.

What is at stake here is not long-standing philosophical questions about the respective priorities and significance of possibility and actuality. That ancient puzzle about the source and scope for novelty has more immediate practical significance when the possibility side is seen to involve a dimension of obligation. It is not just that some things might be the case; there is a sense that they ought to be. Altruism does not loom on the horizon as a possibility, but in some sense as an obligation. Indeed, some of the most prominent modern treatments of morality almost amount to equating morality with altruism. In spite of different views of how it is to be understood and practiced, morality is often seen as a matter of our responsibility to others. For some this responsibility exists precisely because our inclinations are so naturally in the opposite direction. Morality is the check on our own interests represented by the claims of others. For other modern ethicists, the responsibility is a more natural expression of our inherent interconnection with others through social arrangements as well as through the intrinsically social nature of our being. These different approaches not only reflect a fundamental division that runs through modern ethics; they also reflect different answers to an issue that has been central for the whole ethical enterprise in the modern era. What is at stake in the difference between Spencer and Dawkins is not only a matter of how far possibility is tied to or can be separated from actuality, but the question of how facts and values relate. Spencer reflects the older tendency to equate the two, or at least to see them as closely related. The possibilities for life were given; to ignore natural indicators was to invite disaster. Dawkins reflects the tendency that has grown over the past century or so in particular to assume a fundamental gulf between fact and value. Whatever is the case, or has been the case up to now, represents no barrier or restriction to

what might be done in the future. What we would like, what we
value, is essentially independent of what is the case, or what the
facts are.

It is surely one of the amazing anomalies of the modern era
that obsessive pursuit of factuality should have resulted in such
an arbitrary treatment of value. Although it was crucially
important to establish the facts, these facts had no essential
connection with matters of value. Because facts had to be totally
objective, values ended up being essentially subjective. The
issue was posed most directly in the realm of moral values in
terms of the relation between is and ought. In this realm, the
fact–value dichotomy became the argument that ought cannot
be derived from is. The rationale and motivation of morality
must be moral, a matter of ought, and so, as Hume suggested,
fundamentally different from affirmation of what is the case, or
distinctively and independently authoritative in its moral
demand, as Kant held. What is at stake in these most central
versions of modern ethics is illustrated, and possibly illumi-
nated, in the issue of altruism. From this perspective, modern
ethics can be seen as attempts to deal with this moral paradox
of altruism, with how altruism as reality and altruism as ideal
are seen to relate.

The hedonic paradox, that all pleasure, even the pleasure of
altruism, is our pleasure, and the moral paradox, that altruism
as reality makes altruism as ideal unnecessary, while altruism as
ideal implies the unreality of altruism, are both overshadowed
by a third dilemma intrinsic to altruism that we might call the
religion paradox. This paradox brings out central dimensions of
the other paradoxes. The religion paradox is essentially the
paradox of self-consciousness in its starkest form. It is not just
that pleasure in altruism is my pleasure, or that the prospects
for altruism depend on how I seen altruism as ideal and real,
but that acknowledgment of altruistic action is a no-win situation. What is involved may be indicated as an intensification of
the problems represented by the hedonic paradox and the
moral paradox of altruism. The frustrations pointed to by the
paradox of hedonism might open up the moral point of view,
where we see our own happiness tied somehow with the

happiness of others.[44] As we have seen, recognition of the other is often equated with the moral. John Macmurray distinguished between "enjoying the other and enjoying ourselves through the instrumentality of the other."[45] In enjoying ourselves through the other, we remain centered in ourselves, using the other for our purposes. The move from the hedonic to the moral perspective involves taking the other seriously in his or her own right. Susan Wolf designates such an orientation a "necessary condition of moral sainthood." "A necessary condition of moral sainthood would be that one's life be dominated by a commitment to improve the welfare of others or of society as a whole."[46] "Humility and selflessness, we know, are the very center of the moral life,"[47] Ronald M. Green contends. The problem is, that far from leaving the hedonic paradox behind, the move into the moral creates new paradoxes, as well as making the hedonic one more acute. The hedonic paradox remains, as we have seen, in the fact that any pleasure we take in caring about others is our own pleasure, and to this is added the moral paradox of relating how we are and ought to be concerned for others. Within these paradoxes there lies the further dimension, exposed by the frustrations of the moral outlook, the religious paradox of living from beyond ourselves.

The limitations of morality begin to be recognized when the superiority of the focus on the other becomes less satisfying, as we become self-conscious about morality, and ask if it is truly moral if we are so satisfied with ourselves because we are focused on others rather than on ourselves. "Good can exist," Hannah Arendt insists, "only when it is not perceived, not even by its author; whoever sees himself performing a good work is no longer good; but at best a useful member of society or a dutiful member of a church."[48] Since altruism is so readily

---

[44] Peter Singer, *Practical Ethics* (Cambridge: Cambridge University Press, 1979), pp. 217–19.

[45] John Macmurray, *Reason and Emotion* (London: Faber and Faber, 1966), pp. 141–2.

[46] Susan Wolf, "Moral Saints," *Journal of Philosophy* 79/8 (1982): 420.

[47] Ronald M. Green, *Religious Reason: The Rational and Moral Basis of Religious Belief* (New York: Oxford University Press, 1979), p. 188.

[48] Hannah Arendt, *The Human Condition* (Chicago: University of Chicago Press, 1958), p. 74.

equated with the moral, this is tantamount to saying that altruism cannot be self-conscious. "The effort to identify with another cannot authorize and may as psychological praxis even obstruct saintly work."[49] The ideal of altruism would seem to demand an involvement and dedication that is totally unself-conscious. The issue of self and other should not arise at all, except perhaps in retrospect, as it is often posed for rescuers by less altruistically involved individuals.

The religious paradox of altruism is inherent in the reality of altruism itself. It reaches beyond motivation and rationale to the very existence of genuine altruism. As such, it exposes what would seem to be an inescapable contradiction at the heart of altruism, one that is at the same time ontological and epistemo-logical. The ontological dimension is identified by Edith Wyschogrod, in what she refers to as the paradox of saintly self-emptying. The dilemma is that if the "Other fills the place of the self, substituting for the self as a content, then the Other's claim to alterity is undermined," while, from the other side, if "saintliness is a total emptying without replenishment, there is no subject to engage the Other."[50] Altruism requires definite distinction and intimate relation between self and other. This dilemma represents the basis of the epistemological dimension, that altruism is only possible because of the distinction between self and other, but its genuineness depends on lack of focus on that distinction. This is the ontological and epistemological dilemma of altruism, beyond the emotional hedonic dilemma and the motivational moral dilemma. Deliberate focus on the other bears an unstated sense of the goodness of the self that is thus focused. Nor is this dilemma relieved by a deliberate chastening of the self for its surreptitious self-interest. Humility that is deliberate is not humility, any more than altruism that is deliberate is really altruism, as Arendt implies, and Nicholas Berdyaev insists directly. Berdyaev contends that making humi-lity thematic, and worrying about the genuineness of my humility is a sure signal that things have gone wrong. "A

[49] Edith Wyschogrod, *Saints and Postmodernism: Revisioning Moral Philosophy* (Chicago: University of Chicago Press, 1990), p. 85.

[50] Ibid., pp. 33–4.

decadent of humility would ask: How can I, sinful and un-worthy, claim to have love for my neighbour, to have brother-hood? My love will be infected by sin."[51] If love for neighbor depends on my achieving sufficient humility, I will never get around to love for my neighbor, Berdyaev suggests. From both directions, deliberate concern for the other and deliberate concern about the worthiness of the self, altruism as genuine concern for others is inherently compromised by the self-consciousness that allows us to identify it as altruism.

This ontological paradox of altruism can hardly fail to suggest that the whole topic is simply futile. It is bad enough that there is psychological ambiguity because any pleasure I take in being altruistic is my pleasure, and that there is moral ambiguity because of uncertainty about where the line falls between altruism as reality and as ideal; but if altruism is inherently suspect because ideally it should involve a concern for the other that is oblivious to self, whereas its mere identifica-tion raises the specter of self psychologically, motivationally, and ontologically, it would seem to be an unintelligible concept. People do act altruistically, sometimes in heroic ways, but even to try to describe this in retrospect can only distort the reality. It would not do to minimize the difficulties inherent in this very notion of altruism. Yet it points to something in human life that is too important to be dismissed simply because of its elusive-ness. There is one way that altruism might make sense so that the paradoxes can be allowed to stand. This is implicit in calling the most severe form of altruism paradox the paradox of religion.

Religion too is a very elusive reality. Academic definitions often founder on the practiced reality. At the heart of the practice of religion there often lies the phenomenon of worship. In this phenomenon an analogy for altruism might be found. Worship too has its paradoxes. It is evoked, rather than chosen by us, and yet we always face the risk of idolatry, against which we must guard by being deliberate and careful about our

---

[51] Nicholas Berdyaev, "Salvation and Creativity: Two Understandings of Christianity," in *Western Spirituality: Historical Roots, Ecumenical Routes*, ed. Matthew Fox (Santa Fe, New Mexico: Bean and Co., 1981), p. 122.

worship. Altruism is a definite direction that stands in direct contrast to approaching life simply in terms of our own interests and desires, but the distinctiveness of altruism is undermined, not only because it too can be seen to reflect our interests and desires, albeit perhaps on a higher level, but also because it is compromised in the very act of being identified. Worship avoids viciousness in its circularity by embracing the paradox within itself. The vigilance against idolatry is an activity of worship itself; in fact, the whole idea of idolatry makes no sense at all apart from a context of genuine worship. Yet confidence in the genuineness of worship may be one of the surest signals of the dangers of idolatry. Worship and idolatry represent an ongoing process, an unending search for the line of demarcation. Altruism might represent a parallel kind of phenomenon. A sincere focus on the other will be a focus of an independent self who may be expected to, and probably should be expected to, draw satisfaction and inspiration from that focus. Recognition of, much less concentration on, these dimensions, however, is apt to compromise the genuineness of the focus. No theoretical or technical solution can be expected for this dilemma. The paradox is a living one. Its resolution lies in recognizing the transcendent significance of altruism in itself, so that deflections are overcome through renewal of vision, just as inadequacies of worship are themselves perceived, and can only be dealt with, in the context of worship.

Altruism clearly represents a very elusive and intrinsically ambiguous reality. Recognizing that our grasp of reality is metaphoric provides some relief for these difficulties; we do not expect to clarify what altruism entails in impersonal, objective terms. We ourselves are involved in the reality, and so in the end we have to live with the paradoxes. However, it is possible to clarify further why altruism is so ambiguous, and thus to help to clarify the implications of these central paradoxical features.

The dilemmas posed by altruism can be clarified significantly by recognizing that the concept itself is a modern invention. The problem of altruism did not occur for Aristotle, according to Arthur Madigan, S.J.

On my interpretation, the complexity and obscurity of the person or *nous*, and the character of the *kalon* (the noble) as a good jointly constituted by the agent and others (or by the agent regarding himself as another or from the viewpoint of the other) prevent the drawing of simple and straightforward distinctions between self and others, between the self's interests and the interests of others, and so preclude the problem of egoism and altruism in anything like a clear and explicit form.[52]

What we have already seen suggests that the distinctions between self and other prompted by the notion of altruism are anything but straightforward; however, they may well be deliberate in a way that did not present itself to Aristotle, or indeed, to any others who thought about these things prior to the modern period. The issue of altruism owes its origins to modern self-consciousness.

We have seen that Comte coined the term as a social ideal to counteract the divisiveness and anarchy that could replace the repression of ecclesiastical and military authorities that had enforced common bonds in the past. The notion slipped off the agenda of the social sciences, as they coalesced around the assumption of self-interest, which, as we have also seen, charted the course for these developing disciplines without serious deflection until recent questioning of the total adequacy of this assumption. It was left to the side of what had been thought of as the moral sciences to develop the concept of altruism. Moral connotations were one of the principal skins shed by the moral sciences as they became social sciences. The air of objectivity through which they sought to emulate the ideal of the natural sciences made the complexities and humanness of morality a liability. Thus morality found itself occupying a territory of its own that has become what we know in the modern west as ethics. Here altruism found a home. Before Comte coined the term, the sense that morality involved recognition of the claim of others became a defining feature of the dominant streams of this new discipline of modern ethics. "It was in the seventeenth and eighteenth centuries that morality came generally to be

---

[52] Arthur Madigan, S.J., "EN IX 8: Beyond Egoism and Altruism?" *The Modern Schoolman* 62 (Nov. 1985): 17–18.

understood as offering a solution to the problems posed by human egoism and that the content of morality came to be largely equated with altruism."[53] Thus altruism represents a new development. It makes sense only in terms of developments in the modern west.

The development that is most responsible for the notion of altruism is the emergence of self-consciousness. Whether in the form of René Descartes' thinking ego, Adam Smith's individual economic free enterpriser, or Thomas Hobbes' depiction of the political situation as a natural state of war of all against all that is contained only by the authority of the state, the foundational assumption that shaped the modern west isolated individuals as entities in themselves, in contrast to a more communal outlook that had been taken for granted in the past. While this general-ization is easily stated, the reality is only appreciated when these are recognized as foundational visions of life that are taken for granted. People used to take for granted that they were bound up together in various ways; increasingly through the modern period, we have come to assume that we exist in isolation, and far from being connected with others, they are more apt to be seen as competitors for the goods, possibilities, or recognition we seek for ourselves. Altruism emerges and makes sense only in this latter context. "The notion of self-interest therefore has application not to human behavior in general but to a certain type of human situation, namely, one in which behavior can be either competitive or non-competitive. Equally, in this type of situation alone can the notions of benevolence and altruism have application."[54] The possibility, as well as the problems, of altruism are peculiar to our era. This is not to say that people in other times and places have not struggled, or do not struggle, with these moral, and ultimately religious, issues. The difference is that others do not seem to have struggled with them in the self-conscious, competitive atmosphere, where they get posed as issues of self-interest and altruism.

[53] Alasdair MacIntyre, *After Virtue* (South Bend: University of Notre Dame Press, 1981), p. 213.
[54] Alasdair MacIntyre, "Egoism and Altruism," in *The Encyclopedia of Philosophy*, vol. 2, ed. Paul Edwards (New York: Macmillan, 1967), p. 466.

PART TWO

Ideal altruism

CHAPTER 4

Contract altruism

The self-interest vision may require something like altruism to establish its own distinctiveness, but for the vision itself, altruism is an embarrassment. This is evident in the all out assault on altruism in sociobiology, an assault that extends to the ordinary, as well as the biological, sense of the term. It is also buttressed by attempts to understand ethics without reference to anything like altruism. From various directions attempts have been made to base ethics on self-interest, in the conviction that this is the only serious motivation that people can be expected to respond to today.

MOTIVATIONS BEHIND SELF-INTEREST ETHICS

The infamous instance of self-interest ethics is the social Darwinism championed by Herbert Spencer. "Survival of the fittest" became not only a summary of the understanding of the processes that made life possible, but also an ethical mandate indicating the inevitable course that would be sustained by the future unfolding of these processes. This biologizing of ethics has been refined and reinforced through the much more precise mechanisms of sociobiology. The most prominent pioneer of this development, E. O. Wilson, proposes that "the time has come for ethics to be removed temporarily from the hands of philosophers and biologized."[1] He expects that this will produce "a biology of ethics, which will make possible the selection of a more deeply understood and enduring code of

---

[1] Edward O. Wilson, *Sociobiology: The New Synthesis* (Cambridge, Mass.: Harvard University Press, 1975) p. 562

moral values."[2] The basis for such a biology of ethics is sketched by Richard D. Alexander in *The Biology of Moral Systems*. The foundation of this ethics is, of course, the genetic concept of inclusive fitness. The rationale of all behavior is the promotion of the genes of the actor and of his or her immediate kin. This accounts for parental care and the altruism directed to others who can pass on a significant portion of the genetic legacy we possess. Why parents should not be disposed of themselves when they have passed their child-rearing years is probably encompassed in the next layer of explanation. The fact is that people do care for their parents as well as their children, and, in fact, even perform apparently altruistic acts for complete strangers. So reciprocal altruism is added to kin altruism to explain this wider version. The apparent altruist is not serving his or her own genes directly, but is doing so indirectly through the expectation of reciprocation in the future. But what if the recipient is not in a position to reciprocate? Well, it does not have to be direct reciprocation. The apparent altruist is contributing to a kind of general assistance pool from which he or she can draw when the need arises. If you think there is still a dimension of altruism that is too real to be subject to such self-interested explanation, you are advised to look more closely and see if it is not really calculated to raise the regard in which the apparent altruist is held, resulting in greater long-term benefit to this individual because of the trust elicited. But surely there are people who really do things simply for the benefit of others, without any kind of ulterior motive at all? The saddest specimens of all! They deceive themselves as well as others.

The key to the biological ethics outlined by Alexander is the notion of reciprocal altruism. Failure to appreciate that it is reciprocal, and thus self-serving, is what has allowed morality to develop.

The key lies in the argument that systems of indirect reciprocity cause some (indeterminate and adjustable) amounts of indiscriminate altruism to be reproductively favorable to the altruist or to relate to people's proximate feelings and attitudes as if this were the case, and that misrepresentation of this indiscriminate altruism as costly, rather

---

[2] Edward O. Wilson, "Altruism," *Harvard Magazine* (Nov.–Dec. 1978): 196.

than as social investment likely to be profitable to the investor, has been responsible for a widespread if not universal misinterpretation of what it means to be moral.[3]

A morality of misunderstanding might not seem very promising, but for Alexander and Wilson it is the opportunity to become truly scientific about morality. Awareness and acknowledgment of the self-interested motivation behind morality can allow us to fashion a morality of self-interest that leaves no ambiguity about motivation. "True selfishness, if obedient to the other constraints of mammalian biology, is the key to a more nearly perfect social contract."[4]

Although evolutionary ethics pioneered self-interest ethics, the cutting edge of self-interest today, and the background of evolutionary ethics, lies in economics. Before Charles Darwin there was Thomas Hobbes. In the seventeenth century, Hobbes anticipated the understanding of life that has taken shape especially through the instrumentality of modern economics. David Gauthier explores an ethic of self-interest in light of three basic economic principles he takes to be indicative of the Hobbesian vision: "the subjectivity of value, the instrumentality of reason, and the non-truism of interest."[5] Value is a matter of private preference, what economists call utility, what individuals consider useful to them. Reason is the instrument for calculating and conniving to get as much as we can of what we want, or what economists call utility maximization. In pursuing our own interests, we take no interest at all in the welfare of others.

The primary motivation behind Gauthier's version of morality is realism. He does not profess to be presenting the richest exposition of morality possible. What he offers is the only viable approach to morality for us in this time and place. He disavows knowledge of morality as pursuit of human ideals, and seems to be at best ambivalent about morality as concern for others. The

---

[3] Richard D. Alexander, "A Biological Interpretation of Moral Systems," *Zygon* 20 (1985): 16.

[4] Wilson, "Altruism," p. 25.

[5] David Gauthier, "Thomas Hobbes: Moral Theorist," *Journal of Philosophy* 76 (1979): 558.

only approach he has confidence in is a morality that involves "concerns arising from the negative externalities endemic to restricted interaction."[6] Or more directly: "Morality emerges from market failure."[7] If individuals could engage in free exchange, with each seeking his or her own welfare with impunity, there would be no need for morality. But the market produces externalities, conflicts that are counterproductive to such free exchange. This is why it is necessary to develop morality, and it constitutes the only base for a morality that is likely to carry conviction in our situation. "Thus the contractarian finds the basis of morality neither in our fellow feelings (although he does not deny that we have such feelings), nor in any purportedly objective duty independent of our individual concerns, but in the intelligent ordering of our mutual affairs in ways that benefit each, and so are rationally acceptable to each."[8] Neither Humean sympathy nor Kantian duty afford a solid base for morality today. Only a Hobbesian "conception of morality which addresses the condition of the self-interested, secular individual who faces the conflicts of naked egoism" is viable today.[9] The problem with most modern moral philosophers, as Gauthier sees it, is that they seem to be under the illusion that they can combine a secular Hobbesian morality with a religious Lockean morality to produce a secular Lockean morality.[10] They think, in short, that they can build a morality of religious proportions from a secular base. Gauthier's realism insists on recognizing that this is impossible. Having dispensed with the religious vision that informed Locke, our only basis for morality is a Hobbesian one.[11] We can only start with ourselves as self-interested seekers of our own advantage. Morality can only be a matter of contract, negotiated to further our respective individual interests.

The most celebrated version of self-interest ethics does not find things as bleak as evolutionary or economically based

---

[6] David Gauthier, *Moral Dealing: Contract, Ethics, and Reason* (Ithaca: Cornell University Press, 1990), p. 145.

[7] David Gauthier, *Morals by Agreement* (Oxford: Clarendon Press, 1986), p. 84.

[8] Gauthier, *Moral Dealing*, pp. 1f.

[9] Ibid., p. 35.   [10] Ibid., p. 27.   [11] Ibid., pp. 43f.

ethics. For John Rawls, our rationality extends beyond utility maximization to encompass a measure of Kantian moral sensibility. The challenge we face, as Rawls sees it, is not primarily biological or economic, but political, the diversity of views of the good that we hold as moral beings. If our learning to live together peacefully depends on achieving consensus among these diverse views, the prospects are indeed not good. But perhaps it is possible to achieve enough consensus to promote mutual respect for our differences, a political arrangement, rather than metaphysical agreement. To this end, John Rawls invites us to assume an original position, behind a veil of ignorance, that precludes us from knowing who we actually are, what beliefs we hold, what social position we occupy. If we pare down to this common denominator, Rawls is convinced we will find that there is a common core shared by all rational beings. This core includes a political conception of ourselves as "free and equal persons," with a common requirement for certain basic goods – "the same basic rights, liberties, and opportunities," the means for following our vision represented by income and wealth, and a basic self-respect.[12] These goods can best be secured by a system of justice that assures fairness in guaranteeing basic liberties and economic opportunity, along with protection from exploitation. As long as they support this common base, citizens are free to pursue whatever vision and way of life appeals to them.

MOTIVATIONS WITHIN SELF-INTEREST ETHICS

If I become convinced that life is characterized fundamentally by self-interest, why should I bother with ethics at all? The adequacy of its answers to this question constitutes the test of self-interest ethics. On the surface, the prospects for the evolutionary version would not seem great. To take ethics seriously is to give credence to a misinterpretation. Admiration of apparent altruism is due to failure to realize that if it is not directed to immediate kin, it is at best reciprocal, an investment antici-

---

[12] John Rawls, "The Priority of Right and Ideas of the Good," *Philosophy and Public Affairs* 17 (1988): 256f.

pating the possibility of future withdrawal on the part of the supposed altruist. Put bluntly, "ethics as we understand it, is an illusion fobbed off on us by our genes to get us to cooperate."[13] But why should we live by illusion? This crucial question receives several answers from sociobiology. Some of these are versions of the childhood " 'cause, that's why!" Even though morality, as our own subjective illusion, has no objective reality of any kind, we live as though it did. "Even the most hard-lined sociobiologist conducts his or her daily life as though there were such objectivity."[14] The respect for empirical evidence that defines scientific method would seem to dictate serious consideration for a phenomenon that predates recorded history and continues to elicit devotion even from those who regard it as illusory. But this contradiction is ignored or overlooked in uncompromising reaffirmation of the illusion designation. Equally unilluminating is another " 'cause, that's why" answer that appeals to the authority of biology itself. What grounding there is for morality is biological, and because morality is biologically useful, biology maintains it. "Even though we have insight into our biological nature, it is still our biological nature," Michael Ruse reminds us.[15] "The genes hold culture on a leash," Wilson tells us.[16] But if biology has constructed what we know as morality as a grand illusion, how do we know that the sociobiological vision does not have similar sponsorship? Once we begin regarding major portions of our experience as illusory, where do we stop? The prospects are particularly precarious when the exposers of the illusion continue to live by it.

It may be some sense of the special pleading involved in these non-reasons that leads to a further rationale for the resilience of the illusion that is morality. What really accounts for the continuation of the morality that has emerged through misunderstanding is social pressure. "If you cease to play fair, then

---

[13] Michael Ruse and Edward O. Wilson, "The Evolution of Ethics," *New Scientist* 108 (1985): 52.

[14] Michael Ruse, "The Morality of the Gene," *The Monist* 67 (1984): 192.

[15] Michael Ruse, "Evolutionary Ethics: A Phoenix Arisen," *Zygon* 21/1 (1986): 104.

[16] Wilson, "Altruism," p. 28.

before long I and others will chastise you or take you out of the moral sphere."[17] Social pressure suggests a more credible explanation for moral conformity, but the more significance is attributed to this dimension, the more we are moving away from the biological and into the cultural sphere. The extent to which the social is dependent on the biological is, of course, one of the perennial debates of sociobiology, and the lack of consensus among sociobiologists themselves is evident in this area of morality. For in contrast to the strict biological derivation of morality advocated by Spencer, Wilson, Alexander, and Ruse, there are others who see morality as a rebellion against biology. Where Spencer championed "the survival of the fittest," Thomas Huxley looked toward a morality such that "in place of thrusting aside, or treading down, all competitors, it requires that the individual shall not merely respect, but shall help his fellows; its influence is directed, not so much to the survival of the fittest, as to fitting as many as possible to survive."[18] To promote this direction, Huxley advocates rebellion against our biological heritage: we must "refuse any longer to be the instruments of the evolutionary process."[19] We have noted the sociobiological parallel in Richard Dawkins' summons to defy our selfish genes, issued in a book dedicated to the thesis that we are only vehicles for the selfish genes that use us for their own replication. In the Preface, Dawkins assures us: "we are survival machines – robot vehicles blindly programmed to preserve the selfish molecules known as genes."[20] But in the Conclusion, we blind robot vehicles are challenged to rebel against the genes that make us what we are. "We have the power to defy the selfish genes of our birth and, if necessary, the selfish memes [Dawkins' term for cultural counterparts of biological genes] of our indoctrination. We can even discuss ways of deliberately cultivating and nurturing a pure, disinterested altruism – something that has no place in nature, some-

---

[17] Ruse, "Evolutionary Ethics," p. 105.
[18] Thomas Huxley, *Evolution and Ethics and Other Essays* (New York: Appleton, 1894), p. 82.
[19] Ibid., p. 63.
[20] Richard Dawkins, *The Selfish Gene* (London: Granada, 1978), p. x.

thing that has never existed before in the whole history of the world."[21] Some sociobiologists cultivate the moral illusion themselves.

The most sustained attempt to bridge this gulf in sociobiology has involved the adoption of the social science method of modeling situations through game theory, the most prominent example of which is the model of the prisoner's dilemma.[22] Two prisoners are being questioned separately, and each can improve their prospects if they give evidence on the other. If one remains silent and the other talks, the silent one will receive a stiffer sentence, and the talker will receive a shorter one, or actually be released, depending on which version is followed. If both refuse to talk, they will each receive moderate sentences. If both talk, they will each receive long sentences. The essence of the dilemma is summarized in a sociobiological application by Robert Axelrod and William D. Hamilton. "No matter what the other does, the selfish choice of defection yields a higher payoff than cooperation. But if both defect, both do worse than if both had cooperated."[23] Defection here, of course, means telling on the other, and cooperation refers to cooperation with each other, not with the authorities doing the questioning. In the jargon of game theory, defection is the dominant strategy. As Axelrod and Hamilton indicate, it always yields a higher payoff than cooperation. But mass defection, in this case defection of the only two players in the game, yields a deficient equilibrium, a situation in which everyone involved is worse off. Thus selfishness always pays for the individual, but cooperation can pay more, if others cooperate as well – the fundamental dilemma of self-interest and altruism. The question it poses is – why should I as an individual take the risk? Why not play it safe, and take the course that I know will leave me better off, even if that means not being as well off as I could be by risking the chance that others will cooperate with me? Better to risk

---

[21] Ibid., p. 215.
[22] A. Rapport and A. M. Chammah, *Prisoner's Dilemma* (Ann Arbor: University of Michigan Press, 1965).
[23] Robert Axelrod and William D. Hamilton, "The Evolution of Cooperation," *Science* 2 (1981): 1391.

spending three years in prison by assuming that my partner in crime is going to tell on me, than to keep quiet on the chance of getting a one-year sentence, if she too remains silent, but in so doing risk getting five years if she talks while I remain silent. The issue becomes more complex if future encounters can be anticipated; if there is to be a series of questionings, for example. This opens up the possibility of different results. It also raises the question of the possibility of communication, if not directly between the prisoners in this case, at least in terms of the results of previous rounds.

In game simulation, the most stable strategy to emerge is what has been called tit for tat. "This strategy is simply one of cooperating on the first move and then doing whatever the other player did on the preceding move. Thus TIT FOR TAT is a strategy of cooperation based on reciprocity."[24] Motivation clearly remains fixed on a self-interest basis, but the strategy is not reciprocal, at least in terms of the sociobiological understanding of reciprocity. On that view, reciprocal altruism refers to the non-genetic investment an individual makes with the genetic motive of having that reciprocated in the future. The tit for tat strategy follows that pattern on only the first move. After the initial cooperation, the strategy is reactionary rather than reciprocal in the anticipatory sense intended by reciprocal altruism. This leaves the mystery as to how significant cooperation could ever become established. The tit for tat strategy is the most stable one for the self-interested individual. How it moves beyond self-interest, even in illusory terms, is not so clear. The inadequacy of such direct game analogies becomes even more apparent when we consider that social reality rarely, if ever, involves direct one-on-one interactions, with no wider influences or repercussions.

The leap from the base reality of self-interest to the social pressure morality hinted at by Ruse is accounted for more directly by Gauthier. In presenting an early and, Gauthier confesses, confused, account of that leap, it was pointed out to him that what he was really talking about was the prisoner's

---

[24] Ibid., p. 1393.

dilemma.[25] The model allowed him to clarify what the leap involved. It can be seen as a move from Hobbes' natural reason to his conventional reason, or, in economic terms, from direct utility maximization, where we look out only for our immediate self-interest, to restrained utility maximization, which takes a more long-range perspective. Rationality means individual utility maximization, but rationality also involves the ability to reflect on utility maximization and to see the futility of it when pursued directly because of the conflicts this involves. Reflection can see that it would be much more profitable to work out ways of cooperating to avoid the worst of these conflicts. In this way, straight utility maximization is restrained in the interests of avoiding the obstacles to utility maximization. "Thus we suppose it possible for persons, who may initially assume that it is rational to extend straightforward maximization from parametric to strategic contexts, to reflect on the implications of this extension, and to reject it in favor of constrained maximization."[26] This is how the motivation for morality is derived from self-interest. The constrained maximizer is no less self-interested than the straightforward maximizer. She is a more efficient maximizer.[27] That is the self-interested appeal of the constraint that morality involves. This provides the link between naked self-interest and the social pressure view of morality to which Ruse so mysteriously leaps.

But if morality exists to promote more effective realization of self-interest, would this really be a promotion of morality or of a semblance of morality? The truly rational utility maximizer would surely be not the one who took morality seriously, but the one who pretended to, and thereby gained a real advantage over those foolish enough really to live by moral principles. Gauthier replies to this challenge through the examples of Hobbes' Foole and Hume's Sensible Knave, who think they can use morality as a public relations image exercise, rather than taking it seriously. Society needs morality, says the Foole or Knave, and I intend to take full advantage of this by pretending

[25] Gauthier, *Moral Dealing*, pp. 254f.
[26] Gauthier, *Morals by Agreement*, pp. 183f.
[27] Gauthier, *Moral Dealing*, p. 232.

to take morality seriously the better to assure my own interests. The problem with this is that the Foole or Knave thereby fails to appreciate the real advantage of morality. "For in being a knave she makes herself unfit for society – a person to be excluded from, rather than included in, the mutually advantageous arrangements that society affords."[28] To look out for number one most effectively, you must recognize how morality is essential to your self-interest. It allows for arrangements that overcome the worst obstacles that arise from everyone pursuing their interests in a straightforward manner. To benefit from this, you must actually participate, respect the moral principles agreed to, or risk the ostracism that will result from exposure of your insincerity. Thus morality is derived and motivated in a manner totally consistent with the self-interest base.

When that base already includes recognition of the moral dimension, as in Rawls, the prospects for significant derivation of morality from self-interest would seem to be much more promising. Rather than attempting to draw morality from naked self-interest, Rawls is moving in the other direction, paring down full-scale visions to a common base. Rawls' approach is commended on the basis of its neutrality in comparison with the competing visions of the good life that people actually hold. In contrast to these visions, this is essentially a procedure, a political means to provide people with the social and economic wherewithal to pursue their diverse visions in mutual respect. One of the principal means Rawls uses to establish the contrast between his political proposal and the more substantive visions among which it mediates is his insistence on the priority of the right over the good. This allows him to avoid the chaos of Hobbesian self-interest risked by Gauthier and the tyranny of comprehensive visions of the good. His ability to negotiate between these extremes constitutes the measure of Rawls' accomplishment. He avoids the tyranny of comprehensive visions of the good by paring them down to the level of right: "the aim of justice as fairness as a political concept is practical, and not metaphysical or epistemolo-

[28] Ibid., p. 144.

gical."[29] This means that "justice as fairness deliberately stays on the surface, philosophically speaking."[30] At the same time, this procedure is more than a Hobbesian *modus vivendi* that allows individuals and groups to go their separate ways. There is an understanding of justice involved, and this makes it a moral matter. It is a matter of right, and not simply of expediency. This is what distinguishes Rawls from the Hobbesian base on which Gauthier seeks to build. Because it is a matter of right, rather than a full-blown vision of the good, it allows for moral consensus rather than the stalemate of competing visions of what makes life worthwhile.

What allows Rawls to maintain his broader view of self-interest morality is not only this assumption of right, in contrast to prudent expediency. Recognition of right presupposes and reflects some vision of the good, a kind of common denominator of prevailing visions. What Rawls is proposing is an understanding of the right as a consensus drawn from the competing visions of the good themselves. Thus to some extent, far from being neglected, the good defines the right. This is essential to ensure the stability of the system of justice that is developed because it means that those who affirm this vision of the good will have a stake in the system: "in such a consensus each of the comprehensive metaphysical, religious, and moral doctrines accepts justice as fairness in its own way."[31] But while the right is defined from the good, in this sense, this does not contradict the opposite direction already noted; for purposes of justice as fairness, the good is defined by the requirements of right: "the ideas of the good it draws upon must fit within the limits drawn – the space allowed – by that political conception itself."[32] The result may be seen as a complementarity of the good and the right, as Rawls suggests, where "justice draws the limit, the good shows the point."[33] The ethics thus permitted would be more conventional, at least in terms of modern ethics, than the evolutionary or economic varieties, but it would still be an

---

[29] John Rawls, "Justice as Fairness: Political not Metaphysical," *Philosophy and Public Affairs* 14 (1985): 230.
[30] Ibid.   [31] Ibid., p. 247.
[32] Rawls, "The Priority of Right and Ideas of the Good," p. 252.   [33] Ibid.

ethics of self-interest. The main difference is that the interests of the selves would be expected to be more comprehensive than the acquisitive ones assumed to characterize the more primitive versions.

MOTIVATIONS FOR ACCEPTING SELF-INTEREST ETHICS

At first sight, misunderstanding and illusion would not appear to offer much incentive to adopt the sociobiological version of self-interest ethics. When to this is added the contradiction among sociobiologists over the significance of morality and the presence of contradiction even within an individual sociobiologist as to whether we are at the mercy of genes or free to chart our own course, the case for morality is confused at best. The overall impression conveyed by sociobiological treatments of morality suggests that philosopher of science, Michael Ruse, is closer to the truth in his earlier reaction to Wilson than in his later defence of the illusion thesis. "Wilson's arguments therefore do not work," Ruse contended, and went on: "This is perhaps just as well, for he himself blithely ignores his conclusions as soon as he has drawn them, arguing quite inconsistently that our present existential predicament demands, that we start planning for the good of the whole, putting aside selfishness."[34] Yet Ruse himself indulges in the same romanticization of sociobiological ethics, contending that "no evolutionist says that we have no obligation to the world's starving poor."[35] Whence such obligation for self-interest ethics? Garrett Hardin draws the implications of a strict biological self-interest ethics much more consistently, when he says of poor countries: "The greatest gift we can give them is the knowledge that they are on their own."[36] Gauthier too does not hesitate to face the implications of self-interest ethics, concluding that on this basis, we in the developed world have no incentive to cooperate with impoverished countries, and stating the rationale directly. "My neighbor, according to our ideology, is the man with whom I

[34] Michael Ruse, *Sociobiology: Sense or Nonsense?* (Dordrecht: Reidel, 1979), p. 209.
[35] Ruse, "Evolutionary Ethics," p. 106.
[36] Garrett Hardin, "Discriminating Altruisms," *Zygon* 17 (1977): 165.

can make a mutually profitable agreement. Everyone else is my enemy – to be exploited if I can, to exploit me if he can."[37] Mutual exploitation, not concern for victims, is the mandate of self-interest ethics.

If this seems offensive in its implications, Gauthier asks us to look at the directions in life as we live it. However much we may think we operate with standards of civility, and even of graciousness, the reality is that more and more life is being lived by contract. Consider the escalation in law suits and the claims of rights exerted by individuals and interest groups (the term itself is telling in this context). A chief exhibit in this area is marriage and the family. Gauthier cites "the arrangements and practices of those who seek to divest the marriage contract of its religious and moral overtones," to treat it as an ordinary contract.[38] In this way of stating it, he adds ironic weight to his own thesis, because, of course, the stronger contrast involves the recognition that marriage historically was not a contract at all, but a sacrament or a covenant. Whatever we may think of the merits of the causes involved in these developments, they confirm the Hobbesian form of contemporary life.

Consistent and courageous though he is in facing the implications of self-interest ethics, Gauthier also claims to provide a way of transcending these implications. He offers an explanation for the sociobiological appeal to social pressure as an ethical mechanism not only through elaboration of the self-interest dimension of this, but also through his emphasis on the importance of sincerity in this compliance. This latter aspect has received even greater emphasis from Robert H. Frank,[39] through his contention that insincerity will be detected and thus rebound to the detriment of the present-day counterpart of the Foole or Knave. Thus serious moral concern is derived from pure self-interest. Yet even if this explanation deals with the social complications encountered by self-interest ethics, it still leaves the moral problem itself. The more the importance of

---

[37] Gauthier, *Moral Dealing*, p. 350.   [38] Ibid., p. 330.

[39] Robert H. Frank, *Passions Within Reason: The Strategic Role of the Emotions* (New York: Norton, 1988); "A Theory of Moral Sentiments," in *Beyond Self-Interest*, ed. Jane J. Mansbridge (Chicago: University of Chicago Press, 1990).

moral sincerity is stressed, as essential to this self-interest operation, the more we have to wonder why we should not simply recognize the importance of morality as such. Perhaps self-interest is the illusion, in the foundational and comprehensive sense in which it is intended here. What this analysis is uncovering, then, is not mechanisms for promoting self-interest, but evidence of the inescapable reality of the moral dimension.

There are indications that this is really what Gauthier finally thinks himself. He concedes that the morality that can be erected on a Hobbesian base is a minimalist one. This confinement is inescapable as long as we are restricted to the three Hobbesian principles of value as utility or subjective preference, rationality as the maximization of utility, and non-tuism which stipulates complete lack of interest in the utilities of others.[40] A more substantial morality could only emerge through the relaxation of at least one of these principles. Gauthier's own preference is for a relaxation of the non-tuism preference.[41] But that is tantamount to the abandonment of the whole framework. If genuine interest in others is allowed, value can no longer be equated with utility in the sense of individual preference, except in the formal sense that concern for others can be regarded as an individual preference. However, that concern will also modify the equation between rationality and utility maximization, unless we are prepared to regard whatever tuism is permitted as irrational. In short, it would seem that Gauthier has talked himself out of his own position. Self-interest is not so adequate as a characterization of humanity as he, and probably also we, have been inclined to take it to be.

There seems to be little room for doubt that this is Gauthier's fundamental vision. He acknowledges that the market system, which appears to represent the heart of his system, really depends on more fundamental levels of trust, and that the progressive erosion of this foundation, precisely through the explicit contractarianism that he seems to stand for, portends dire consequences for the future: "the effect of extending contractarian ideology is and will continue to be to corrode all

[40] Gauthier, "Thomas Hobbes: Moral Theorist," p. 558.
[41] Ibid., pp. 558f.

of those bonds which in the real world have been the under-
pinning of the market. Bereft of its framework, the bargaining
order will collapse into competitive chaos."[42] Gauthier's
mission seems to be to appeal to people from within this
desperate situation to recognize the folly of their ways. What he
seems to demonstrate, despite his intentions, is that this contractarian approach cannot be expected to regenerate the kind
of foundation it is rapidly eroding. The altruism derived from
self-interest is at the mercy of its origins.

The prospects for basing morality on self-interest thus do not
seem promising, unless the self-interest itself includes a moral
dimension. This is the possibility proposed by Rawls. Because
he does not profess to extract morality from naked self-interest,
Rawls does not face the obstacles confronting evolutionary
ethics and the Gauthier economic version. However, Rawls'
approach raises its own kind of questions. For while he does not
assume Hobbesian self-interest, he does claim to be operating
with a metaphysically neutral understanding of the self. "If we
look at the presentation of justice as fairness and note how it is
set up, and note the ideas and conceptions it uses, no particular
metaphysical doctrine about the nature of persons, distinctive
and opposed to other metaphysical doctrines, appears among
its premises, or seems required by its arguments."[43] For Rawls
to make good on this neutrality claim, his view of the self has to
be acceptable to the various full-blown visions of the good that
actually prevail. The most direct test of his success is to ask
whether there are selves that would be excluded by the political
limits that justice as fairness prescribes. An obvious candidate
to consider would be an ascetic who lived according to an
approach to life like medieval monasticism or stricter forms of
Buddhism that involve renunciation of at least some of the
primary goods that Rawls regards as universally required. It
might be suggested, as indeed it has been by Rawls himself,[44]
that ascetics can be accommodated in a system of justice as
fairness, so long as they do not insist that their way must be

---

[42] Gauthier, *Moral Dealing*, p. 353.
[43] Rawls, "Justice as Fairness," p. 240.
[44] Rawls, "The Priority of Right and Ideas of the Good," p. 268.

adopted by others. If they want to renounce the goods to which justice as fairness entitles them, they are free to do so. What they cannot do, under this system, is expect others to do so. By the nature of the system, people have a right to these basic goods.

Although the system, once established, can thus accommodate even the ascetic, the real question is why an ascetic would accept it in the first place. Why would someone whose vision of the good involves renunciation of possession assume an original position designed to secure possessions? If asceticism seems like an extreme case, this may be as much a comment on our age, and the anchorage of Rawls' vision of justice within it, as on the merits of asceticism. However, the point applies to less strenuous religious stances as well. What incentive is there for a devout religious believer to enter the original position? Like the ascetic, the religious believer can be tolerated by the system as an eccentric, but how can such a person be expected to own the system in the way that Rawls requires to ensure its stability? They are expected to do this on the understanding that all views of the good are the choices of free and equal persons.[45] This is possible because "as free persons, citizens claim the right to view their persons as independent from and not as identified with any particular conception of the good, or scheme of final ends."[46] This reflects directly the view of persons that we saw Rawls designating as metaphysically neutral, but we can now see that this neutrality depends on excluding religious views of persons. Persons with religious convictions can hardly "view their persons as independent of the good, or scheme of final ends." What can be expected of religious believers politically is that they do not require others to accept their beliefs. This is the import of religious liberty entailed by modern democratic recognition of the fallibility of finite humanity. But what Rawls requires is something different. For religious believers to adopt his system, they would have to disavow their central convictions, including their understanding of themselves. They would have to see themselves existing as

---

[45] Rawls, "Justice as Fairness," p. 235.
[46] Ibid., p. 241.

independent choosers, contrary to their convictions that life is God's gift, for example.

What is particularly insidious about Rawls' position is that, in spite of the widespread application of the liberalism label it has garnered, seen from a position that takes religious conviction seriously, he can be seen to represent the antithesis of liberalism in his imposition of his own view of humanity under the guise of neutrality. If Rawls really represents what he promises, a functional way of allowing people with various views of the good to pursue and promote their own vision, while respecting those who differ, it would not be unreasonable to expect Rawls to offer some indication of the wider vision of the good to which he himself subscribes. If we ask whether Rawls ever does this, two answers are possible. I am not aware of any place where Rawls articulates anything that could be thought of as his own vision of the good, in the sense of one of these competing visions for which his procedure is supposed to make room. However, in another sense, everything he writes is an articulation of his vision of the good. Many, including Thomas Nagel[47] and Michael Sandel,[48] have argued that that vision is essentially that of modern liberal humanism. It is certainly a clear reflection of modern secular humanism. In effect, Rawls offers us a means of cutting through the complexities and controversies that beset us today, if we are willing to accept not only the procedure he outlines, but the vision of the good that informs this. The veil of ignorance excludes any acknowledgment of religious veneration precisely because it prescribes the vision of autonomous human beings exercising what amounts to an ability for absolute choice.

The import of this in the present context is that Rawls represents an even more strident version of self-interest ethics than Gauthier. Where Gauthier is straightforward, if ultimately inconsistent, in his depiction of self-interest ethics, the greater subtlety involved in Rawls' common view of the good and professed neutrality obscures the primacy of his own view of the

---

[47] Thomas Nagel, "Rawls on Justice," *Philosophical Review* 82 (1973): 220–4.
[48] Michael J. Sandel, *Liberalism and the Limits of Justice* (Cambridge: Cambridge University Press, 1982).

self. This is particularly significant because the ultra-free chooser stands at the opposite extreme from the genetic dupe of sociobiology. As the epitome of perfect impartial rationality, Rawls' chooser is the secularized God we are warned about by Gauthier. If we are intrinsically capable of such heights of philosophical nobility, we would hardly need ethics at all.

These three prominent versions of self-interest ethics, then, suggest that ethics is either illusory, contradictory, or unnecessary. If we are as completely characterized by self-interest as modern commercial culture and evolutionary ethics assumes, the only rational course is to forget about ethics. We may be duped by our genes, but now that we know this, we shall be on our guard, and resist any tendencies toward consideration of others, or, heaven forbid, nobility. Of course, we will not be blatant about our dismissal of ethics. We will make an effort to give the appearance of ethical seriousness. And we might even get caught up in this and be duped by the social phenomenon. However, in our more reflective moments, we see through the mystification, and recognize again that self-interest is all there is. If this picture of isolated selves looking out for their own interests becomes too depressing, we can play Rawls' let's-pretend-we-are-noble-sophisticates game. The jarring note struck by the notion of self-interest ethics is thus well founded. The most concerted attempts to account for ethics on a self-interested base indicate "self-interest ethics" is an oxymoron.

CHAPTER 5

Constructed altruism

Attempts to derive altruism from a base in self-interest leave any semblance of altruism thus derived vulnerable to this origin. So much is this the case that it is dubious whether the term altruism can be legitimately used at all in this context. The observation that Christopher Jencks makes about the socio-biological version of altruism is apt. "What Trivers calls recipro-cal altruism is not really altruistic in my sense of the term; rather, it is a matter of 'enlightened self-interest.'"[1] In this state, the enlightenment may be sacrificed to the self-interest at any moment. As a recent advocate of evolutionary ethics admits, something more is needed. "If an evolutionary ethics is based on kin selection and altruism, then it will require supplementa-tion to be complete, because rationality must be added to biology and evolution."[2] The altruism referred to here is the widest form recognized in biology, reciprocal altruism, the kind that we have just suggested is not deserving of the name. By the same token, the rationality that is to be added might be equally inadequate if it is the instrumental rationality exemplified by Gauthier's rational expansion of self-interest. If reason means the cleverness to calculate what is in my self-interest, even the cleverness to see that some approximation to altruism might be in my self-interest, this is more a refinement on enlightened self-interest than an endorsement of altruism, and still leaves the

---

[1] Christopher Jencks, "The Social Basis of Unselfishness," in *The Gift: An Interdisciplinary Perspective*, ed. Aafke E. Komter (Amsterdam: Amsterdam University Press, 1996), p. 183.

[2] Lewis Petrinovich, *Human Evolution, Reproduction and Morality* (New York: Plenum Press, 1995), p. 175.

putative altruism achieved at the mercy of its origins in self-interest.

As we suggested in considering this move, acknowledgment of the possible usefulness of the appearance of altruism poses the mystery as to why those who reach this position do not go all the way and actually advocate altruism in its own right. The answer might be that such advocacy becomes possible only through a change of vision, where the self-interest base is transcended in a recognition of a more intrinsic connection with one another. This may be thought of as the difference between an instrumental rationality, where reason is a means to realizing the aims of self-interest, and a more reflective rationality, where reason has more elevated scope and goals. Instead of my interests, for example, it might involve reflection on the interests of humanity as a whole. Today, in light of environmental awareness, it might be seen to involve the welfare of the whole natural order. The difference may also be thought of as the difference constituted by morality in its distinctiveness. Rather than being a biological legacy, either as a direct imposition or a restriction to be opposed, or an expansion of that legacy through contracts designed to secure ourselves against each other, morality may be seen to constitute a distinctive approach to life in its own right. This brings us to what Kurt Baier calls "the moral point of view," which involves something very different from claims of self-interest. "Consistent egoism makes everyone's private interest the 'highest court of appeal'. But by 'the moral point of view' we *mean* a point of view which is a court of appeal for conflicts of interest. Hence it cannot (logically) be identical with the point of view of self-interest."[3] If there is to be any adjudication among all the claims of self-interest, the possibility for this would seem to require some such wider and deeper vision. If the moral point of view constitutes a court of appeal for such adjudication, it represents such wider vision, one where altruism may not only be admitted but required.

This fundamental difference, however, also suggests that the

[3] Kurt Baier, "The Moral Point of View," in *The Definitions of Morality*, ed. G. Wallace and A. D. M. Walker (London: Methuen, 1970), p. 191.

wider perspective will not be readily accessible. It may be that this "moral point of view" is so different from an outlook of self-interest that it can only be appreciated in its own terms. This would mean that between self-interest and the moral point of view there stands a form of conversion. There is no justifying morality at the bar of self-interest. As F. H. Bradley warned: "it would be well to remember that we desert a moral point of view, that we degrade and prostitute virtue, when to those who do not love her for herself, we bring ourselves to recommend her for the sake of her pleasures."[4] If this is not clear enough, Peter Singer spells it out in contemporary terms: "we can never get people to act morally by providing reasons of self-interest, because if they accept what we say and act on the reasons given, they will only be acting self-interestedly, not morally."[5] Morality requires and offers its own peculiar perspective. It constitutes its own rationale. Nobody was more insistent about this than the pioneer of modern approaches to morality, Immanuel Kant. In his uncompromising promotion of the autonomy of morality, he was advocating the distinctiveness of the moral point of view. Since there has been a tendency to equate the moral with an altruistic outlook in the modern west, we will not be surprised to find that Kant's pioneering work in ethics also involves a rationale for altruism.

KANT'S ALTRUISM OF IMPARTIALITY

It would not represent a major distortion of Kantian ethics to see it as an attempt to acknowledge the demand for altruism. The main complaint that might be made against such a characterization is that, while this may be the effect of Kant's approach to ethics, the intention comes more from the other direction; the concern is not so much to promote altruism as to check self-interest. Philippa Foot sees Kant's rational ethic as a defence against the possibility that desires might change, especially one's own: "one wants as it were to make sure that one is stuck with the idea of acting morally whatever one's

---

[4] Peter Singer, *Practical Ethics* (Cambridge: Cambridge University Press, 1979), p. 209.
[5] Ibid.

concerns have become."[6] Morality protects us, and humanity at large, from being led by whatever inclination or attraction happens to appeal to us. It checks such temptations with the voice of reason. In this way, Kant's morality of duty remains as the echo of the voice of the God which has been replaced by the rational perceptiveness of mortals whose rationality somehow transcends the limitations of their emotional and passional natures.

The central concepts of Kantian morality are too familiar to require more than introductory recollection.[7] The pivotal notion of the categorical imperative provides the identification for the divine echo of the voice of duty. Kant's depictions of this provide the mechanism for substitution of a human calculation for the divine command. The way to determine whether a proposed course of action satisfies the requirement of the categorical imperative is to consider whether you would be willing to see that action performed by everyone in similar circumstances. Moral requirements are by their very nature free and uncoerced, but the test of the rightness of a possible action is to consider whether you would be willing to have it become as inescapable as a law of nature. If the action you are considering could be conceived to be as fortuitous in the moral realm as the law of gravity is in the natural realm, you could ask no higher warrant for assurance of the categorical nature of the imperative under consideration. The other widely noted version of the categorical imperative makes its function as a human rationale for morality more directly explicit in its admonition that we are to treat human beings, fellow possessors of rationality, always as ends and never merely as means. The rationality that we know in ourselves is to be respected in others. The overtones of altruism are already beginning to emerge, even in this brief sketch of the central direction of Kant's ethics.

---

[6] Philippa Foot, *Vices and Virtues and Other Essays in Moral Philosophy* (Berkeley and Los Angeles: University of California Press, 1978), p. 171.

[7] Immanuel Kant, *Critique of Practical Reason*, tr. Thomas Kingsmill Abbott (London: Longmans, Green & Co., 1927) represents the authoritative statement on Kant's ethics, but, as indicated in the succeeding notes, what is most relevant to the issue of altruism tends to appear in his other ethical writings.

The direct application of the approach to the issue of self-interest and altruism shows that it is impossible to extend self-interest to the status of a universal principle. "The maxim of self-interest contradicts itself when it is made universal law, that is, it is contradictory to duty."[8] To refuse to help others is to dismiss the possibility of help for anyone, including oneself. "If he lets his maxim of not willing to help others in turn when they are in need become public, i. e. makes this a universal permissible law, then everyone would likewise deny him assistance when he needs it, or at least be entitled to."[9] It could be said that this shows how refusing to help others would be inconsistent with self-interest. How it is inconsistent with duty might not be so clear. If I refuse to help others, I have to expect that they will not be inclined to help me. That is the consideration that underlies the reciprocal altruism of the sociobiologists. Kant takes this a step further, however, by suggesting not just that they would not be inclined to help, but that they would be entitled not to. Why would they be so entitled? That is where the rational consideration comes in, beyond the pragmatic consequence of the probability of tit-for-tat behavior. What is involved here is not anticipating possible consequences, but identifying courses of action that could be endorsed with rational consistency, courses of action that would be expected of anyone in similar circumstances. If I decide that the course for me is not to help, then I must allow that this is the appropriate course for everyone.

What Kant appears to offer, through his rational morality, thus might seem to represent not so much an alternative to the self-interest, contract ethics that takes others into account in one's own interest, as a refinement on more crass versions of this. Such a conclusion throws in serious question the concern and claim for the distinctiveness and autonomy of morality. So much is this the case that we must suspect that we have missed something crucial in Kant's position. What we have missed might be the way in which Kant's ethic requires us to approach

---

[8] Immanuel Kant, *The Doctrine of Virtue*, tr. Mary J. Gregor (Philadelphia: University of Pennsylvania Press, 1964), p. 121.
[9] Ibid.

morality impersonally, and thus to subordinate our own interests to the moral law. The distinctive note of morality, in these
terms, is impartiality. In asking whether we would be willing to
have every other moral agent act in the way we are considering,
we are submitting ourselves to the impartial adjudication of the
moral law. In a sense, we ourselves are an other; we view
ourselves impersonally, rising above our own particular desires
and ambitions. This is how Kant's ethic makes altruism possible, and indeed necessary: ". . . I ought to endeavour to
promote the happiness of others, not as if its realization
involved any concern of mine (whether by immediate inclination or by any satisfaction indirectly gained through reason),
but simply because a maxim which excludes it cannot be
conjoined as a universal law in one and the same volition."[10]
Kant's morality is thus ultra-altruistic, but in the most abstract
rational terms.

In this sense, morality and altruism coincide also for Kant.
The impartiality that allows us to bring ourselves and others to
the bar of rationally consistent behavior is what constitutes the
moral point of view and allows moral sensitivity. Such impartiality identifies concepts of moral virtues. "We use these concepts
to identify, understand, and evaluate our experiences of our
own inner states as well as those of others' as we naturally
imagine them."[11] As one among others, we are prevented from
the indulgence of self-interest that would ignore the reality of
others except insofar as recognizing them and their interests is
seen to be in our self-interest. The imaginative process entailed
in this pursuit of impartiality also allows us to appreciate the
presence and claims of others. The requirements of reason thus
place us on the same level as other human beings and raise the
moral claim of others to the level of our own. In this way,
morality checks the extreme individualism of what is often
regarded as natural self-interest.

The altruism of impartiality can be seen to represent a giant

[10] Immanuel Kant, *Fundamental Principles of the Metaphysic of Morals*, tr. Thomas Kingsmill
Abbott (London: Longmans, Green & Co., 1927), p. 60.
[11] Adrian M. S. Piper, "Impartiality, Compassion and Modal Imagination," *Ethics* 101
(1991): 756.

leap beyond the self-centered outlook. However, Kantian altruism is far from a heroic endorsement of self-sacrifice for
others. The impartiality between self and others that it identifies
represents essentially a morality of justice. The fundamental
direction is not one that enjoins concern for others; it is more a
matter of not infringing on others. The restrictions that this
morality would impose on inclinations of self-interest are primarily ones of non-interference. The rational morality reflects
and promotes the modern liberal vision of individuals making
their own way in life with as little regard for one another as
possible. The primary virtue is what has come to be called
justice as fairness; one is to accord to others the same opportunities that one expects for oneself. This is the direction represented by the impartiality that rationality makes possible.

The altruism required of a Kantian rational morality is thus
essentially a negative one. Positive concern for others, or a sense
of any requirement to come to the aid of others, amounts to
doing more than rationality requires. Such behavior involves
acts of supererogation, in a strict Kantian scheme. In a sense
they are more than morality demands, and yet morality represents the supreme human opportunity and achievement. Works
of supererogation may even be something of an embarrassment
in the Kantian scheme. They may appear to constitute a kind of
super morality. However, they also have a dangerous element in
that they can represent an infringement on the autonomy of the
moral agent who is the recipient of the benevolence. Thus acts
of benevolence can actually be immoral, undermining the
moral independence of the putative beneficiary.

The result of Kant's rational approach to morality thus
challenges preferential treatment of the self by the impartiality
requirement that the self be recognized as an other, and so
subject to any moral expectations we would have of others.
However, because it puts such a premium on the independence
and integrity of the moral agent, it also establishes expectations
of altruistic concern at a minimal level; primary duties involve
avoiding infringing on other moral agents. Positive acts of
benevolence are essentially above the call of duty. On these
terms, the prospects for serious altruism would not seem to

extend much beyond the reciprocal variety of sociobiology. The Kantian version of altruism is about recognizing the self as an other, rather than treating others as ourselves, and this rational requirement of impartiality subordinates benevolence to justice as a matter of principle.

A more positive reading of the Kantian approach to altruism sees it distinguished by the virtue of realism. It offers a modest range for recognizing the presence and claims of others that avoids the extremes of isolated self-interest and a naive assumption of a natural altruism that inclines us toward concern for others automatically. "The Kantian position, by contrast, is that, once we see the reasons for doing so, we can guide our conduct by a limited principle of benevolence, no matter how warm or cold our feelings toward others may run."[12] The scope may be modest, but it is realistic. We are not left in a Hobbesian state of total competition; nor are we expected to devote ourselves to others in disregard of our own aims and interests. We are expected to recognize that others are moral agents like ourselves; to extend them the courtesy of scope for their own living, and to come to their assistance in circumstances where we would want them to come to our aid. This realistic portrait illustrates how assumptions about our natural condition and understandings of our moral prospects are intimately intertwined. What is at stake may be seen more clearly by considering a contemporary variation on the Kantian approach that depicts how a common life might be constructed on such a base.

RAWLS' POLITICAL ALTERNATIVE TO ALTRUISM

The moderate avoidance of extremes of self-interest and altruism is represented in recent scholarship in the work of John Rawls. The justice morality of Kant is the main inspiration behind Rawls' central concept of justice as fairness. Of course, it is not the only inspiration. Rawls also draws heavily on social

---

[12] Thomas E. Hill, Jr., "Beneficence and Self-Love: A Kantian Perspective," in *Altruism*, ed. Ellen Frankel Paul, Fred D. Miller Jr., and Jeffrey Paul (Cambridge: Cambridge University Press, 1993), p. 5.

contract theory as a method of implementing the Kantian ideal.
The combination has been seen as an attempt "to retain Kant's
principle of moral autonomy while substituting the pursuit of
self-interest for Kant's universal rationality."[13] As a result of
this combination, Rawls not only addresses the challenge of
self-interest more explicitly than Kant did, but this is also what
allows him to be compared to the self-interest focus of sociobiologists. His position thus straddles the contractarian exten-
sions of self-interest, reflected in evolutionary ethics and in the
contractarianism of Gauthier, and the explicitly rational, constructivist approaches that remain closer to Kant's insistence on
the distinctiveness of morality.

The contractarian orientation allows Rawls to be claimed by
advocates of evolutionary ethics. In the assumed vision of the
human situation as one that is characterized by a natural
inclination to look out for ourselves and in the direction of
solution envisaged in terms of enlightened self-interest, Rawls
and evolutionary ethics can be seen to operate in basic agreement.[14] The deficiency in Rawls, from the evolutionary point of
view, is that he wastes effort on the hypothetical construction of
a contract; the human reality has been shaped directly by
natural selection.[15] From the Kantian side, the deficiency is in
conceding scope to self-interest; morality involves the rational
transcending of all inclinations and interests of the self. Rawls
can be seen to represent "the expression of a highest order
rational interest . . ., but that does not join the question of the
relationship between morality and interests per se, and motives
of connection in particular."[16] The dilemma of contract ethics
remains: on the basis of self-interest, why enter the contract?
Even if that can be answered in terms of advantages over the
vulnerabilities of naked self-interest, there remains the question:
why honor the contract, when it is to our advantage not to?
Refinements of self-interest reasons beg the question of why it

[13] James E. Will, *The Universal God: Justice, Love, and Peace in the Global Villiage* (Louisville,
Ky.: Westminster John Knox Press, 1994), p. 109.
[14] Michael Ruse, "Evolutionary Ethics: A Phoenix Arisen," *Zygon* 21/1 (1986): 100–1.
[15] Ibid.
[16] Barbara Herman, "Agency, Attachment, and Difference," *Ethics* 101 (1991): 779.

would not be easier and more adequate simply to acknowledge the moral claim. That, however, would challenge the self-interest base, and thus probably entail something of the conversion we suggested that appreciation of morality might require and provide.

The position that Rawls proposed in his influential *A Theory of Justice* has been refined after more than two decades in his *Political Liberalism*. Here Rawls explains how issues like moral positions can be avoided when the Kantian vision of justice as fairness is limited to the political dimension. This can be seen to offer a procedure for implementing the limited altruism afforded by Kant:

the reasonable (with its idea of reciprocity) is not the altruistic (the impartial acting solely for the interests of others) nor is it the concern for self (and moved by its ends and affections alone). In a reasonable society, most simply illustrated in a society of equals in basic materials, all have their own rational ends they hope to advance, and all stand ready to propose fair terms that others may reasonably be expected to accept, so that all may benefit and improve on what everyone can do on his own.[17]

The key premise of this position is the concept of reasonableness. Reasonable people can be expected to accord consideration to other people. They can hardly expect to have the freedom to pursue their own priorities, if they are not willing to accord that same freedom to others. This is essentially the liberal political alternative to altruism. This political version makes the limited altruism of Kant even more avoidable. The claim of the other is addressed at the level of political procedures.

We saw that the distinctive feature of Rawls' version of social contract is its requirement for the veil of ignorance in the original position, so that each person in the social contract does not know what position he or she will occupy in the resulting arrangement. This is how justice as fairness is to be assured. One major difference between the articulation of this approach in *A Theory of Justice* and the developments reflected in Rawls' subsequent essays, and consolidated in *Political Liberalism*, is that

[17] John Rawls, *Political Liberalism* (New York: Columbia University Press, 1993), p. 54.

theory is now replaced by a political focus. "The ambiguity of theory is now removed and justice as fairness is presented from the outset as a political conception of justice."[18] Rawls' determination to avoid metaphysical debates is solidified in an uncompromising concentration on the political. What is more, the political is conceived purely in procedural terms. It is an arrangement by which understandings of reality and direct contact with others can be avoided. No public vision is required in a political arrangement that allows individuals to respect each other's visions. Nothing as extravagant as altruism is required in a political arrangement that establishes space for one another as a matter of impersonal structural agreements.

The significance of Rawls' developed position for an understanding of altruism, especially of the rational Kantian version, is illustrated by the difference it represents from the crass commercial contract approach represented by David Gauthier. Although he represents a more pessimistic view of the human condition, seeing morality as at best a matter of arrangements to further our self-interests, in contrast to Rawls' affinity with the Kantian assumption of a more intrinsic moral sensibility, Gauthier is much more ambitious than Rawls in his expectation that the morality that is feasible should be defensible in rational terms. The insistence on restricting the focus to the political is expressed by Rawls in terms of a distinction between the rational and the reasonable. "The best one may be able to do is to show that serious attempts (Gauthier's is an example) to derive the reasonable from the rational do not succeed, and so far as they appear to succeed, they rely at some point on conditions expressing the reasonable itself."[19] All that reasonable people can do is agree to disagree. Gauthier's attempt to justify morality from a basis in rational self-interest is a lost cause. The problem is not the reservation we noted, the distinctiveness of morality, but the limits of rationality. Rationality defies conclusive agreement. The realistic course is to settle for reasonableness. People who cannot agree at the level of reason can be expected to act reasonably and respect the other person's right to differ.

---

[18] Ibid., p. xvii.   [19] Ibid., p. 53.

The position advocated by Rawls would answer the issue of altruism by rendering it superfluous, except in the "rational" sense of reasonable respect for others. Among possible reservations about this means of avoiding the direct challenge of altruism, two in particular seem to stand out: one is the assumption that reasonableness is intelligible and accessible apart from considerations regarding the rationality of the visions of the people involved and the other is the assumption of reasonableness itself. The increasing insistence on the purely political nature of "justice as fairness" involves seeing this political liberalism as "free standing." "Political liberalism, then, aims for a political conception of justice as a free standing view."[20] It is a political agreement that allows people with all sorts of religious and philosophical views to live together in spite of those differences. This is possible because they can agree on the purely political level that reasonable people should respect people who hold views that differ from their own. In this sense, political liberalism, as Rawls promotes it, is, as he says, an extension of the movement for toleration that marked the transition from the Church-controlled uniformity of the pre-modern era to the acceptance of religious diversity in the modern period. "Were justice as fairness to make an overlapping consensus possible it would complete and extend the movement of thought that began three centuries ago with the gradual acceptance of the principle of toleration and led to the nonconfessional state and equal liberty of conscience."[21] Agreement at the level of basic convictions is impossible; modern political toleration of different views is far preferable to clashes over convictions that provoked the religious wars that preceded the acceptance of toleration and that are still all too evident today, as close to the locale in which the acceptance of toleration was forged as Northern Ireland.

On the political level, to which Rawls seeks to confine himself, it is difficult to do anything but endorse the direction he proposes. The question is whether the political level can be separated from wider visions as cleanly as Rawls assumes. He

---

[20] Ibid., p. 10.   [21] Ibid., p. 154.

recognizes that his proposal for a free-standing political toler-
ance derives from a Kantian vision, but he is confident that that
background can be ignored in concentration on the political
level. "The problem is this: in order to work according to a
Kantian conception of justice it seems desirable to detach the
structure of Kant's doctrine from its background in transcendental idealism and to give it a procedural interpretation by
means of the construction of the original position."[22] In the
context of modern liberal democracy, the procedural direction
Rawls advocates seems obvious. In spite of his disavowal of
theory, what Rawls seems to be doing is offering theoretical
backing for this political compromise. Yet precisely because of
the democratic atmosphere, it is easy to overlook that what is
being called for is compromise. Holders of various visions of life
are being asked to disregard what is most distinctive in those
visions in the interest of endorsing a common political compromise that will allow them all to function privately, or in groups
of like-minded citizens, out of those visions. Rawls would state
his expectation in more positive terms; his claim is that the
political agreement should represent a consensus that is possible
out of those varied visions. "Since we assume each citizen to
affirm some such vision, we hope to make it possible for all to
accept the political conception as true or reasonable from the
standpoint of their own comprehensive vision, whatever it may
be."[23] Such acceptance may well appear reasonable in a
modern western context, but that may be because of the
homogenization of visions that has resulted through seculariza-
tion. It would not be so easy for people who hold visions that
contrast with the western Kantian outlook assumed by Rawls.
To take one extreme example, an implication of Rawls' position
is that no basic vision is worth civil disagreement; for some
people, visions are not only worth civil disagreement but also
worth dying for. Such a possibility would seem to be precluded
by Rawls' position, except as an eccentric personal stance.
Anyone who would go to such extremes would not be reasonable, after all. Yet that is precisely the point: what is reasonable

[22] Ibid., p. 285.   [23] Ibid., p. 150.

can hardly be separated from how reason is understood. Basic visions may not be as detachable as Rawls' political alternative to altruism would require.

We can hope that it is more than modern western prejudice that would lead us to favor an extension of the principle of toleration to the whole world. For people to be willing to die for their convictions is one thing; to be ready to kill for them is another. Yet what is at stake in such clashes of basic vision is hardly something amenable to political compromise. The compromise that Rawls suggests is clearly preferable to violent clashes between proponents of differing visions; that is the merit and basis for endorsing his direction. If it is to be more than a compromise, however, it will have to allow for engagement of competing visions themselves. Insofar as such engagement is precluded, either deliberately or by default, through a concentration on supposedly independent political procedures, those visions will smoulder and erupt in ways that can only be destructive for the reduced agreement achieved. The ideal would seem to involve a working compromise, such as Rawls depicts, along with ongoing public discussion among, and where possible celebration of, different fundamental visions. Without this added dimension, the separation of the political that Rawls advocates is apt to amount not so much to an avoidance of involvement in wider visions as to a surreptitious endorsement of the modern secular anthropocentric vision. Without this public dialogue, which has been seriously lacking in the modern western compromise, fundamental visions can only be private or interest group options that are overshadowed by the unofficial, but for that reason all the more influential, vision of modern secularity.

The virtue of Rawls' proposal, as of its Kantian precedent, is its apparent realism. "The reasonable society is neither a society of saints nor a society of the self-centered. It is very much a part of our ordinary human world, not a world we think of much virtue, until we find ourselves without it."[24] In the spirit of Aristotle, and in the direct lineage of Kant, Rawls offers

---

[24] Ibid, p. 54.

us a middle way between the extremes of altruism and egoism. It might not seem spectacular, but its importance may be appreciated the more life varies from that state of basic civility. Who would not prefer to live among reasonable people, rather than among religious fanatics or acquisitive and aggressive egotists? The ordinariness of Rawls' proposal may lead us to underestimate its significance. However, that danger must not be allowed to divert us from its defects as a position of compromise. Those defects concern both the understanding of life that underlies this compromise proposal and the possibilities for life that the proposal affords.

As an assessment of the human condition, the Kantian rational approach as it is refined by Rawls may be naive and optimistic. We may not be as reasonable as his requirement for reasonableness assumes. To be rational, in Rawls' scheme, is to hold some view of life that we seek to live by, and presumably, because it is seen to be rational, one we would also like to see others adopt. In a sense, this is what distinguishes humans as rational beings. If we are also reasonable, we will recognize that people who hold different views are in the same position. The success of Rawls' proposal depends on the combination of rationality and reasonableness. "Merely reasonable agents would have no ends of their own they wanted to advance by fair cooperation; merely rational agents lack a sense of justice and fail to recognize the independent validity of the claims of others."[25] The rational views and interests of individuals who are pursuing their own ends must be qualified by the reasonable recognition of the similar right of others. What is more, there seems to be a basic assumption that such reasonableness can be expected to follow. If views are rational, people holding them will be reasonable. That assumption extends beyond any formal connection between reasonableness and rationality to cover the view of the human condition as such. The liberal democratic project assumes that people are and will be reasonable. Any consideration that they might be egotistical and self-serving is not given much scope. "All that is known in the original position

[25] Ibid., p. 52.

is that each of the conceptions of justice available to the parties have consequences superior to general egoism."[26] This might be taken to imply that without the contract people are taken to be fundamentally egotistical, perhaps even in a Hobbesian sense. However, the very possibility of the contract is premised on the assumption that people are ready and willing to rise above any egoistic inclinations in a spirit of general reasonableness. Rawls offers a more optimistic view of humanity than the self-interest vision of sociobiologists and commercial contractarians like Gauthier, but the very assumption of moral sensibilities may lead to overlooking some of the propensity to self-interest that these narrower visions assume.

To some extent, this is a variation on the fundamental problem we noted in Rawls in considering the contract approach he advances in *Theory*. His assumption of a minimum consensus may not be as inclusive as he thinks. His equation of rationality with self-interest, even in a broad sense that is supposed to encompass the moral and even the religious, may be too restrictive. Even if a formal rationality is conceded, in the sense that by definition everyone wants to advance their own position, there may be some positions that directly contradict the primacy of self-interest that Rawls' rationality continues to assume. In short, his position may not be as neutral as he assumes and requires. The difficulty we are facing here is, in some ways, the other side of this picture. Not only may individuals hold visions that defy the self-interest platform; in practice they may be more driven by self-interest than Rawls' rational version would allow. For while Rawls assumes a basic characterization of humanity in terms of self-interest, he understands this self-interest in very rational terms. It is a self-interest from which cooperation is readily derivable, because the selves involved are basically reasonable. There is as much reason to wonder about Rawls' anthropology, whether human beings are as reasonable as he assumes, as there is to wonder about his metaphysics, whether self-interest can afford a sufficiently broad base to encompass all possible visions of reality.

[26] Ibid., p. 279.

These reservations are closely connected; indeed, they are two sides of a common reservation. What is at stake ultimately is Rawls' view of reality; his metaphysics and the anthropology that goes with it. The issue is not as straightforward as this, though, because Rawls insists that he is not involved in metaphysics. Especially in the more recent writings, culminating in *Political Liberalism*, Rawls contends that his focus is purely political, a procedural approach for allowing reasonable people to cooperate without regard to metaphysical commitments. Richard Rorty contends that the kind of reservations we have been considering reflect a basic misunderstanding of Rawls because not only does he not intend to make pronouncements in the areas of metaphysics, his position does not involve any particular view of the self either. Rorty contends that Rawls' post-*Theory* writings indicate that he intends to move a step beyond the Enlightenment vision represented by Kant. As the Enlightenment eliminated the theological dimension as a source of controversy, so, Rorty claims, Rawls is proposing the elimination of controversy about the human dimension. "As citizens and as social theorists, we can be as indifferent to philosophical disagreements about the nature of the self as Jefferson was to theological differences about the nature of God."[27] The later writings of Rawls, which have since been encompassed by *Political Liberalism*, indicate, according to Rorty, that the focus is completely immediate. "When reread in the light of such passages, *A Theory of Justice* no longer seems committed to a philosophical account of the human self, but only to a historico-sociological description of the way we live now."[28] Then far from sidelined religious issues obtruding on the sanitized political scene, we do not even have to be concerned about different understandings of ourselves. Yet if this is what Rawls is about – if he is telling us how we actually live – why does his work have such a prescriptive tone? Even Rorty's own prose is laden with an admonition to avoid persis-

---

[27] Richard Rorty, "The Priority of Democracy to Philosophy," in *Prospects for a Common Morality*, ed. Gene Outka and John P. Reeder, Jr. (Princeton: Princeton University Press, 1993), pp. 259–60.

[28] Ibid., p. 261.

tent errors and to follow the way of wisdom he detects. And just as such postmodern claims to simple description ring hollow because of the undertones of prescription, so the prescription also reflects a vision both of how life is and of how it ought to be. If these elements are lacking, it is difficult to imagine why people like Rawls and Rorty would be worth reading or why they would take the trouble to write. It may be that Rorty can see Rawls' position not to require a view of the moral subject because the view of the moral subject it contains is the one that he also assumes, namely the modern Enlightenment-sponsored view of humanity as basically reasonable.

That this procedural approach involves a view of humanity, not to mention a metaphysical vision that places humanity at the center of reality that is optimistic, if not naive, in the reasonableness it expects of human beings, is only one side of the difficulty posed by a Rawlsian refinement of the rational Kantian approach. This problem is that we may be more selfish than this rational, moral view of humanity assumes. The other side is that this vision also has an almost opposite effect in terms of the possibilities it affords for expression of human initiative. Just as its assessment of human nature may be unduly opti-mistic, so its prospects for human improvement may be unduly restrictive. It assumes that human beings will be reasonable, but it does not expect more than this. In fact, in his political refinement of Kant, Rawls may even seem to be approaching the reciprocity stance of evolutionary ethics: "the idea of reciprocity lies between the idea of impartiality, which is altruistic (being moved by the general good), and the idea of mutual advantage understood as everyone's being advantaged with respect to each person's present or expected future situa-tion as things are."[29] In these terms, justice as fairness can be seen as a reasonable counterpart to the reciprocal altruism of the sociobiologists; it is a procedure by which we can each expect to be better off than we would be if we pursued our own self-interest directly. What Rawls might be seen to add to the sociobiology version is the claim that as rational beings we can

---

[29] Rawls, *Political Liberalism*, pp. 16–17.

be expected to appreciate the reasonableness of this position. What the position does not allow for, any more than socio-biology does, is the reality of genuine altruism. As a compromise position, justice as fairness remains in the middle. It expects people to be reasonable, rather than crassly self-interested; but it also does not expect more than this.

Once again, it might be said that we are failing to appreciate what Rawls intends. He does not mean to exclude genuine altruism, it might be said; in fact, his promotion of justice as fairness could be seen to be intent on providing a basis on which genuine altruism might flourish. The point is that it cannot be expected to flourish without this common reasonable base. "Reasonable persons, we say, are not moved by the general good as such but desire for its own sake a social world in which they, as free and equal, can cooperate with others on terms all can accept."[30] The purely political procedure of justice as fairness will allow the altruist scope to advance her or his cause of altruism. Of course, this also allows people scope to pursue their self-interest. This is where the Machiavellian machinations arise, posing the question of whether it would not be more profitable to appear to be cooperative rather than actually to cooperate. The answer of procedural justice would seem to be that reasonable people would not act this way. This brings us back to the issue of the accuracy and adequacy of the anthropological vision involved; it is also indicative of the limit on expectations of reasonable people. Far from proving a base for altruism, such purely procedural justice would seem to be as exclusive of altruism as it is vulnerable to manipulation by people who are less reasonable than the position assumes.

Rawls can be seen to reflect the illusion of "preliminarity" that has characterized modernity. A large part of the authority exercised over the popular imagination by science was due to its promise that it was in process of building a totally secure factual picture of reality, piece by empirical piece. Any reservations about this assurance were met with the rejoinder that the issue posed represented an area that science had not yet managed to

[30] Ibid., p. 50.

encompass; the implication, if not outright assertion, being that its incorporation in the authoritative scientific picture of reality was only a matter of time. Rawls is offering us a procedural political platform on which reasonable people can construct any form of life they wish. The illusion emerges from two dimensions of this focus, which are directly parallel to the positivistic reading of science. On the one hand, the explicit focus never gets beyond the platform. The possibilities of procedural justice remain the dominating topic of considera-tion. Rawls can never get beyond reciprocity to altruism. At the same time, however, the treatment of this limited focus entails all sorts of metaphysical and anthropological assumptions and expectations. Far from being left as a possible goal to be pursued on the basis of the social arrangements effected through procedural justice, altruism recedes and reciprocity becomes definitive of human prospects.

Thus, through his refinement of the rational approach, Rawls can be seen to reflect a Kantian realism. Avoiding the extremes of bestiality and moral heroism, he outlines a way for reason-able people to live together despite their differences. As he says himself, this would be no small accomplishment in a world of such diversity and hostility. Unfortunately, his approach presup-poses that people are reasonable and ultimately allows nothing more than the compromise of rationality. Having likened Rawls to the advocates of natural science, a more adequate character-ization of his position might be found through comparison with the social sciences. His proposal can be likened to the modeling done by economists, for example, so that the limitations of those models is also indicative of the limitations of Rawls' purely political procedures. Economic models are often ingenious in their own terms; the difficulty is that the real world so seldom conforms to the patterns they prescribe. In the end, the greatest difficulty with Rawls may be that his realistic approach is so unrealistic. His proposal remains as remote from unreasonable people as economic models are removed from real buyers and sellers; and unfortunately many of us are much more unreason-able than a Rawlsian society can tolerate. At the same time, the overly optimistic view of human reasonableness results in imposing a limitation on expectations for human goals and behavior, whereby transcending of reasonable reciprocity is an aberration. Thus the import of Rawls' refinement of Kant may be that the rational approach to altruism is too broad and too narrow at the same time, too broad in failing to appreciate how self-interested humans can be, and too narrow in assuming a horizon that does not exceed the possibilities of a reciprocal broadening of self-interest. Human beings may be more selfish and more altruistic than the outlook of the rational middle can appreciate. Further clarification of this approach may be possible through consideration of a direct attempt to assess the possibility of altruism from this rational perspective.

NAGEL ON THE RATIONAL POSSIBILITY OF ALTRUISM

A direct articulation of the meaning of altruism, from a Kantian rational perspective, has been attempted by Thomas Nagel, in *The Possibility of Altruism*. In keeping with its Kantian lineage, Nagel's approach to altruism is in terms of rational impartiality. "To apply a principle to oneself impartially, one must be able to apply it to the person who one is, in abstraction from the fact that it is oneself."[31] Altruism, in this approach, amounts to seeing oneself as an other, as we saw in Kant. The point, as Nagel presents it, is to be able to rise above natural inclinations for personal preference and to treat oneself as any other person. The claim of ethics, in its characteristic Kantian authoritative autonomy, depends on this ability to see oneself as subject to the same requirements as all other rational beings. Where Nagel makes his distinctive contribution is in seeking a rationale for such moral motivation. Why should I be concerned about others at all? Rather than leave the answer at the level of a Kantian confidence in the rationality of serious human beings, Nagel risks entering the murky realm of self-interest and motivation.

While morality itself may be seen to derive its authority from the requirements of rational consistency, so that the possibility

[31] Thomas Nagel, *The Possibility of Altruism* (Princeton: Princeton University Press, 1979), p. 108.

of altruism depends on the ability to treat ourselves impersonally, this rational requirement is not obviously and immediately compelling in itself. Some link is required between that rational level of morality in itself and the level of activity where the moral requirement is felt by the individual and translated into practical terms of action. "What can be asserted with some confidence is that in so far as rational requirements, practical or theoretical, represent conditions on belief and action, such necessity as may attach to them is not logical but natural or psychological."[32] We are not purely rational beings; what we do and why we do it is determined by the particular being we are and the feelings and aspirations that prompt our action.

At the risk of compromising the rational purity of a Kantian approach to morality, Nagel seeks to find an anchor for ethical motivation in the self. "The more central and unavoidable is the concept of the self on which the possibility of moral motivation can be shown to depend, the closer we will have come to demonstrating that the demands of ethics are inescapable."[33] The particular form of the risk that Nagel takes involves combining what for Kant were contradictory, if not contrary, categories, the moral and the prudent. He seeks to find a parallel between the fact that we have reason to be concerned about our future selves and a sense that we should also have some concern for other selves. However, this is not simply a prudential grounding, as it could be if it were simply a matter of seeking to broaden self-interest. The claim that is being made is ultimately a metaphysical one. "A person's future should be of interest to him not because it is among his present interests, but because it is *his future*."[34] A person's total well being, Nagel argues, should be more important than any desires that happen to be present at the moment. Present desires represent an appeal from the outside; consideration of future desires, on the other hand, involve "an acknowledgement that certain things are not outside to begin with, and that events in his future hold an interest for him now because they belong to a single person of whom his present significance is merely one

stage."[35] Looking beyond the appeal of present desires to
desires of the future represents a reasonable extension for
outlooks that are inclined to remain narrow and short-range, to
the detriment of those who hold them. A person who neglects
long-term desires for indulgence in desires of the moment is not
acting prudently.

It is Nagel's contention that this reasoning can be expanded
to encompass the scope of altruism. Just as I can expect to exist
in the future as a variation on the self that I am now, so too I
must recognize that there are other selves now. In looking
beyond my present self temporally, Nagel seems to be saying, I
should be prepared to look beyond my present self spatially.
The parallel that is being proposed is not only not entirely
clear; it also appears to be very precarious. Future versions of
my self are precisely versions of *my*self. Even if I can be
persuaded to be rational enough to take my future prospects
into account, it is not clear how this opens the way for any
serious recognition of the claim of selves that are truly other.
The difficulty is the one that Kant avoided by insisting on a
categorial distinction between the moral and the merely
prudent. It is prudent to take a broad view of my interests, one
that encompasses future prospects for myself. But no amount of
prudence, Kant would contend, can add up to morality.

This brings us back to the issue with which we began this
consideration of constructivist approaches to morality – does
morality reflect a distinctive outlook that is accessible only
through some type of conversion? Nagel wants to mitigate such
a contrast by providing a link between our natural concern for
ourselves and acknowledgment of the claims of others. His
reason for doing this would seem to lie in a recognition that
rational impartiality is too far removed from our basic human
reality to represent a serious goal for us. Even if we could be
induced to consider our interests in the long term, and if this
were to extend to recognition of the presence of other selves
with similar interests, for this to result in actual altruistic
behavior is something else again. Nagel himself is not optimistic

[35] Ibid., p. 43.

about the prospects. "The manner in which human beings have conducted themselves so far does not encourage optimism about the moral future of the species,"[36] are the words with which he closes the book. In his later book, *The View from Nowhere*, Nagel is ambivalent about the prospects for morality, to the point of actual contradiction. The gap between our own interests and the demands of morality is seen to be so great that he is forced to conclude: "I doubt that an appealing reconciliation of morality, rationality, and the good life can be achieved within the boundaries of ethical theory, narrowly understood."[37] Success in the articulation of a persuasive moral account remains as unpromising as the prospects for altruism appeared in the earlier book. Yet he is now considerably more optimistic about the prospects for the actual practice of morality than in the conclusion of his consideration of altruism. "I do not think it is utopian to look forward to the gradual development of a greater universality of moral respect, an internalization of moral objectivity analogous to the gradual internalization of scientific progress that seems to be a feature of modern culture."[38]

If Nagel risked transgressing the crucial distinction Kant drew between morality and prudence in his earlier book, in this later one, he could be seen to be overlooking the even more pervasive distinction to which Kant also contributed, that between the evaluative moral realm and the descriptive factual realm, this latter being epitomized particularly by science. It is one thing for humanity to internalize scientific progress, with the conveniences it provides, although even this is not so obvious today in light of increasing awareness of overlooked environmental costs; however, it is another matter for humanity to internalize new possibilities which come as claims and demands upon us. This newfound optimism could be indicative of a shift from assumptions of Kantian insistence on the

---

[36] Ibid., p. 146.
[37] Thomas Nagel, *The View from Nowhere* (New York: Oxford University Press, 1986), p. 205.
[38] Ibid., p. 187.

autonomy and authority of morality to one where the claims of morality are taken to be less foreign.

The pessimism of the earlier Nagel is readily explained in terms of the outlook he broadly shares with Kant and with Rawls. This outlook not only makes altruism elusive because of its elevation as a rational ideal; it renders it virtually impossible because of the egotistic view of rationality that is assumed. To be rational is to be concerned with self, so that everything, including altruism, can be reasonable only by satisfying the requirements of this egocentric vision. "Only if we know what people have reason to do for themselves can we discover what, if anything, others have reason to do for them,"[39] Nagel insists. The assumption reflected here is the rationalistic one that insists on the integrity of the individual above all. That is what underlies Kant's insistence on the autonomy of morality; moral autonomy is essential finally because morality is a matter for individuals to appreciate in their own autonomy. This is what underlies Rawls' assumption of the necessity for a social contract; reasonable people can be expected to be cooperative, but to be reasonable is essentially to be an independent individual.

This assumption of the importance of the individual is the strength of the rational approach. It is surely true that serious altruism must depend on an ability to recognize the claims of others as having a legitimacy similar to our own. It is also the case, however, that the isolation of the self in this outlook makes such recognition difficult, if not impossible. The prospects for altruism may thus depend not only on such a recognition of others, rationally, as on direct encounter with others. This may also extend to a challenge to this view of our situation in terms of an essential individualism. It may be that we are not finally isolated individuals so much as inherently social beings. Perhaps the links that rationalists seek to establish are there naturally to some extent. This is the view of the other dominant approach to ethics in the modern west, and the other distinctive approach to altruism.

---

[39] Ibid., p. 17.

CHAPTER 6

Collegial altruism

Thomas Nagel's Kantian exploration of the prospects for altruism in *The Possibility of Altruism*, has its counterpart in a description and promotion of a more immediate version of altruism by Lawrence Blum in *Friendship, Altruism and Morality*. "Impartiality, fairness, and justice are personal virtues, but they are merely some virtues among others," Blum contends. "They are not definitive of moral virtue altogether."[1] To equate these qualities with moral virtue is to see morality in abstract terms. This overlooks two central dimensions of morality in particular. It does not consider the actual situation in which the moral agent operates, and so is deficient in accounting for motivation for moral action in general, and for altruism in particular.[2] Moral issues emerge not by standing back and reflecting on reality in impersonal terms, but through claims that are made on us directly by people to whom we are connected and with whom we come into contact. Failure to consider the moral agent's real situation points to the other basic defect in the rational approach to altruism, the neglect of the emotions. "Our feelings and emotions are as much a part of our moral self as are the actions we perform and the moral views to which we give assent."[3] Rational deliberation, on its own, is not only ungrounded in human life, but also unmotivated for human beings. As well as being rational beings, we are also constituted by emotions and the attachments that trigger these. Such attachments, and our vulnerability to them, are the main source

---

[1] Lawrence A. Blum, *Friendship, Altruism and Morality* (New York: Routledge & Kegan Paul, 1980), p. 55.
[2] Ibid., pp. 139, 133, 137.   [3] Ibid., p. 185.

of moral sensitivity and motivation, and the basis of a living, as opposed to an abstract, altruism, according to this direct approach.

DIRECT ALTRUISM

This approach to altruism draws on the other main version of morality that has enjoyed prominence in the modern west. Although the Kantian approach to morality has been very influential throughout the modern era, it has not been the only approach. Kant's duty morality has had to share the stage with the utilitarian approach formulated by Jeremy Bentham and John Stuart Mill. In contrast to Kant's insistence on the autonomy and purity of morality, the utilitarian approach determines moral priorities in terms of consequences. Not pure rational justification, but prospects for improving life are to constitute the determinative direction of ethical reflection. What is more, the focus of that reflection is to be not the moral propriety of the acting individual but the benefaction of those affected by the action. Achieving "the greatest good for the greatest number" was the way that Mill stated the moral objective. The utilitarian approach thus offers a fundamentally social perspective, in contrast to the individualism of Kant. As a result, its version of ethics would seem to hold the promise of much more scope for altruism. Where, on Kantian assumptions, altruism represents an alien objective for individuals who exist in essential isolation, a utilitarian vision would see individuals as social beings whose destinies are interlocked from the start. Altruism, then, is not only an objective, but to some extent a reality. Our welfare is bound up with the welfare of others, as is theirs with ours.

Although utilitarian consequentialism has been the main alternative to Kantian duty ethics in the modern era, it is not this form as such that is the direct inspiration for this more immediate approach to morality. Utilitarianism also remains too much on the abstract level to capture the full effect of this more direct approach to altruism. Like Kant's duty ethics, it too is an ethics of principle. It involves standing back and deciding

on the right course of action. That this takes possible consequences into account makes it more socially responsive than the
Kantian rational approach, but not necessarily that much more
personal. Alasdair MacIntyre illustrates the further dimension
that is needed through the example of Huckleberry Finn. As a
matter of principle, Huck knows what he should do; he should
turn in Miss Watson's slave, Jim. But Huck finds, what many of
us have discovered, that sometimes you have to forget your
principles and do what is right. Huck decides that he cannot
inform on his friend Jim, even though all his training and moral
insight tells him that is what he ought to do. That is his duty;
but Huck is led by another route. "He finds his way morally by
means of a half-hearted sympathy. But he does not find it by
universalizable maxims or indeed by maxims at all."[4] From a
Kantian perspective, this amounts to the abandonment of
morality; Huck makes his situation an exception to the universal
demands that everyone else is expected to honor. Slaves are
property, their whereabouts to be reported if they are at large;
Huck knows this, but Jim is not just a slave, but his friend. He
has allowed his own desires to cloud his rational obligation to
duty.

Huck's action would have been right, on a Kantian basis, if
slaves were recognized as persons; whether that would happen
on a Kantian basis itself is a debatable point. It might be that it
would take something of the utilitarian sense of consideration of
consequences of actions to trigger the recognition that would
result in such change of social vision. Yet whether an expansion
of the utilitarian range of consequences would be sufficient
either is also debatable. It may be that the change could only be
effected by people like Huck, who get to know actual slaves like
Jim, and discover that they are people. If this is so, then
morality involves something much more immediate and personal than rational duty or ranges of consequences. Actual
relations and the emotions that go with them may have to be
recognized as part of the moral domain, rather than as dangerous deflections to be avoided by rational defences. Such a

[4] Alasdair MacIntyre, "What morality is not," in *The Definition of Morality*, ed.
G. Wallace and A. D. M. Walker (London: Methuen, 1970), p. 38.

possibility has its own modern classical advocate in the person
of Kant's Scottish predecessor, David Hume. Altruism is not a
matter of rational impartiality, for Hume, but of a feeling for
others that Bernard Williams calls "the slide towards morality."
"For Hume, there are desires of different degrees of generality,
involving objects with different degrees of remoteness and
independence from the subject: the slide towards morality is a
slide along these continua."[5] For this approach, morality and
altruism are more immediate and natural than the Kantian
rational account can recognize.

Unfortunately, how Hume understands morality is not as
clear as some who appeal to him would tend to suggest.
Because he did not isolate morality for its distinctiveness, as
Kant did, there is a less deliberate focus. Because he saw
morality to involve emotions, rather than identifying it with
rationality as a bulwark against the emotions, as Kant did, his
treatment is inherently more ambiguous. It also seems that
Hume's views on the subject changed. Alasdair MacIntyre
points out that in the *Treatise*, he seems to link any tendency in
the direction of altruism to our own self-interest. "In general, it
may be affirm'd that there is no such passion in human minds
as the love of mankind, merely as such, independent of personal
qualities, of service, or of relation to oneself."[6] However,
MacIntyre notes, in the *Enquiry Concerning Human Understanding*,
Hume recognizes a tendency to concern for the welfare of
others as a direct source of motivation, independent of concerns
of self-interest.[7] Yet such differences may be encompassed by a
more consistent view of human nature that informs Hume's
basic outlook. In the next section of the *Treatise* after the one
MacIntyre cites, Hume observes: "So far from thinking, that
men have no affection for anything beyond themselves, I am of
opinion, that tho' it be rare to meet with one, who loves any
single person better than himself; yet 'tis as rare to meet with

---

[5] Bernard Williams, *Problems of the Self* (New York: Cambridge University Press, 1976),
p. 260.
[6] David Hume, *A Treatise of Human Nature*, ed. L. A. Selby-Bigge (Oxford: Clarendon
Press, 1928), bk. III, pt. II, sec. I., p. 481.
[7] Alasdair MacIntyre, "Egoism and Altruism," in *The Encyclopedia of Philosophy*, vol. 2,
ed. Paul Edwards (New York: Macmillan, 1967), p. 464.

one, in whom all the kind affections, taken together, do not over-balance all the selfish."[8] It is this optimistic reading of human nature that accounts for Hume's expectation that morality can be expected to develop and be refined from natural human sympathy.

Central to Hume's approach to ethics is the conviction that sympathy is "the chief source of moral distinctions."[9] In contrast to Kant's rational moral agents, who seek to rise above the siren call of desires and the competing clashes of self-interest, Hume's moral agents expand from the particular location in which they find themselves toward the wider welfare that became the focus of utilitarianism. Humean individuals do not become moral beings as adults who are capable of rational abstraction, but rather as members of families who learn to recognize the claims and concerns of other members of the family. Morality grows from expansion of these natural sympathies. "Morality, on Hume's account, is the outcome of a search for ways of eliminating contradictions in the 'passions' of sympathetic persons who are aware both of their own and their fellows' desires and needs, including emotional needs."[10] Although Hume starts from the particular circumstances, in contrast to Kant's direct engagement of the individual in determining the universal demands of rationality, he is no less intent on the universal scope of morality than Kant was. This too is the aim of practical education in sympathy. This is implicit in the nature of morality itself, for Hume no less than for Kant. "It [the notion of morals] also implies some sentiment, so universal and comprehensive as to extend to all mankind, and render the actions and conduct, even of persons the most remote, an object of applause or censure, according as they agree or disagree with that rule of right which is established."[11] Morality emerges from the real relations in which we

---

[8] Hume, *A Treatise of Human Nature*, bk. III, pt. II, sec. 2, p. 487.
[9] Hume, *A Treatise of Human Nature*, bk. III, pt. III, sec. 6, p. 618.
[10] Annette C. Baier, "Hume, the Women's Moral Theorist?" in *Women and Moral Theory*, ed. Eva Feder Kittay and Diana T. Meyers (Totowa, NJ: Rowman & Littlefield, 1987), p. 41.
[11] David Hume, *An Enquiry Concerning the Principles of Morals*, in *Enquiries Concerning Human*

find ourselves; what is at stake in these relations, however, is something that concerns humanity as a whole.

More than two decades ago, Paul T. Menzel was detecting what he described as "a growing movement in contemporary philosophical circles toward granting that a Humean step of sympathy for others may be the only way to start moving the egoist out of his pure egoism toward some altruism."[12] The intervening period has provided considerable confirmation of Menzel's anticipations, especially in the directions advocated in feminist ethics. That the proposals can be attributed to Hume, however, is not so clear. There would seem to be a significant gap between recent promotions of sympathy ethics and the direction indicated, however ambiguously, by Hume, and not least in the very matter of the central concept of sympathy itself. "Sympathy" has received a lot of bad academic press in recent years. In ordinary usage, it can carry connotations of pity and condescension. One who feels sympathy for another is then asserting their superiority to that other person, however unintentional that assertion may be. However, these elements of pity and condescension should not be characteristic of sympathy.[13] To avoid such connotations, some have abandoned the term entirely for the more recent alternative, "empathy."

A fundamental distinction between the two is that empathy involves taking the other seriously. In generalizing from their experience of interviews with rescuers of Jews under the Nazi regime to propose how we might move toward a caring society, Pearl and Samuel Oliner find the distinction between sympathy and empathy crucial. "Sympathy," they suggest, "means pity or commiseration *for* another's condition. It implies looking at another person from one's perspective and at a distance." This leaves sympathy as "basically self-centered"; contrary to the moral connotations it would have for a follower of Hume's direction. The preferred alternative for the Oliners, and many

Understanding and Concerning the Principles of Morals, third edition (Oxford: Clarendon Press, 1986), p. 272.

[12] Paul T. Menzel, "Divine Grace and Love: Continuing Trouble for a Logically Norm-Dependent Religious Ethics," *Journal of Religious Ethics* 3/2 (1975): 261.

[13] Philip Mercer, *Sympathy and Ethics: A Study of the Relationship between Sympathy and Morality with Special Reference to Hume's Treatise* (Oxford: Clarendon Press, 1972), p. 19.

others today, is empathy. "Empathy, on the other hand," the Oliners claim, "means feeling *with* the other person. It implies looking at others from their own perspective and responding to them on their own terms."[14] The significance of the difference emerges in the result, according to the Oliners. Those who help others out of sympathy are really primarily helping themselves, and this is detected by the recipients. The notes of pity and condescension are not far off, however little the helper is aware of them. The aid of the empathizer, on the other hand, tends to be more appreciated because people find themselves taken seriously in their own right. The moral would seem to be that if Hume's more direct approach to altruism is to be followed today, it must be followed more strictly. It must be deliberately altruistic, taking the other seriously in her or his own right. Practitioners of sympathy ethics must first be empathizers.

"The Other" has become a prominent theme in academia of late. Emphasis on the reality and claim of the other is central to several strands of the amorphous movement labeled post-modernism. "The real face of postmodernity, as Emmanuel Levinas sees with such clarity, is the face of the other,"[15] says David Tracy. The merit of this assessment is attested in one of the most prominent schools of postmodernity, deconstruction, by one of its most prominent representatives, Jacques Derrida: "deconstruction is, in itself, a perceived response to an alterity which necessarily calls, summons or motivates it."[16] This focus of postmodernity emerges in contrast with a perceived homogeneity that is taken to characterize the modern outlook. The point of modernity was to relate everything to a common denominator, to reduce everything to a manageable sameness. Kant's preoccupation with the universal is a case in point. According to Mark Taylor, this uniformity is what evokes the

---

[14] Pearl M. Oliner, *Toward a Caring Society: Ideas in Action* (Westport, Conn.: Praeger, 1995), p. 32.

[14] David Tracy, "Theology and the Many Faces of Postmodernity," in *Readings in Modern Theology: Britain and America*, ed. Robin Gill (Nashville: Abingdon Press, 1995), p. 228.

[16] Jacques Derrida, "Deconstruction and the other," in *Dialogues with Contemporary Continental Thinkers*, ed. Richard Kearney (Manchester: Manchester University Press, 1984), p. 118.

interest in alterity. "When thought and action tend toward homogenization and hegemony, the question of otherness becomes critical."[17] Such recognition of the importance of otherness cannot help but have significance for any attempt to appreciate the place and role of altruism in human life. That significance is even more directly relevant than such insistence on attending to otherness in itself, however, in that the focus on otherness also has received direct ethical statement. The first authority cited here in illustration of this focus on alterity, Emmanuel Levinas, takes a pointedly ethical direction in his explication of the importance of the other. "I am trying to show that man's ethical relation to the other is ultimately prior to his ontological relation to himself (egology) or to the totality of things we call the world (cosmology)."[18] Through the ethical encounter with the other, we discover ourselves and we are driven to the political, because more than two of us are involved, and from there to the ontological, Levinas claims. The ethical claim of the other is the basis of entry into these other dimensions.

Making the claim of the other the center of ethics, and ethics the center of human experience, accords ethics a very high status. Whether it can fulfill this role is a serious question that would involve more direct consideration of Levinas' position than we can begin to contemplate in the present context. What is clear from others who take up this strain is that it could lead to very significant transformations in ethics. On the surface, it sounds like a realization of the dream cherished by Kant, of according ethics its own foundational role. The result, however, might amount to the elimination of ethics as anything that would be recognizable to Kant. John D. Caputo follows the direction of attending to the claim of the particular other to the point of dispensing entirely with the universal claim that was so central for Kant and assumed even by Hume. "I leave the hermeneutics of excellence to Greeks and other connoisseurs," Caputo sneers. "But I think the claim of victims, who are

---

[17] Mark Taylor, *Alterity* (Chicago: University of Chicago Press, 1987), p. 178.
[18] Emmanuel Levinas, "Ethics of the Infinite," in *Dialogues with Contemporary Continental Thinkers*, ed. Kearney, p. 57.

usually the victims of somebody's Good, is singular, compelling, claiming."[19] In place of ethics of virtue, right, or good, Caputo advocates an ethics of disaster. He asks us to consider the case of a child born with AIDS. What is at stake here, Caputo contends, is not questions of who is to blame or of what vision of good or right is to be followed. This child exerts her own ethical claim directly. This is ethics of the other, ethics of empathy, that cannot do anything but attend to the needs of the other who confronts us in such glaring reality,

The drama of Caputo's example makes it unavoidable, but then that is why he chose it. That drama can also obscure a basic ambiguity in the sympathy–empathy distinction. The advantage of empathy over sympathy is supposedly that it takes the other seriously, where sympathy ultimately amounts to using the other for our own ends, however much the other may benefit in immediate, usually material, terms. Yet the contrast between sympathy and empathy can also be presented in terms that virtually reverse this reading. Empathy can involve treating the other as a case, as an object of investigation, to be understood, where sympathy involves identification with the plight of the other.

In a direct comparison of sympathy and empathy, L. R. Wispé defines the two terms in ways that contrast with, if they do not actually contradict, the comparison proposed by the Oliners. "Sympathy," Wispé contends, "refers to the heightened awareness of the suffering of another person as something to be alleviated."[20] The implication, that the primary focus is altruistic, concern for the other person, is strengthened by the contrasting definition of empathy. "Empathy, on the other hand, refers to the attempt by one self-aware self to comprehend unjudgementally the positive and negative experiences of another self." On this reading, empathy is the more isolated approach. "In empathy, the self is the vehicle for understanding, and it never loses its own identity." Here it is sympathy that really relates to the other person. "By contrast, sympathy is

---

[19] John D. Caputo, *Against Ethics* (Bloomington: Indiana University Press, 1993), p. 34.
[20] L. G. Wispé, "The Distinction between Sympathy and Empathy," *Journal of Personality and Social Psychology* 50 (1986): 318.

concerned with communion rather than accuracy, and self-awareness is reduced rather than augmented." Wispé puts his reading in a succinct form, which brings out how dramatically it contrasts with the earlier reading considered. "In empathy, we substitute ourselves for the others. In sympathy, we substitute others for ourselves." Far from using others for our own purposes, however unwittingly, sympathy here appears as the approach that takes others seriously for themselves. It involves real identification with their plight. Empathy, by contrast, does involve focusing on others, but this is an abstract focus, the motivation being to understand the other in themselves, without personal involvement.

In spite of the contrast between these interpretations of empathy and sympathy, they may not be as contradictory as they first appear. In fact, they might even be complementary. On the surface, the message could be that the Oliner reading shows that sympathy is indulgent, while empathy represents real caring for others, whereas the Wispé reading suggests that it is sympathy that involves caring, while empathy remains inherently aloof. A fuller appreciation of what is at stake in altruism may be achieved by closer attention to the focus of these two treatments, noting how they agree as well as where they differ. Both imply that empathy involves a more direct focus on the other than sympathy. The Oliners draw from this a warning about the dangers of untutored sympathy. Feeling sorry for people, and rushing to aid them in ways that we think they need, can be counterproductive precisely because of failure to take these people seriously themselves, precisely what Thoreau feared in those who were out to do him good. Sympathy without empathy is dangerous, the Oliners suggest. On the other hand, Wispé warns that concern to understand the other may become such a preoccupation that we never get around to offering any assistance: "empathy might impede helping behavior."[21] Empathy without sympathy is sterile, Wispé warns. Constructive altruism would seem to demand that delicate balance of sympathetic identification and em-

---

[21] Ibid., p. 319.

pathic distance, for the sake of both givers and recipients of caring.

In advocating an approach to ethics in terms of expansion of sympathy, Hume did not get involved in analysis of the nature of sympathy as such, and certainly did not have available the rather clinical twentieth-century notion of empathy. However, as we have noted, the legacy of Hume has been reclaimed in recent years, particularly in feminist ethics. From its origins in the 1960s, this phase of feminism reflects two basic shifts in terms of ethical orientation: "from an attachment to ideals of androgyny to a debate over norms of difference" and "from a commitment to ideals of individual rights to an insistence on moralities of caring."[22] While prominent feminists can be found advocating androgyny and individual rights, there has been a dramatic emphasis in feminist ethics in particular on the distinctiveness of women, a distinctiveness that is expressed in ethical terms by contrasting an approach of caring to the more standard focus of western ethics on establishing justice. The approach could signal a revolution in ethics as such, and a more deliberate focus on altruism in particular. "The region of 'particular others' is a distinct domain, where it can be seen that what becomes artificial and problematic are the very 'self' and 'all others' of standard moral theory."[23] Rights and justice are issues because we are seen to exist in constant competition with one another. Prominent stands of feminist ethics challenge this assumption and the vision behind it: "above all else a feminist moral theology insists that relationality is at the heart of all things."[24] Far from constituting a foreign ideal, altruism represents a lived reality insofar as we are inextricably interconnected with one another. This does not mean, however, that altruism is, or indeed should be, automatic. There is still the

[22] Mary Fainsodkatsenstein and David DeLaitin, "Politics, Feminism, and the Ethics of Caring," in *Women and Moral Theory*, ed. Kittay and Meyers, p. 262.

[23] Virginia Held, "Feminism and Moral Theory," in *Women and Moral Theory*, ed. Kittay and Meyers, p. 117.

[24] Beverly Wildung Harrison, "The Power of Anger in the Work of Love: Christian Ethics for Women and Other Strangers," in *Weaving the Visions: New Patterns in Feminist Spirituality*, ed. Judith Plaskow and Carol Christ (San Francisco: Harper & Row, 1989), p. 221.

matter of the relation between sympathy and empathy, concern and appropriate distance. This matter is central for the ethics of caring that has been developed in feminist ethics.

CARE MORALITY AS DIRECT ALTRUISM

Through interviews with women, Carol Gilligan came to realize that she was in touch with a view of morality that cast doubt on the adequacy of the ideal of moral maturity implicit in the moral stages of her mentor in moral psychology at Harvard, Lawrence Kohlberg. The three-level, six-stage, measure of moral maturity worked out by Kohlberg follows the psychological categories of Jean Piaget, tracing progress from dependence through conformity to independence, with the implication that the moral ideal is seen in terms of a Kantian autonomous moral agent. By this criterion, women tend to get stuck at level-two, stage-three conformity, appearing generally to be incapable of the abstraction that appreciates moral principles in their own right, which is taken to be reflective of mature moral development. What Gilligan discovered through studies with female subjects was that this result indicated more about this scale, and the view of morality assumed in it, than about women's moral maturity. This scale was not really appropriate to women because, rather than worrying about general moral principles, women tend to identify with the moral dilemma and the people in it. Their moral orientation is one of care and responsiveness, in contrast to the morality of abstract justice and responsibility.

This fundamental difference in orientation lends itself to the delineation of more specific contrasts between the two moralities.[25] Somewhat to Gilligan's chagrin, the contrast that is apt to suggest itself first is the stereotypical one between male

---

[25] Lawrence Blum, "Gilligan and Kohlberg: Issues for Moral Theory," *Ethics* 98 (1988): 474ff., identifies seven differences between the Gilligan and Kohlberg approaches to morality. Cf. also Nona Plesser Lyons, "Two Perspectives: On Self, Relationships, and Morality," in *Mapping the Moral Domain: A Contribution of Women's Thinking to Psychological Theory and Education*, ed. Carol Gilligan, Janie Victoria Ward and Jill McLean Taylor, with Betty Bardige (Cambridge, Mass.: Center for the Study of Gender, Education, and Human Development, Harvard University Graduate School of Education, 1988), pp. 33 and 35, for tables comparing care and justice moralities.

rationality and female emotion. However, Gilligan rejects the charge that she is perpetuating this stereotype, and counters with the suggestion that ignoring gender differences, while considering factors like social class and education, in assessing moral development, may be more revealing about views of development than about morality and gender.[26] The reference is to claims that the reason women subjects have not fared so well on the Kohlberg scale is due to their being from lower social classes and lacking the educational level of male subjects. How far cultural factors account for differences in outlook between men and women is a complex and unresolved issue. Gilligan contends that it is premature to foreclose that issue by ignoring evidence of gender differences as an element in that complexity. There is evidence that women do tend to react to moral concerns with emotional identification, whereas men tend to react more reflectively.

The reason–emotion contrast is directly suggestive of a contrast of levels between these two moralities. Reflective, justice morality tends to operate on a second-order, abstract level, standing back from particular moral dilemmas, seeking common principles and standards. The way of identification of care morality involves entering into the situation, imaginatively if not literally, and seeking the best solution for the persons involved. Thus the orientation of care morality is practical and active, in contrast to the more theoretical and detached stance of the justice approach.

The difference between detached deliberation and direct identification is indicative of a still more fundamental contrast between these two moralities. Justice morality is essentially individualistic in orientation and method, whereas care morality is inherently social. The model of moral maturity in the justice approach is the competent individual, capable of identifying moral principles that will ensure that justice is done. From the care perspective, moral maturity involves identification with the persons involved in a moral dilemma. These different views of maturity reflect different basic visions of humanity. Human

---

[26] Carol Gilligan, "Reply," *Signs* 11 (1986): 327.

beings are separate, ideally independent individuals, for the justice outlook; human beings are inherently interrelated, as the care perspective sees life.

The orientations of these fundamental visions can be contrasted more specifically in terms of their central focus. The individualistic, justice outlook is focused principally on the moral agent. The socially oriented care approach is concerned more directly with the other, or others, with whom our lives are bound together. The difference may be one of emphases, rather than of absolute contrast, as Diana T. Meyers implies: "Whereas Kohlberg's vision of moral maturity might be characterized as one of decent respect for others while pursuing one's own good, Gilligan's alternative might be characterized as a vision of concerned involvement with others while respecting oneself."[27] Yet, if the difference is a matter of emphases, it is by no means an insubstantial one. For the justice view, the trick is to see oneself as another; for the care approach, it is more a matter of being oneself among others.

The source of the difference between care and justice moralities appears as an empirical one. Gilligan's discovery came from listening to the experience of women. Their accounts suggested that for them morality was not seen to involve stepping back and seeking impartial adjudication by identifying a principled justice, but rather to entail a caring identification with the persons facing a moral dilemma. Thus care morality is an empirical morality in this double sense. It arose from empirical investigation, through listening to what women were actually saying about how they functioned morally. What emerged, the distinctive characterization of care morality itself, was an empirical morality, focusing on experience and direct involvement in moral dilemmas.

To anyone familiar with twentieth-century western ethics, "empirical morality" is apt to sound like an oxymoron. For to claim that morality is a matter of direct experience implies contravention of what has come to be the cardinal rule of twentieth-century ethics, avoidance of what G. E. Moore

---

[27] Diana T. Meyers, "The Socialized Individual and Individual Autonomy," in *Women and Moral Theory*, ed. Kittay and Meyers, p. 141.

termed the "naturalistic fallacy," and what has more generally been identified as the impossibility of deriving "ought" from "is." The implication of the care orientation is that sufficient identification with the persons involved in a particular situation will yield moral direction. If the "is" of identification is strong enough, the moral "ought" will follow. If we care enough about persons in a moral crisis, we will find the right direction.

It may be that such a violation of the sacredness of the is/ought gap is not unwarranted. Although it has increasingly dominated ethical thinking in this century, particularly where the influence of English ethicists has been strong, the absolute nature of this gap has not gone unchallenged. It is surely not unreasonable to hold that evidence and experience are relevant, and even indispensable, for reaching moral insight. Yet, while the is/ought distinction has been overstated by its more absolutist exponents, its dominance among ethicists is indicative of more than professional conformity on their part. It reflects the basic realization that morality, by definition, involves more than the circumstances of the immediate moral situation. Although the prohibition against deriving "ought" from "is" is overdrawn, if this is taken to mean that descriptive evidence and first-hand involvement are irrelevant, it is pertinent as a reminder that moral direction is not reducible to appreciation of what is the case, whether this is achieved through sophisticated analysis or profound first-hand identification. Morality involves more than understanding and appreciation of any situation or circumstance; it entails a vision of what ought to be that is not reducible to, or derivable from, the immediate context.

Although the care morality introduced by Gilligan may be seen to challenge the standard fact/value dichotomy, there are also indications that such challenge is not a major concern. In fact, in some ways, Gilligan's moral outlook remains quite conventional. On the level of vision, it seems that she remains significantly under the influence of the outlook that informs justice morality. Although she can be seen to subordinate the concerns of justice morality to her own care approach, in a way that is comparable to Kohlberg's acceptance of care morality on his own justice terms, the much more striking impression

from Gilligan's proposals is that she really remains firmly under
the influence of the justice morality vision. The revision to
women's experience that she prescribes will sound familiar to
anyone aware of prevailing patterns in developmental psychology. As she observes herself, "the sequence of women's moral
development follows the three-level progression of all social
development theory, from an egocentric through a societal to a
universal perspective."[28] The difficulty is that the sequence is so
faithful to standard development theory that the overall picture
looks very much like the view assumed in justice morality. The
sequence is from selfishness, to care for others, to independence.
The independent integrity of the self is qualified by recognition
of the importance of relation with the other, but the mature
person is essentially the independent person. The suggestion
seems to be that the person is defined primarily in terms of
independence, as the justice outlook assumes, with involvement
with others seen as something that becomes possible for the
independent person.

This could be taken as an indication that Gilligan falls into
the same trap as her critics; in the end she too ultimately
assumes the prevailing, male understanding of humanity. Then,
contrary to the charges of her critics, the problem would be not
that she focuses on the distinctiveness of women's experience,
but that she does not do this consistently enough. She recognizes that contrary to the equation of moral maturity with
autonomy and emotion-free rationality, women experience life
in terms of care, but she draws back from this insight, and falls
in with her critics, when it comes to the matter of self-sacrifice.
Because self-sacrifice has been assumed for women, it must now
be precluded even as a possibility. But how can serious care be
assumed to exclude self-sacrifice? It can be for the carer who is
so absorbed in caring that she is unaware of self. Cases of
conspicuous altruism could be said to preclude self-sacrifice for
the carer herself. But what Gilligan is talking about is almost
the opposite of that. The motive for excluding self-sacrifice is

---

[28] Carol Gilligan, "In a Different Voice: Women's Conception of the Self and of
Morality," *Harvard Educational Review* 47 (1977): 482f.

not that the carer is unconcerned with self, but precisely the conviction that the carer should be concerned with self.

On this reading, Gilligan's insistence on taking women's experience seriously stops short of seeing this experience as truly altruistic. At this point, she joins her critics in seeing women's caring as an imposition of patriarchal social structures. Back in 1960, Valerie Saiving pointed out that self-sacrifice was destructive for women because it did not allow them to develop a self to sacrifice.[29] By internalizing the male understanding of sin as self-assertion, women are prevented from seeing that they are really subject to an opposite form of sin, denial of self.[30] Susan Dunfee calls it "the sin of hiding."[31] Her description of this in terms of acquiescing in the roles and expectations of others, rather than facing up to responsibility for oneself, sounds very close to Gilligan's second stage of moral development. "The conventions of feminine goodness encourage women in the sin of irresponsibility and hiding under the guise of being responsible (meaning responsive) to the needs of others."[32] Hiding and altruism are virtually synonymous. This is what requires a third stage in order to achieve moral maturity: "for women, true human integrity, honesty, maturity, and liberation lie not through service and altruism – attendance to the voices of others, putting the needs of others and the community first – but through a threshold beyond altruism."[33] This is what Gilligan's third stage recognizes and advocates – "a new concept of goodness which turns inward in an acknowledgment of the self and an acceptance of responsibility for decision."[34] But how distinctive is care morality, when its highest stage of moral development "turns inward in an acknowledgment of the self"? This certainly sounds very similar to the assumed perspective of the justice morality it is intended to correct.

[29] Valerie Saiving, "The Human Situation: A Feminine View," *Journal of Religion* 40 (1960): 100–12.

[30] Judith Plaskow, *Sex, Sin and Grace: Women's Experience and the Theologies of Reinhold Niebuhr and Paul Tillich* (Lanham, Md.: University Press of America, 1980).

[31] Susan Dunfee, "The Sin of Hiding: A Feminist Critique of Reinhold Niebuhr's Account of the Sin of Pride," *Soundings* 65 (1982): 316f.

[32] Susan Dunfee, *Beyond Servanthood: Christianity and the Liberation of Women* (Lanham, Md.: University Press of America, 1989), p. 89.

[33] Ibid., p. 96.   [34] Gilligan, "In a Different Voice," p. 500.

If the vision of care morality remains essentially that of justice morality, how then does it differ? One of the clearest points of contrast is the adoption of a social, as opposed to the essentially individualistic outlook assumed by modern ethics generally. The grounding implied by Gilligan's treatment of care morality is a social one. She sees morality as a kind of social consensus, or at least a matter of insights that a person arrives at through discussion with others – "dialogue replaces logical deduction as the mode of moral discovery, and the activity of moral understanding returns to the social domain."[35] Where morality has come to be thought of as a matter for experts, reflecting on comprehensive principles and systems, Gilligan sees it operating first-hand among people in their daily lives. People make moral decisions not by consulting principles and systems, but by consulting each other. Morality is much more a social than a philosophical matter.

This social horizon affects the substance as well as the form of morality. Morality is not so much about right and wrong, but about co-feeling with one another. Co-feeling designates a concrete morality that avoids the extremes of isolation from one another and identification with the other. It thus avoids the worst, and captures the best, of the extremes of sympathy and empathy. "Co-feeling, then, depends on the ability to *participate* in the other's feelings (in their terms), signifying an attitude of engagement rather than an attitude of judgment or observation."[36] In contrast to the assumption of an identity of feelings in sympathy, co-feeling involves experiencing something of the feelings of others. This requires more distance from the other than sympathy allows. However, the real experience of the feelings of the other reflects an engagement with the other that contrasts with the distance, and implicit superiority, of empathy. Thus co-feeling reflects a morality of social balance, just the

---

[35] Carol Gilligan, "Do the Social Sciences Have an Adequate Theory of Moral Development?" in *Social Science and Moral Inquiry*, ed. Norma Haan, Robert N. Bellah, Paul Rabinow, and William M. Sullivan (New York: Columbia University Press, 1983), p. 45.

[36] Carol Gilligan and Grant Wiggins, "The Origins of Morality in Early Childhood Relationships," in *Mapping the Moral Domain*, ed. Gilligan et al., p. 122.

right combination of connection and distance between the self and others.

So congenial is this result, that it would be easy to forget that the balance involved is an ideal, rather than a realized fact. Since "social" designations can refer both to present circumstances and to ideal arrangements, it is easy for the gap that makes morality necessary, and possible, to collapse in this kind of reference. The caring of women could be taken to represent the final realization of morality. This may be mitigated to some extent by Gilligan's dissatisfaction with the caring that is "natural" to women, and her proposal for modifying this. However, not only does this raise the question about the direct significance of this modification for care morality; it leads to the more basic question of the adequacy of society as the source of the ideal that informs and motivates this proposal. From the justice perspective, or other views of morality that do not operate with such a direct focus on the social level, this social version of morality could appear to collapse morality into social convention. For these established approaches, morality has to do not simply with what is taken as normative in any given society, or through dialogue among any number of co-feeling persons, but with a sense of rightness that transcends the social level. An obvious flaw in care morality, from a justice perspective, is that it allows no scope for ideals to guide persons, individually and collectively. How do even the most sensitive practitioners of co-feeling know which feelings are worthy and which are not, or is there no such thing as unworthy feelings, if those feelings are truly mutual?

It is interesting that in sketching the dangers of care morality, Gilligan does not raise this concern. It sounds like she is approaching this problem when she says that "the potential error in care reasoning lies in the tendency to forget that one has terms," but it turns out that this is not referring to ideals which one recognizes, but to loss of one's independence, "a tendency to enter into another's perspective and to see oneself as 'selfless' by defining oneself in other's terms."[37] Again, the

---

[37] Carol Gilligan, "Moral Orientation and Moral Development," in *Women and Moral Theory*, ed. Kittay and Meyers, p. 31.

horizon is strictly social. There is no recognition of the importance of ideals, as assumed by the justice perspective.

A basic difference between Gilligan and Kohlberg, at this
point, is that between a social science and a philosophical
outlook. For Kohlberg, "social perspective taking levels" are
"necessary but insufficient to define the structure of the moral
stages."[38] Morality, by its very nature, transcends the social
horizon. It involves a reaching beyond what we can control or
what can be expected to emerge through dialogue. This re-
bounds on attempts to portray moral activity, and, for Kohlberg, the depiction that fails to recognize this disqualifies itself
from serious consideration. He castigates social science approaches to morality for failing to realize that "conceptions of
morality cannot themselves be morally neutral."[39] Although he
does not aim this critique at Gilligan's work directly, her
treatment of morality invites this application. For in spite of the
fact that she presents morality in very personal terms, as
involving the actual engagements of co-feeling, this presentation
itself has the impersonal air of neutrality befitting the aspirations of social science through its avoidance of moral affirmation. Where the line is to be drawn between good and bad, right
and wrong, is not considered directly, but is expected to emerge
through dialogue among those who engage in genuine co-
feeling.

While he too operates from the vantage point of a social
scientist, Kohlberg does not envisage a social science account of
morality. The fundamental motivation behind his attempt to
identify sequential stages of moral development was his
Kantian view of the transcendent significance of morality. This
conviction underlies, and is seen to be confirmed by, the
progressive inclusiveness and reversibility of the ascending
stages.[40] Each stage contains and can refer back to previous
stages in the sequence. This progression is possible because of
the sense that morality is leading somewhere, and ultimately
coming from somewhere. Kohlberg's compromise on the hard-

[38] Lawrence Kohlberg, *Essays on Moral Development*, vol. 2 *The Psychology of Normal
Development* (New York: Harper & Row, 1984), ch. 4, p. 384.
[39] Ibid., ch. 3, p. 279.   [40] Ibid., ch. 3, p. 317.

ness of the stages and his acknowledgment of the lack of clear evidence for the sixth stage could suggest a weakening of this conviction. However, that sense of the significance of morality remains as firm as his commitment to the justice framework itself.

While he is less certain of the characterization of the sixth stage, and has rejected the suggestion of Jürgen Habermas for a seventh dialogue stage (a stage that would seem to be closer to the depiction of morality Gilligan presents), Kohlberg not only remains convinced of, and committed to, the belief in progressive stages, but even proposes his own version of a seventh stage, which is metaphysical or religious. As he sees it, morality cannot be taken seriously simply in terms of a series of psychological types or stages. What Kohlberg is attempting "requires a terminal stage to define the natural end and point of the kind of development we are studying."[41] For Kohlberg himself this terminal stage looks very much like the justice morality articulated by John Rawls.[42] He describes it as a type of natural law framework.[43] But Kohlberg's acknowledgment of the need for such a seventh stage is significant in itself, even apart from his own particular characterization of it. He finds it necessary to allow for it in order to detect the stages of moral sensitivity that represent approximations to it – "we believe that the development of soft stages toward the cosmic perspective just described informs us of trends in human development which cannot be captured within a conceptual framework restricted to the study of justice reasoning per se."[44] Morality itself, and attempts to define gradations of moral maturity, assume a cosmic vision that identifies a fundamental shape and thrust that defines and supports moral direction.

Gilligan's recognition of the importance of perspective reflects something of this direction, but in the articulation of her own moral vision, she relies so completely on an assumed social horizon that the issue of the shape of the fact–value dialectic required by morality is posed in a particularly direct way. On the one hand, it is the question as to whether she really allows

---

[41] Ibid., ch. 3, p. 271. [42] Ibid., ch. 3, p. 272.
[43] Ibid., ch. 3, p. 250. [44] Ibid.

enough scope for the ideal in her proposal for moral revision. Is it really morality she is concerned with, or social engineering, albeit of a personal mode? Does she really address the moral dimension, or essentially transpose the moral into the social? Implicit in this is the other issue that festers under the surface in modern ethics – does the moral ideal, however it is conceived, not assume a grounding in reality? As Kohlberg's treatment suggests, this is really the question of whether morality does not in the end reflect some metaphysical, if not actually religious, vision. Not only must the ideal be anchored in the real, as Gilligan's initial proposal for a more practical and empirical approach to morality suggests, but the real must be seen to be adequate to sustain the ideal. Gilligan's treatment highlights this further question that could be directed to much contemporary ethicizing – is the social metaphysically capable of grounding the moral?

LIMITATIONS OF DIRECT ALTRUISM

The love–hate relationship between Gilligan's care morality and the justice morality of Lawrence Kohlberg, against which it is reacting, provides a convenient case study of rational and sympathy approaches to altruism. From its location on the sympathy side, care morality challenges the is–ought gap that has been promoted by the rational tendency to confine morality to its own specialized domain. Morality is not so much a matter of principles to be worked out at the abstract level of rational consistency as of direct involvement with others in concrete situations where difficulties are experienced. In this way, care morality illustrates the direct approach to altruism characteristic of sympathy ethics. Thus the contrasts noted between care and justice moralities can be seen to elucidate further what is at stake in these different approaches to morality. These views of altruism differ on both sides of the is–ought distinction. In challenging extremes of the distinction, the sympathy approach, illustrated by care morality, brings the is and the ought closer together than the rational approach would accept. Reflected in this are different views of both the is and the ought, of what the human condition is and of the direction in which resolution of our difficulties is to be found.

Rational and sympathy approaches differ in their assessments of our situation. On the whole, the rational view is more somber, if not actually pessimistic, as reflected in Nagel's restricted expectations for serious altruism. The sympathy approach, on the contrary, not only holds more hope for altruistic behavior; it does this because it sees such behavior as an integral part of the way life is. We are fundamentally social beings, so that our well-being is inescapably linked with the well-being of others. This is especially true of our most immediate relatives, and beyond that, of those individuals with whom we associate most routinely. Altruism is a present reality through these relationships; what is at stake in its promotion, for the sympathy approach, is the expansion of these circles of mutual interest and caring. From the other perspective, the suspicious eye of the rational approach is cast on the breakdown of relationships, often in the most intimate circles. It is precisely those with whom we are most closely associated who are our most direct rivals. Are any animosities more intense than family quarrels? Is anyone better placed to evoke my envy and ambition than a coworker or a neighbor? It is those closest to me who are in line for the same promotion that I want. Where would commercial culture be without the very real "mythical" Joneses who demand emulation? Real life is ambiguous, showing evidence of altruism and of selfishness, often in the most surprising places. The rational outlook tends to be more surprised by the altruism, even when it is where the sympathy outlook expects to find it most readily, among those who have most in common.

Although the rational approach reflects a more pessimistic view of humanity, and holds considerably lower expectations of altruistic behavior, it does not extend that pessimism to the rational side of humanity. If people would exercise their rational capacities, the situation would be dramatically different, according to this approach. The inconsistency is noted by the advocate of the contrasting sympathy approach, Lawrence Blum. Blum challenges Kant because in his position "the emotions are criticized for how they actually operate (although we have seen that the Kantian view does not get this right), whereas the rationalistic motives are not scrutinized for how they do operate, but are put forward only for how they are capable of operating."[45] Kant exempts reason from the limitations he detects in the emotions. The emotions easily lead us astray, encouraging us to indulge our own desires and prejudices, whereas reason, for the Kantian outlook, represents the reliable assessor that treats our own case with the impartiality that puts it on the same level as that of any other human being in similar circumstances. However, the conclusion that is generally drawn by the sympathy approach to this exposed inconsistency in Kant is not to demand of reason the kind of suspicion that Kant directs to the emotions, but, quite the contrary, to extend Kant's exemption of reason from need for scrutiny to the emotions as well. How the emotions actually operate is no more a subject of investigation for this approach than how reason actually operates is for Kant; the focus here is just as firmly on how the emotions are capable of operating. The natural goodness that Kant accords reason is extended to the emotions in this approach that looks for altruism in immediate forms, with the result that the sympathy approach tends to see the human condition in very positive terms.

This assessment of humanity is illustrated, as we have noted, particularly in prominent feminist treatments such as those of Saiving and Dunfee, at least for feminists themselves. Altruism is something of an artificial problem, in these accounts, because the emphasis on egoism that has been so prevalent reflects a patriarchal outlook, and is not at all representative of women and their experience. However, this is not the only reading of the human condition within feminism. There is another view that challenges this widely accepted vindication of the innocence of women as complacent and self-serving. Through her experience of the rivalries and pettiness in the women's peace movement at Greenham Common during the 1980s, Angela West experienced what she came to identify as a fundamental

---

[45] Blum, *Friendship, Altruism and Morality,* p. 34.

flaw in feminist thought generally, a flaw that she labeled *Deadly Innocence*. The fatal flaw of much feminist rhetoric, West claims, is that "feminism shared the hope of all post-Enlightenment ideologies from the crudest ethno-fascism to the most benign and high-minded idealism, that somehow through conversion of our minds, and the affirmation of our intrinsic goodness, we could be freed from the effects and implications of sin."[46] West detects a particular irony in the way in which feminists exempt themselves and their positions from the taint that they find elsewhere. The irony is that this really represents a new version of traditional female purity; "gender purity has been substituted for sexual purity."[47] Women are characterized by total innocence, because they are women. Indeed, this could be seen as a double irony, because in assuming their own purity, feminists could be seen to be engaging in the ancient sin of Adam, buck-passing.[48] The source of difficulty is always somewhere else. Feminists readily employ this supposedly male device to assure others and themselves of their own innocence.

West's critique of feminism is not intended to obscure the legitimate complaints and real gains that feminism has involved. Among these are the exposure of ways in which altruism has been prescribed for women, often with expectations of self-sacrifice from which men generally were exempt by birth. Conversely, that the antidote to this situation involves encouraging women to care about themselves and to recognize and pursue their own right to dignity and respect must also be applauded. Even the contention that sin is different for women than for men can also be acknowledged. Where their power base has exposed men to the sin of pride, women have been more prone to the acquiescence and subservience that Saiving calls the sin of "hiding." However, it must also be recognized that characterization of sin in terms of acquiescence and lack of aggression is a very convenient one in a competitive and acquisitive society. It is especially convenient when self-assertion is approved for one particular group. For feminists to dissociate

---

[46] Angela West, *Deadly Innocence: Feminism and the Mythology of Sin* (London: Cassell, 1995), p. 205.
[47] Ibid. p. 37.   [48] Ibid. p. 110.

themselves entirely from the sin of pride is precisely to entertain that very prospect. To characterize pride and acquiescence as typically male and female forms of sin, respectively, is at best a generalization, subject to all the limitations of generalizations, so that allowance must always be made for significant exceptions. Women can be guilty of pride and men can settle for unworthy ambitions in life. What is more, the limitations of this generalization must be applied to the corrective itself. The more this diagnosis is accepted, and the more scope women have for self-assertion, the more inaccurate the diagnosis becomes. The cause of feminism would gain wider credibility, West believes, if feminists were to acknowledge their own involvement and implication in the mess that humanity has made of life.

Although there are indications that some feminists would accept this direction, it is also clear that there are prominent strains that would not. Such acknowledgment would be seen by some as a compromise of the most basic insights of feminism. It could threaten to blur the distinction not between guilty men and innocent women so much as between oppressive patriarchal structures that shape society, language, and thought and the natural affinities and cooperativeness of which women are capable. This brings us to the prescriptive side of feminism. Its claim is not only that women are innocent victims, but that apart from this victimization, and its legacy, the natural goodness of life would flourish. Theologian Carter Heyward provides a compact statement of the solution side. "To live with integrity, we live *with* others: We are 'for' ourselves and 'for' others. In fact, the more we are genuinely for others, the more we are authentically for ourselves; and the more we are for ourselves, the more we are for others."[49] There is no barrier to altruism; altruism is natural because there is no egoism. Mutuality would flourish, if we did not impose this promotion of egoism. Without egoism, there would be no need for anything like self-sacrifice. Clashes between self and other will disappear in a context of mutual support where everyone wins.

[49] Carter Heyward, *Touching Our Strength: The Erotic as Power and the Love of God* (New York: Harper & Row, 1989), p. 26.

The catch, of course, is that egoism will not go away by closing our eyes to it. Such a state of mutuality may be pleasant to contemplate, but it must reckon with the reality of egoism. People do look out for their own interests, and they are very apt to disregard or actually violate the interests of others in doing so, rather than engaging in mutually beneficial compromises. How can this portrayal of idyllic mutuality overlook the reality of egoism, and the consequent barriers to altruism that this represents? The answer may be that it does not. This promotion of mutuality is accompanied by a parallel promotion of self-assertion. Feminists who display such confidence in the prospects for mutuality also challenge women to recognize how they have been institutionalized into subservience and to rebel against this condition by recognizing and pursuing their own dignity and claim to self-respect. We have seen how Gilligan finds no inherent incompatibility between such a demand for self-assertion on the part of women and the ethic of care that she finds so natural for women. How do these two apparently contradictory dimensions go together? How can mutuality and self-assertion be combined? The expectation would seem to be that women cannot fail to be care-givers. It would seem that this is natural rather than the result of patriarchal imposition. So deeply does this run, that people like Gilligan seem confident that it can be counted on to continue along with women's redirection of this care toward themselves. "In the daily realm of love and friendship, we seldom face a zero-sum choice," Carter Heyward assures us. "The more I love you, the better able I am to love myself, and vice versa."[50] Love is not a zero-sum game, where there is only so much to go around. The more it is exercised the more there will be.

This pleasant prospect depends on love being thought of as some kind of uniform phenomenon that is parceled out under different labels. Self-love and love of others are two versions of the same thing. If this were true, why would egoism be a problem at all? Why would egoism not lead to altruism? Abundant evidence of a fundamental distinction between love

---

[50] Ibid.

of self and love of others leads to posing a parallel question of this expectation. It is the question posed by Ted Peters with regard to a similar proposal by Ernest Becker. "How does accentuating the self-orientation of individuals serve to make them selfless?"[51] If love were this uniform, it is difficult to see why there would be a problem in the first place; since there obviously is a problem with self-love and egoism, how can accentuating that feature be expected to provide a solution? The apparent confusion of diagnosis and prescription is so thorough that it is difficult to make sense of this stance as either a depiction of the human condition or a proposal for its betterment.

At the same time, this position is held so passionately and so broadly among people who deal with ethical matters today that it can hardly be dismissed so easily. There must be some foundation for this confidence that has so far not been exposed. One possibility is the influence of the social horizon that has gained such prominence in recent decades. This seems to be indicated in another statement of this expectation, one without particular feminist sponsorship. In this instance, a depiction of a naturalness of moral evolution is contrasted with morality as intuition of transcendental truths or as a direct derivation from facts of nature. "Moral thought, it would seem, is instead the gradually more inclusive form of decision making motivated by those life circumstances that encourage nonegoistic commitment to an ideal community of care."[52] Morality is not a matter of transcendent ideals, or of natural biological impulses, but rather develops out of social relations. This orientation of Gilligan's care morality, and the insistence in feminist ethics generally that what is at stake is relationships, supports this reading. Sociality is expected to provide moral motive and substance. The mutuality of actual relations will dispose of the deficiencies of hierarchical forms of life and the extremes that they elicited. Mutuality will dispense with egoism. And since

---

[51] Ted Peters, *Sin, Radical Evil in Soul and Society* (Grand Rapids, Mich.: William B. Eerdman's, 1994), p. 51.

[52] Robert C. Fuller, *Ecology of Care: An Interdisciplinary Analysis of the Self and Moral Obligation* (Louisville, Ky.: Westminster/John Knox Press, 1992), p. 53.

there will be no egoism, there will be no need for self-sacrifice. Where self-love and love of others reinforce one another, mutuality reflects the way life should and could be.

The mutuality of sociality is expected to destroy the need and motivation for concern for self, except in the healthy sense that involves a corresponding concern for others. In a context where one is accepted, self-assertion should not be necessary. Self and other will be affirmed in the ongoing relations of mutuality. Whether this expectation recognizes the devastating reality of egoism, however, remains a central issue. It is difficult to regard the outlook as anything but naive as a depiction of the human condition. From the other direction, it would appear to be equally unpromising as a solution, and not only because its diagnosis fails to address the depths of the challenge of egoistic self-interest. It is deficient as a solution also in regard to the positive alternative it offers. It can claim the virtue of limiting the prospects for self-righteousness by keeping the focus social. Mutual enhancement and caring define virtue, rather than the kind of individual action that might be represented by conspicuous altruism. This minimizes the temptation to make virtue an end in itself, and to encourage individuals to claim to exemplify it. "High virtue is suspect precisely because of its claim to superiority."[53] However, this danger is avoided at the price of virtually eliminating high virtue. The virtues of mutuality crowd out the heroic virtues. Self-sacrifice and altruism in its strongest forms are as redundant as egoism is expected to be. The result, then, appears to constitute a great leveling down of moral horizons.

Social ideals are intended to be to everyone's benefit, but the ideal itself seems to have severely slipped in the process. Consequently the range of moral vision ends up being as restricted as the diagnosis of the human condition is naive. As Iris Murdoch observes, ethics is meant to point to high ideals. "Ethics should not be merely an analysis of ordinary mediocre conduct, it should be an hypothesis about good conduct and about how

---

[53] Jonathan B. Imber, "Social Exchange: A Sociological Theory of Satisfaction," in *Sociology and Human Destiny: Essays in Sociology, Religion and Society*, ed. Gregory Baum (New York: Seabury Press, 1980), p. 141.

this can be achieved."[54] It might be said that there would be nothing mediocre about mutuality. It would be a major improvement over the destructive pursuit of self-interest that has prevailed. But this is precisely the point. How would it be such an improvement if self-love and love of others are simply versions of the same thing? In this leveling of the moral horizon, the rational, Kantian approach of Rawls and the sympathetic, Humean approach of Gilligan meet in a political or social compromise that excludes serious altruism and endemic self-ishness. It may be that the modern and postmodern secular horizon does not permit more radical assessments of the human plight and of human prospects. The devastating difference between self-love and love of others may be recognizable only from the perspective of an ideal that transcends the social horizon. Beyond mutuality as an endorsement of self, along with other selves, a more radical diagnosis of our condition and prescription for its remedy finds a basic contrast between self-interest and self-transcendence. Not mutuality of selves, but overcoming of self, is seen to be required before there can be any hope of significant mutuality.

[54] Iris Murdoch, *The Sovereignty of the Good and Other Concepts* (Cambridge: Cambridge University Press, 1967), p. 2.

PART THREE

Real altruism

CHAPTER 7

Acute altruism: agape

Although altruism is a modern concept, it is, of course, not entirely novel. Despite the secular context of its emergence and submergence, the basic notion behind it, of a concern for others, was integrated into the fabric of western culture through the influence of the Christian gospel. The sense that God reaches out to humanity in love, and seeks to elicit an emulating caring from us for one another, represents an obvious inspiration for a concept isolating other-regard. The obviousness of the Christian source is enhanced by an apparent lack of other prominent candidates. The notion seems to be missing from the other major pillar of the western outlook, Greek civilization. "In classical times at any rate, the Greeks seem to have had no inkling of a notion of brotherly love that could extend to all humanity."[1] It seems clear that in western culture, Christianity is the ultimate source of the modern concept of altruism. It might be the case that there are parallels in other major religious traditions; however, that is a very large subject, and one that does not need to be pursued here. What does seem clear is that Christianity is the wider source of this modern western concept, and that that source is definitive of the Christian vision itself.

The focus in Christianity that provides the background for the concept of altruism is reflected particularly in the peculiar Christian concept of love as *agape*. In a book that has become a modern theological classic, *Agape and Eros* (the first volume of which was published in 1930), the Swedish theologian, Anders

---

[1] Charles H. Kahn, "Aristotle and Altruism," *Mind* 90 (1981): 20.

Nygren, established the uniqueness and total sufficiency of *agape* as "the Christian fundamental motif *par excellence*, the answer to both the religious and the ethical question."[2] The central message of Christianity is that God is *agape*; the central requirement of Christians is to live by *agape*. Although this reading has been widely acknowledged as capturing the fundamental thrust of the Christian gospel, it has also evoked strong criticism. In recent years the criticism has come to drown out the appreciation, as both *agape* and the altruistic extreme that it promotes have been challenged as unrealistic or positively counterproductive. Complaints against Nygren's thesis have focused on two basic alternative understandings of love, *eros*, the acquisitive love of flesh-and-blood human beings, and *philia*, the social love of exchange between givers and recipients of mutual care and support. In considering these alternatives to *agape*, we shall be delving further into the motivation behind the suspicion in which extreme altruism is held.

THE DISPLACEMENT OF *AGAPE* BY *EROS*

Nygren made his case for the uniqueness of *agape* by contrasting it in absolute terms with *eros*. *Eros* is the term ancient Greeks used to designate their aspiration and desire. It could cover sexual desire and thirst for the divine. Its distinguishing characteristic is this reaching out from need and craving. *Agape*, by contrast, as the overflowing of divine plenitude, operates in the opposite direction. It is essentially God reaching out to humanity, providing the assurance and inspiration that accounts for any love that we might express. For Nygren, these two kinds of love represent fundamental motifs, what we would be inclined to refer to today as paradigms – comprehensive perspectives that provide total ways of understanding and living. As he sees it, the two motifs are totally separate in their origins, the one in Greek thought and the other in Christianity, but over the centuries they have become so intertwined that it is almost

---

[2] Anders Nygren, *Agape and Eros: The Christian Idea of Love*, tr. Philip S. Watson (Chicago: University of Chicago Press, 1953), p. 48.

impossible to distinguish them.[3] That almost impossible task is the one Nygren undertakes.

His emphasis on the uniqueness of *agape* was undoubtedly what gave Nygren's proposal its attractiveness, but this absolute contrast has also been the target of much of the dissatisfaction with his approach. One form of this dissatisfaction centers on his neglect of the concrete physical reality of love. He notes Plato's distinction, in the *Symposium*, between "vulgar *eros*" and "heavenly *eros*," and he follows Plato in concentrating on the heavenly variety.[4] Where the vulgar *eros* remains tied to the world of sense and sensation, the higher *eros* uses the physical as a springboard for launching into the higher realm of the spirit. From Nygren's point of view, this is treating *eros* at its best. For his critics, it amounts to ignoring the importance of the physical. In this, Nygren reflects a long tradition, which Sam Keen traces back to Augustine's guilt over his mistress, in which "Christianity fell into an anti-erotic posture: glorifying virginity, degrading women, linking sex to guilt, discouraging romance, denying the flesh, casting suspicion upon sexuality."[5] The problem here is not anything Nygren says, so much as what he does not say. His sin is essentially one of omission. He avoids the erotic in its most visible form. This neglect is seen to rebound to the significant impoverishment of an exclusively agapistic version of Christianity. "The traditional Christian understanding of love fails to value adequately the embodied human experience of love among friends and sexual partners *because* it assumes the negative, dangerous, and non-spiritual character of sensual, erotic, and sexual feelings and expressions."[6] Historic neglect of positive appreciation of sexual love is hardly unrelated to recent revelations of sexual abuse, at times under direct Christian sponsorship, not to mention the more general confusion and discomfort with sexuality in a culture inundated with the exploitation of sex.

Neglect of "vulgar *eros*" is not the only problem with

---

[3] Ibid., pp. 30f.   [4] Ibid., p. 51.

[5] Sam Keen, *The Passionate Life: Stages of Loving* (New York: Harper & Row, 1983), p. 9.

[6] Carter Heyward, *Touching Our Strength: The Erotic as Power and the Love of God* (New York: Harper Row, 1989), pp. 98f.

Nygren's treatment. The way he deals with "heavenly *eros*" is seen to be equally suspect. Nygren's absolute contrast between *agape* as God's care for us and *eros* as our attempt to deal with God has the effect of eliminating even the human response in the relation to God.[7] Nygren points out that Paul does not use any term for love to refer to the human response to God. His preferred term is faith. Paul does use *agape* to refer to the love of neighbor. This is because here it is really God working though us.[8] In this depreciation of human initiative, the self is particularly devalued. Such devaluation is integral to Nygren's position because he equates *eros* with self-love; *eros* is the self seeking to acquire and possess, whether in crude or refined forms. This is the only way *eros* can be understood from the perspective of *agape*: "it must be regarded as sinful by the Agape that 'seeketh not its own.'"[9] Thus not only the physical dimension, but the human, and in particular the self, fall victim to the absolute contrast between *agape* and *eros*.

The legacy of Nygren's dismissal of *eros* has led to a contrary dismissal of *agape* through the promotion of an all but exclusively erotic theology. So Carter Heyward sees us holding the possibility and responsibility for the redemption of God.[10] This happens through our relating to one another, especially our relating sexually. "My eroticism is my participation in the universe."[11] Not only are we the agents for the redemption of God, but "we are the womb in which God is being born."[12] The New Testament affirmation that God is love is here reversed in the affirmation that love is God. In the reversal, *eros* displaces *agape*.

More typical than this counterdismissal of *agape* in Heyward's lesbian feminist erotic theology has been a plea for balance between the legitimate concerns of *eros* and *agape*. Sallie

---

[7] Martin Cyril D'Arcy, *The Mind and Heart of Love, Lion and Unicorn: A Study in Eros and Agape* (London: Faber & Faber, 1945), p. 79.

[8] Nygren, *Agape and Eros*, p. 129.

[9] Philip S. Watson, "Translator's Preface," in Nygren, *Agape and Eros*, p. xxi.

[10] Carter Heyward, *The Redemption of God: A Theology of Mutual Relation* (Lanham, Md.: University Press of America, 1982), p. 183.

[11] Heyward, *Touching Our Strength*, p. 25.

[12] Ibid., p. 24.

McFague seeks to shift the focus from redemption to creation, so that *eros* is recognized as the inherent need for relation and connection that is characteristic of all life. This is seen to complement, rather than to displace *agape*, which remains as the overarching divine concern for all.[13] Robert Merrihew Adams acknowledges the importance of *agape*, understood as benevolence, but sees this operating realistically only through an erotic desire for relation with the other who is the recipient of the caring concern. The result is what he calls an agapic *eros*.[14] A similar dialectic is proposed by Paul Avis, for whom *eros* represents the pulsating vitality "that makes the world go round," but which, precisely because of its sheer vitality, needs "the guiding, restraining, compassionate hand that *agape* holds out to *eros.*"[15] In this manner, he hopes to encourage the spontaneity of *eros* in such a way that its excesses are checked by the benevolence of *agape*. Such balance he finds endorsed by the Christian understanding of God. "Jesus is the great lover of humanity and shows how we may predicate his 'agapistic *eros*' or 'erotic *agape*' of the ineffable life of God himself."[16] The authority for this plea for a balance of *agape* and *eros* in recent theology is Paul Tillich, who asserted: "If *eros* and *agape* cannot be united, *agape* towards God is impossible."[17] For Nygren, *agape* toward God was impossible. *Agape* is of God. The human response to God is faith. Through faith, the believer may participate in *agape* toward the neighbor. Recent recovery of interest in *eros* questions whether this outlook does justice to either humanity or God in their alterity. Far from *agape* inviting the direct equation with pure altruism, serious altruism might depend on real difference on both sides, human and divine, so that divine *agape* may be appreciated only from the need of human *eros*, and perhaps the fullness of divine *agape* may even

---

[13] Sallie McFague, "God as Mother," in *Weaving the Visions: New Patterns in Feminist Spirituality*, ed. Judith Plaskow and Carol P. Christ (San Francisco: Harper & Row, 1989), p. 143.

[14] Robert Merrihew Adams, "Pure Love," *Journal of Religious Ethics* 8 (1980): 98.

[15] Paul Avis, *Eros and the Sacred* (London: SPCK, 1989), p. 142.

[16] Ibid., p. 137.

[17] Paul Tillich, *Systematic Theology* (Digswell Place, UK: James Nisbet & Co., 1968), p. 312.

imply a divine *eros*, reflecting a genuine need in God for humanity.

The possiblity that an appreciation of *eros* may enrich, rather than threaten, *agape*, will have to be considered more fully. In this survey of this renewed interest in *eros*, however, we must notice the threat that is posed when *eros* is allowed to displace *agape*. An interesting case in point is provided by the way in which Sam Keen interprets – and distorts – the views of Gabriel Marcel, whom he wishes to claim as an authority. Marcel depicts love in *Being and Having* in the following terms: "Love, in so far as distinct from desire or as opposed to desire, love treated as the subordination of the self to a superior reality, a reality at my deepest level more truly me than I am myself – love as the breaking of the tension between self and other, appears to me to be what one might call the essential ontological datum."[18] What Keen sees Marcel doing here is articulating "the basis of an erotic metaphysic."[19] By all historical usage, Marcel is talking about a check on *eros*-love "as distinct from desire or as opposed to desire," "as the subordination of the self to a superior reality," "as the breaking of the tension between self and other." What Marcel is describing is much closer to the basic sense of *agape* than it is to the essential thrust of *eros*. Keen might appeal to the development in Plato where *eros* is transformed from the direct pursuit of acquisitiveness to creativity and love of beauty,[20] but even Plato scholars generally agree that this remains substantially different from the embrace and sustenance of *agape*. If Marcel had been confined to a Platonic background, he could hardly have written of love as he did. To call what Marcel points to *eros* is indicative of the absorption of *agape* by *eros*.

Even more blatant instances of the inversion are readily available. Matthew Fox speaks of "eros as love of enemy."[21] How this distinctive Christian mandate, rooted in the language of *agape*, gets construed as a possibility of *eros* is totally baffling,

---

[18] Keen, *The Passionate Life*, p. 125.   [19] Ibid.
[20] A. H. Armstrong, "Platonic Eros and Christian Agape," *Downside Review* (1961): 107.
[21] Matthew Fox, *Original Blessing* (Santa Fe, New Mexico: Bear & Company, 1983), p. 291.

unless it reflects such antipathy to Nygren's emphasis on the distinctiveness of *agape* that it reacts by attributing the meaning of *agape* to *eros*. What it cannot do is claim biblical sponsorship. The New Testament does not speak of *eros*, much less of *eros* as love of enemies. Unlike Fox, Don Cupitt acknowledges the New Testament references to *agape* at the expense of *eros*, but he explains this away by denying the distinctive meaning of *agape*: "Agape is just ordinary human affection and compassion, such as will flow freely if we can but become liberated from self-concern and its attendant anxieties."[22] The people behind the New Testament developed a special word to designate the ordinary. Furthermore, the whole development was pointless because what they wanted to say could have been conveyed by the familiar Greek word *eros*. Whatever may have been lost by failure to appreciate *eros*, and whatever may be gained by its recovery, the net result is apt to be negative, from a Christian perspective, if it involves the eclipse of the distinctiveness of *agape*.

THE DISPLACEMENT OF *AGAPE* BY *PHILIA*

The confusion over *eros* and *agape* may be due in large part to a missing middle term. In what has become one of the most prominent responses to Nygren, M. C. D'Arcy's *The Mind and Heart of Love*, *philia* is proposed as the missing term. "What then is clear is that the true relation of Eros and Agape must be understood in the light of Philia."[23] For D'Arcy, *philia* refers particularly to the appreciation of personality he sees to be involved in the emergence of Christianity and to the possibilities for community and the deeper meaning of love this can make possible. In short, the missing term that *philia* provides is relation. Where *eros* tends to designate concentration on the self and its needs and desires and where *agape* offers deliverance from self that renders even sidelong glances at the self suspect, *philia* opens up that middle ground of mutual involvement of the self with other selves. The mutual love of equals in commun-

[22] Don Cupitt, *The New Christian Ethics* (London: SCM Press, 1988), p. 57.
[23] D'Arcy, *The Mind and Heart of Love*, p. 122.

ity is what is missing in the individualistic orientations of *eros* and *agape*.

It is striking that Nygren does not deal with *philia* in his exposition of *agape*. He deals with *eros* negatively, *agape* positively, and *philia* not at all. Nor could he appeal to the Protestant authority of Scripture for a mandate for this, for the New Testament does speak of *philia*. It is not as prominent as *agape*. Whereas, according to Young's *Analytical Concordance*, *agape* occurs one hundred and fifteen times in the New Testament, *philia* itself occurs only eighteen times, and compounds like *philadelphia* and *philanthropia*, sixteen times, for a total of thirty-four occurrences of all variations of *philia*. The significance of the references bears considerable relation to this distribution, with *agape* being used in the most enduring sayings and *philia* often tending to be used with a negative connotation. Yet, although it is considerably less prominent than *agape*, quantitatively and qualitatively, *philia* does have significant representation in the New Testament, and this makes its neglect by Nygren particularly striking.

A major problem that critics detect in the insistence on the uniqueness of *agape* is that it characterizes love as unidirectional. It represents overflowing generosity, from God to human beings and from those who experience that generosity on to other human beings. The lovers remain essentially detached from the process, a strange characterization for love. Mutual love is seen to overcome this distance through its direct relational involvement. It is not only giving but receiving. As Stephen Post points out, "Selfless, purely one-way love may be an understandable exaggeration of unselfishness, but its impact is essentially negative in that it undermines the circular flow of giving and receiving in which *agape* is sustained and supported."[24] Love is a living relation, rather than a commodity that can be passed on, or passed down, and as a result its vitality consists in the back and forth exchanges that constitute the relation. There is giving and receiving, in both directions.

Interestingly, the objection lodged by these scholars against

---

[24] Stephen G. Post, *A Theory of Agape: On the Meaning of Christian Love* (Lewisburg, Pa.: Bucknell University Press, 1990), p. 12.

agape is not that it requires the effacement of the self. Ironically, the barrier to the living reality of mutual love is not unwillingness or inability to give so much as unwillingness or inability to receive. The one-sidedness of the unique Christian love is a one-sidedness of giving. Arthur McGill calls this "the illusion of perpetual affluence"[25] and regards this reading as a distortion of the reality seen in Jesus. "Active love," McGill insists, "occurs within the fellowship of neediness, within the neediness of the one who serves and leads, of the one who serves in neediness." The exclusive emphasis on giving as self-sacrificial love presupposes a self-sufficiency that overlooks the need and vulnerability of the care-giver at the same time that it renders the recipient of this love an object of charity.[26] Love as mutuality exposes and addresses needs on both sides of the loving relation. Far from being one-way self-sacrifice, real loving involves the mutual growth of self and others in the reciprocal bonds of community.[27] The self grows through the experience of love, as a person is able to receive and give as circumstances and abilities make possible.

The contemporary case against Nygren does seem convincing. The contrast between the real exchange of mutuality and the abstraction of the independent bestowal of self-sacrificial love gives mutuality an inherent appeal and the traditional reading of *agape* a deprecatory air of unreality. There is even an exposure of a kind of debilitating inversion implicit in the insistence on the independent sufficiency of *agape*; the insistence on self-sacrifice has the effect of emphasizing the self. The result is that the supreme form of caring love idealizes and promotes an isolated self-sufficiency. The real irony is that this recovery of the true gospel of Christian love can be seen to reflect the modern deistic sense of God in terms of detached self-sufficiency and a corresponding human ideal typified by

[25] Arthur C. McGill, *Death and Life: An American Theology* (Philadelphia, Pa.: Fortress Press, 1987), p. 89.
[26] A crucial aspect of this subject is the question of the vulnerability of God. However, in spite of its relevance, and the extensive discussion of this issue in recent theology, consideration of this dimension will be postponed until the next chapter.
[27] Stephen J. Pope, "Expressive Individualism and True Self-Love: A Thomistic Perspective," *Journal of Religion* 71 (1991): 399.

"Promethean man."[28] Recognition of this inversion is promoted particularly from the perspective of mutuality widely endorsed in feminist theology. Beverly Wildung Harrison shudders at recalling the warnings she received from Christian ethicists against confusing real Christian love with mere mutuality. In retrospect, she thinks they had things backwards. "One senses that persons who can think this way have yet to experience the power of love as the real pleasure of mutual vulnerability, the experience of truly being cared for or of actively caring for another."[29] This contemporary account sees the depth of caring that is supposed to be peculiar to *agape* actually being experienced in the mutuality of *philia*. In fact, as condescending bestowal, *agape* is seen as preventing the direct experience of mutuality that is accessible only through acknowledgment of our own vulnerability.

The egalitarian tone of mutuality, and the challenge to face our own vulnerability, evoke a sympathetic response amid the postmodern suspicions of imperialistic overtones of hierarchy. However, the vision of a society of mutually supportive persons, sensitive enough to one another's needs to provide the security for people to expose their own vulnerability, will be doomed to remain a romantic illusion unless there are individuals who are strong enough to initiate these exchanges. Much of the talk of mutuality suggests that the only barrier to the bliss of the give and take of true mutuality is the insecurity that prevents us from exposing our own vulnerability. How positive growth is to be expected from immersion in vulnerability is not made clear. It would seem that the vulnerability required to initiate and sustain the mutuality of *philia* is, in fact, the vulnerability of *agape*, a reaching out that carries no assurance of response, much less of mutuality. "One's love of others remains unilateral in that one does not await, anticipate, or demand a response in kind as a requirement for one's attention and care."[30] In

---

[28] Beverly Wildung Harrison, "The Power of Anger in the Work of Love: Christian Ethics for Women and Other Strangers," in *Weaving the Visions*, ed. Plaskow and Christ, pp. 221f.

[29] Ibid., p. 222.

[30] Gene Outka, "Universal Love and Impartiality," in *The Love Commandments*, ed.

identifying this distinctively agapistic dimension, Gene Outka notes that we are not told whether a friendship developed between the Good Samaritan and the victim he rescued from the roadside. This is not said with cynicism toward the notion of mutuality. Outka recognizes response as desirable, and even contends that "we should say. . . that mutuality is the internal, ideal fruition of *agape*."[31] The point is that such mutuality is elicited and sustained only through the generosity of *agape*. Thus the displacement of *agape* by *philia* as mutuality, in itself, appears to be as problematic as the displacement of *agape* by *eros*.

THE DISPLACEMENT OF NYGREN'S *AGAPE* BY POST-ENLIGHTENMENT *AGAPE*

If proponents of *eros* make their case only by adopting something of the coloration of *agape*, and advocates of *philia* require the initiative of *agape* to achieve the mutuality they prize, this would seem to confirm Nygren's insistence on the indispensability of *agape*. Yet such confirmation remains elusive. The distinctiveness of *agape* can even appear precarious in the treatment of someone as sensitive to its peculiarity as Gene Outka. Where Nygren's emphasis on the distinctiveness of *agape* reflects his background in the Protestant insistence on the indispensability of divine grace, and Darcy's qualification of *agape* by the mutuality of *philia* draws on his background in Catholic theology,[32] Outka's theological focus is qualified by concerns of modern ethics, as indicated by the subtitle of his

Edmund N. Santurri and William Werpehowski (Washington, DC: Georgetown University Press, 1992), p. 89.

[31] Ibid.

[32] D'Arcy has been cited as illustrative of the impression that "the Catholic tradition offers more useful material for a feminist articulation of the meaning of *agape*" (Barbara Andolsen, "Agape in Feminist Ethics," *Journal of Religious Ethics* 9 (1981): 81, n.3; cf. p. 77). A more prominent representative of the mutuality reading in Catholic theology is Karl Rahner. (Stephen J. Pope, "The Order of Love and Recent Catholic Ethics: A Constructive Proposal," *Theological Studies* 52 (1991): 257.) The ultimate authority for this in Catholic theology, of course, lies in Saint Thomas Aquinas, especially in his assertion of the legitimate claims of concern for oneself (Pope, "Expressive Individualism and True Self-Love," p. 393; see also Pope, "The Order of Love and Recent Catholic Ethics," p. 262).

major work in this area, *Agape: An Ethical Analysis.*[33] Because he presents *agape* in relation to the ethical requirements of impartiality, critics complain that his interpretation is restricted by Enlightenment assumptions.[34] As an ethicist, clearly he belongs in this tradition out of which ethics as we know it has emerged. To take this Enlightenment confinement as an adequate characterization of Outka, however, would lead us to miss some broader insights and subtle distinctions that are evident particularly in his recent writings.

Not only does Outka recognize the distinctiveness of *agape* in ways that approximate the priority accorded it by Nygren, as his insistence on the indispensability of *agape* in taking the initiative in caring suggests, he also discusses it in theological terms that exceed anything that would be approved by the canons of post-Enlightenment ethics. In fact, beyond the primacy of agapistic love in initiating human caring, he even alludes to a more primary divine initiative. "Our love for God remains dependent and responsive in a manner that God's love never is."[35] Outka also addresses the most radical requirements of the Christian gospel of *agape*. Even though he employs philosophical language, it is the mandate to repay evil with good that he has in mind when he suggests that *agape* will "strive for reconciliation that forsakes negative equivalence."[36] His distance from enlightenment captivity could not be more clearly attested than in his rebuff of ethicist R. M. Hare's confidence in rational consensus in favor of theologian Reinhold Niebuhr's emphasis on our inevitable bias toward our own interests – a bias that Outka asserts must be counteracted by what he calls an "ameliorative strategy."[37]

While Outka's treatment is certainly theologically much richer than an Enlightenment label would suggest, his ethicist role clearly does influence his own approach to *agape*. The impartiality interpretation he advances can only be understood

---

[33] Gene Outka, *Agape: An Ethical Analysis* (New Haven, Conn.: Yale University Press, 1972).
[34] Post, *A Theory of Agape*, pp. 88f.
[35] Outka, "Universal Love and Impartiality," p. 88.
[36] Ibid., p. 8.   [37] Ibid., pp. 46f.

as a post-Enlightenment qualification of the strong version of *agape* promoted by Nygren. The relevance of *agape* for human beings is seen to depend on how it can be expressed in terms of moral concern with fairness and impartiality in human relationships. Outka begins his case for this qualification by distinguishing between self–other and other–other situations. In the direct self–other context, he qualifies the radical altruism of *agape* with an insistence on the legitimate claims of the self. Here the claims of modern self-consciousness soften the radical focus on the other that characterizes Nygren's reading. *Agape* is understood in terms of the universal love that includes the self, which, in turn, effects a partial alignment with modern ethical requirements of impartiality, rather than in terms of the other-regarding orientation entailed in the sense of *agape* as the initiation of positive relations. The superiority of the former reading is seen by Outka to consist in its ability to do justice to the self, while allowing for what Outka calls a "swerve" away from our own claims to those of others.[38] But a position in which we are not prevented from considering others is far removed from the challenge to put others before ourselves to the point of loving enemies and returning good for evil.

Outka attempts to bridge this gap between the altruistic reading of *agape* and his own reading of *agape* as impartial judgment through the contention that altruists and impartialists are not so different when it comes to other–other situations. In such completely third-party contexts, altruists are almost as likely to approve of rights of self-defence as impartialists.[39] Those who really contrast with impartialists are members of the peace churches who do not make the distinction between self–other and other–other contexts. Since Christian altruists are not willing to embrace the absolute pacifism of this extreme, but rather "distinguish the shedding of blood from the shedding of innocent blood,"[40] Outka proposes that the gap between altruism and the self–other balance of impartiality is not as great as altruists, in particular, are inclined to suppose.

To distinguish between aggressors and victims, and to accord

[38] Ibid., pp. 81–2.   [39] Ibid., pp. 26, 33ff., 80.   [40] Ibid., p. 26.

more concern to the latter than to the former, is, so the implication seems to be, indicative of compromise of the focus on the other. Yet the import of Outka's analysis of the differences in responses to self–other and other–other situations may not be that the altruistic understanding of *agape* has to be qualified in the direction of more manageable impartiality, but that still further distinctions need to be made, such as the distinction between public and private spheres. In some ways, the self–other/other–other distinction corresponds to the distinction between personal relations and impersonal structures. The direct engagement of self–other relations provides more immediate incentive and possibility for *agape* than the impersonal distance of third-person situations. In third-person situations, the self tends to be submerged in an official role or office, and the other is generally an anonymous aggregate of citizens or clients. In this complex situation, some others are bound to be harmed. The sheer number of others and the need for impersonal mechanisms to regulate life at this public level calls for policies and procedures that complicate the direct implementation of an *agape* direction, but this does not automatically imply an adjustment of the radical altruistic focus of *agape*. It will do so only if *agape* is seen to be irrelevant to the complex demands of real life.

Outka charges that this is what happens in Reinhold Niebuhr's relegation of *agape* to the realms of personal ideal, and corresponding advocacy of justice in the name of realism, of justice as the highest virtue in the public or political realm. Outka suggests that he prefers Paul Ramsey's attempt to combine the two so that justice is seen not as an alternative to or approximation of love but as the realization of love. I would argue that Outka's intention may be more readily achieved through the position represented by Niebuhr than through Ramsey's supposed combination. Conventional wisdom (with which Outka seems to concur) is that Niebuhr is guilty of the displacement of love by justice and Ramsey is not because Niebuhr so elevates *agape* that it becomes an unattainable abstract ideal, leaving justice as the only practical possibility, while Ramsey offers the prospect of an integrated approach that preserves the distinctiveness of *agape* in the very pursuit of justice. However, it is by no means clear that this is the case, particularly if we are attending to the mature Niebuhr. The gap Niebuhr posits between love and justice is a function of the realism dictated by his Augustinian-Reformation conviction of the seriousness of sin. Approximations of justice are the best that can be expected of sinful humanity. Agapic love remains as the ideal measure of humanity, an ideal not inherently unrealistic, but rendered so through the distortion of sin. The saints reveal occasional flashes of agapic heights, but for most of us the restraints and arrangements of justice are all that can be realistically expected. Still, agapic love remains relevant as an inspirational ideal that provides motivation and goal for the justice that may be attained. Ramsey's more direct combination of love and justice appears to give more practical expression to *agape*, but this may be at the expense of its distinctiveness as an ideal that stands in contrast to the inclinations of sinful humanity. So choosing to align oneself with Ramsey, as Outka does, turns out to be accepting a subtler but more intractable form of the displacement of love by justice than any advocated by Niebuhr.

There is a second reason for holding Outka guilty of the very activity of displacement of which he (mistakenly) convicts Niebuhr. To understand this second reason, we have to take another look at the relation between Outka's position and that of R. M. Hare. In defending Outka against superficial claims that he is a captive of Enlightenment biases, I pointed out how completely he differs from Hare in some of his fundamental assumptions – he does not, for example, share Hare's assumptions about the power of human beings to govern the moral domain through rational consensus. What we are now prepared to see is that Outka's *motive* for tempering love with justice betrays a deeper similarity to the Enlightenment configuration of commitments than his reservations about its rationalistic extreme might suggest. Outka's concern to balance the claims of the self and the other shares in Hare's Enlightenment outlook despite their differences on the matter of the need for ameliorative strategies. To the degree that Outka refers to the other not as the direct focus of concern but in terms of a "swerve" on the part of the self, he appears to share Hare's assumptions concerning the basic integrity of the self. We are urged to pursue a justice-defined *agape* that demands consideration for self as well as other because it applies to everyone. "In this way justice may have a limiting effect on *agape* qua radical other-regard."[41] Outka holds that justice sets limits on *agape* directly, whereas Niebuhr held that it is only because sin compromises our ability to live out the requirements of *agape* that we must accept justice as the more realistic goal.

While some of the critics of Nygren's reading of *agape* might see *agape* as being subject to some such restrictions, the initiative it represents is possible only on the basis of the renewed life made possible through divine forgiveness. In spite of his references to the dependence of human *agape* on the prior divine *agape* and in spite of his acknowledgment of the necessity for an "ameliorative strategy" to overcome our tendency to self-preference, Outka's program for impartiality seems to allow no integral necessity for divine forgiveness. *Agape*, qualified as impartiality, is more a rational strategy that justifies our concern with ourselves as long as this concern is balanced by an acknowledgment of the reality of other selves, as a concession on the part of the self. Clearly this is very different from the essentially altruistic orientation of *agape* as it is seen through the traditional reading articulated by Nygren. As a reading of *agape*, Outka's reinterpretation might be even more detrimental to the distinctiveness of *agape* than the foreign displacements effected by those who propose *eros* or *philia* as plausible and advantageous models for understanding Christian love.

THE INDISPENSABILITY OF ALTRUISTIC *AGAPE*

The most serious threat to appreciation of the distinctiveness of *agape* today thus may lie not in the obvious alternatives of those who oppose it but in the redefinition advanced by a sympathizer like Outka who finds *agape* compatible with the modern ethical

---

[41] Outka, *Agape*, p. 301.

horizon. There is a fundamental difference between an *agape* that is primary and inherently altruistic and an *agape* that functions as a secondary requirement that qualifies a prior realm of appropriate claims and counterclaims. It is the difference between a theologically based understanding, such as Nygren promotes, and an ethically based agenda, such as Outka pursues. In spite of his own theological interest and sensitivity, Outka's treatment is shaped in decisive ways by the independent ethical agenda that goes with the modern autonomous understanding of ethics.

The comprehensive ambitions of modern ethics can be seen as an attempt to establish the parameters of reasonable responsibility, beyond which we need feel no sense of obligation. In many ways, the focus of modern ethics is the question of what others may reasonably demand of me. The other is a contract partner whose interests have to be recognized, if I am to expect my interests to be acknowledged. Of course, I might do more than morality demands, but that would be an act of supererogation. This extra concession on my part is pure gift. In so far as this vision informs Outka's account of *agape* in terms of universal love and impartiality, the altruistic distinctiveness of *agape*, which he clearly appreciates, is compromised in his own final position.

Such an understanding of life does not make sense from the perspective of the gospel because from that perspective life itself is a gift. We are givers only secondarily, being first and foremost recipients of the gift of life and of its renewal through the gospel. This awareness cuts the ground from under the notion of supererogation. We confront here the gap between, on the one hand, the vision that sees life as a gift, so that we live as recipients, linked in common total indebtedness, and, on the other hand, the vision of life that sees it as our possession, to be shared to some reasonable extent and to be subject to our withholding or bestowal beyond that. This gap confirms Nygren's contention that what is at stake is a matter of comprehensive paradigms. The difference is one between some form of theocentric vision and one determined by a post-Enlightenment anthropocentric perspective.

The difference between theocentric *agape* and the anthropocentric orientation of modern ethics is illustrated in the analysis
of neighbor love undertaken by Garth L. Hallett. His book
provides a carefully constructed analysis of six possible stances
that might be taken on Christian neighbor love – self-preference, parity, other-preference, self-subordination, self-forgetful-
ness, and self-denial – and advocates what he claims is the
seldom noticed option of self-subordination as a more adequate
understanding of the gospel mandate than the extreme of self-
denial. In the course of this exposition, Hallett admits a certain
incongruity in what he is doing.

A Vincent de Paul or a Mother Teresa does not carefully balance pros
and cons or estimate benefits to self versus benefits to others. A need is
seen, the heart is moved, the loving deed is done. By comparison, a
calculative attitude may seem positively pernicious. And a study that
inculcates it, through careful discriminations like those in chapter 1,
may appear a worse than futile enterprise.[42]

This momentary consideration does not deter Hallett in his
analysis. He rightly observes that the New Testament includes
precepts as well as parables. What he does not consider is that
the focus on precepts, on drawing boundaries between reasonable claims of self and others, has a way of constituting its own
parable, a vision of life that is just as total and foundational as
any theistic vision. This is what modern ethics represents, and,
as such, threatens to compromise the distinctiveness of *agape*, if
it approaches it at all, even in theologicallly sensitive expositors
like Outka. Part of the problem is that ethics, as the distinct
discipline it has become in the modern era, reflects a secular
outlook, and while this involves visions that are as comprehensive and absolute as any theological ones it displaces, this basis
and its implications are more often assumed than noticed.

The relation between morality and religion is a complex and
debatable issue, but the main options are neatly summarized by
Charles W. Kegley in terms of four basic directions.[43] In

---

[42] Garth L. Hallett, *Christian Neighbor-Love: An Assessment of Rival Versions* (Washington,
DC: Georgetown University Press, 1989), pp. 114–15.

[43] Charles W. Kegley, "Religion and Morality, Relations of," in *A Dictionary of Christian
Ethics*, ed. John Macquarrie (London: SCM Press, 1967), pp. 290–1.

classical religious traditions, the two were taken as indistinguishable, as illustrated particularly in early Judaism, Confu-
cianism, and some forms of Buddhism. Secondly, philosophers
tended to accord morality an independent significance, a tendency which can be seen to become progressively more pro-
nounced as we move from Plato to Aristotle to the modern era
as represented particularly by Kant. A third variation sees
religion as a dimension of morality. Kegley cites Matthew
Arnold's notion of religion as "morality tinged with emotion";
he might also have mentioned R. B. Braithwaite's view of
religion as stories illustrating and inspiring moral commitment.
But it is the fourth position that has come to dominate the
present, one that takes morality to be autonomous and capable
of fulfilling the functions formerly performed by religion. This
identifies the heart of the dilemma. In the modern secular
perspective, morality not only stakes out its own territory,
independent of religion; it completes the inversion from its
traditional anchorage in religion to become the assumed
context in which religion itself must find any credibility it may
be able to claim.

As this dialectic of religion and morality constitutes the
context for the compromise of the distinctiveness of *agape*,
consideration of the problematic of this displacement from the
point of view of religion can help to indicate what that compromise involves. Morality may be demanding, but it does not
challenge us at the level of religion. Ronald M. Green has made
an heroic effort to expose the rationality of religion as the
logical completion of morality. What finally distinguishes religion from morality, he suggests, is the matter of forgiveness;
"the suspension of strict justice required by forgiveness is the
most complex element in the deep structure of religious reasoning."[44] The justice orientation of modern ethics finds its
completion in, but is also in fundamental ways contradicted by,
religious forgiveness. The awkwardness is suggested in Green's
depiction of the ambivalence about the reality of forgiveness
that characterizes the moral point of view.

[44] Ronald M. Green, *Religion and Moral Reason: A New Method for Comparative Study* (New
York: Oxford University Press, 1988), p. 104.

That question, "How can I ever be morally worthy?" finds its answer, we now see, in the belief that there possibly exists a perfect moral causal agency, supreme over all reality, which is not strictly required always to act or judge morally as we are, and which, in its very supremacy, stands as the final objective ground and arbiter of moral worth. By means of this belief, the individual's self-condemnation is relieved and he is given the possibility – however slight it may be – of rationally doing what his moral reason commands: renewing at every moment of time his commitment to the strict priority of morality.[45]

Green's analysis discloses the incompleteness of morality as an attempt to justify ourselves. The frustrations and failures of our best moral efforts may lead us to consider the need for some wider basis of reassurance. However, such a basis can only be one that "possibly exists" and consequently one that offers at best a "slight" possibility of inspiring renewed commitment to morality. Even such a "slight" possibility must be doubted, when the source itself is hypothetical. How can a "possible" God (the perfect moral causal agency) provide assurance of anything? The attempt to invoke a hypothetical religion to complete an assumed moral base is inherently problematic. Green's exposure of the inner logic of morality points to morality's grounding in religion. However, the modern emergence of ethics has pointed morality in the opposite direction, seeing it as independent of religion, and ultimately as the grounding for any credibility religion may be able to claim.

The inability of morality to ground the forgiveness that it anticipates is indicative of the fate of *agape* within its horizon. *Agape* is no more accessible within the parameters of morality than forgiveness. As a moral ideal it can only produce failure and frustration. This inherent danger in every moral ideal is pushed past the breaking point with an ideal as lofty as *agape*. In this way, it exposes the need of morality for religion, as intimated by Green's analysis. To appreciate this, however, presupposes the insights of religion itself. From the perspective of the gospel, *agape* is a reality before it is an ideal. It reflects the basic reality of God. It is because God is *agape* that we are

---

[45] Ronald M. Green, *Religious Reason: The Rational and Moral Basis of Religious Belief* (New York: Oxford University Press, 1978), p. 106.

challenged to pursue that way. The challenge is rooted in and renewed by the assurance of its divine endorsement and encouragement. This religious' vision is very different from any moral stance, however elevated. As John Whittaker has rightly remarked:

Those who believe in the promises of God are unbound from the task of achieving their happiness. They have replaced the struggle for happiness with the trust that it will be given to them in God's way. Thus, they are free to show others a pale copy of the concern that they believe has been shown to them. Their fundamental disposition has changed from preoccupation into gratitude, the fountainhead of all Christian charity. This is the reason that the second great commandment of Christianity depends on the first. And it is the reason why there is something distinctively Christian in the ideal of *agape*.[46]

The appreciation of *eros* and *philia* among theologians in recent years and the concern for justice in contemporary theology and ethics have much to commend them, not least of all their function as correctives to isolationist spiritualization of Christian thought and practice. But that corrective is fraught with the danger that these dimensions of concern will be allowed to displace rather than to express the indispensable theological context of *agape*. It is this theological context that permits the recognition of the feebleness of our efforts and prevents that recognition from degenerating into despair and defeat. The reality of religion, as represented in the Christian tradition through faith in God and the renewal of life through the rites of worship, constitutes the basis for the confidence that affords some motivation for caring about others in spite of our inclination to the contrary. Green can look for this in an extension of morality, and see what supposedly thus emerges as restoring confidence in morality only because of a previous and pervasive confidence in morality that is of religious proportions. That confidence is undermined, however, by Green's own intimations of the incompleteness of the moral horizon.

This humanistic, moral horizon is taken for granted by the champions of *eros* and *philia* when these are presented as

---

[46] John H. Whittaker, "'Agape' and Self-Love," in *The Love Commandments*, ed. Santurri and Werpehowski, p. 238.

adequate replacements for *agape*. I contend, for example, that it is just such a humanistic horizon that frames feminist claims that the vitality of *eros* and the mutuality of *philia* provide sufficient representations of Christian love, without recourse to anything like what is intended by *agape* as outlined by Nygren; my contention is confirmed from within the ranks of feminist theology by Daphne Hampson:

What strikes me about much modern theology – and this is not least true of feminist theology – is how profoundly secular it is. It is as though theology has lost its moorings. In the case of feminist theology, what seems to have replaced talk of God is largely talk of women's experience. It is not even women's experience of God; it is simply women's experience.[47]

In contrast to this theological neglect, Outka seeks to implement the explicit theological agenda of *agape*. Yet his attempt to qualify *agape* as universal love that embraces the ethical demands of impartiality endangers the distinctiveness of *agape* even more, precisely because he professes to leave *agape* intact. The gospel promise of the establishment of self through abandonment of self is displaced by the direct concern for self characteristic of the post-Enlightenment perspective. From this rational perspective, the claims of the self are as legitimate as the claims of others. After all, the self *is* other to other selves. But *agape* is not a rational, anthropocentric concept. It represents the divine extravagance of giving that does not take the self into account. Clearly this is impractical. Common sense demands that the needs of the self be taken into account. If they are not, how can there be a self to be concerned with others? The answer of the gospel is: "through *agape!*" The commonsense responsibleness of balancing the claims of self and others represents a compromise of the distinctive thrust of *agape*, rather than being an application of it.

Beyond his aid in identifying the religious pretensions of contemporary morality, Kegley's summary also identifies this theological distinctiveness of *agape* as a further option beyond the conventional lines of demarcation between religion and

---

[47] Daphne Hampson, *Theology and Feminism* (Oxford: Basil Blackwell, 1990), p. 170.

morality. "Among those of theistic persuasion morality and
religion would appear to join in some version of the biblical
doctrine of *agape*."[48] Far from being amenable to the categories
of modern ethics or a dispensable diversion from the real
desires of *eros* and the mutuality of *philia*, *agape* is the indispensable theological basis and direction of gospel living. Daniel
Day Williams sounds the essential note: "*Agape* is identification
with the neighbor and meeting his needs, but it is identification
at the level of confession of our betrayal of the divine image,
and hope for the possibility of renewal through the grace of
suffering love."[49] The reality of *agape* is only identified through
the horizon of theological conviction and sustained through the
apparatus of religion. In spite of his disservice to *eros*, and his
neglect of *philia*, Nygren deserves to be heard clearly in his
insistence on the distinctively theological significance of *agape*.

[48] Kegley, "Religion and Morality, Relations of," p. 293.
[49] Daniel Day Williams, *The Spirit and Forms of Love* (New York: Harper & Row, 1968),
   p. 262.

CHAPTER 8

Absolute altruism

If the modern concept of altruism derives from the Christian concept of *agape*, the ultimate source of the concept is in the Christian understanding of God. Nygren contends that *agape* is only a human possibility at all because it is the divine reality. Human *agape* results from participation in the overflowing divine *agape*. Unselfish love of neighbor is inspired by and sustained through faith in the unselfish love of God. On this reading, God is the absolute altruist. Our existence is due ultimately to the overflowing generosity of God. Our continued existence is due to the persistence of that generosity in the redemption that reaffirms us in spite of our rejection and abuse of that generosity through sin.

Reservations about Nygren's total contrast between *agape* and *eros* extend beyond concern with the loss of the erotic dimension of human life, and the neglect of the mutuality of *philia*, to a questioning of the adequacy of this understanding of God exclusively in terms of *agape*. The total generosity of *agape*, on its own, may not represent the epitome of altruism. Although this vision sees the distinctiveness of God in terms of ultra-altruism, this altruism is possible only because God is characterized by an intrinsic self-sufficiency. The aseity of God constitutes the ontological basis of the character trait of love. The generosity of overflowing and undeserved *agape* is a reflection of the divine plenitude. This implicit side of Nygren's version, and indeed of much conventional theological thinking, raises the disturbing prospect that the more basic characteristic of God may not be altruism, but egoism. The generosity and condescension of God entailed by *agape* may imply a more basic isolation and even arrogance.

This dilemma may be avoided, if *agape* reflects not simply the overflowing plenitude of self-sufficiency, but is an expression of genuine caring that takes the otherness of creation seriously in its own right. If *agape* represents sympathy in the negative sense, creation is a divine plaything; if *agape* reflects empathy in the negative sense, creation is understood but essentially alien. *Agape*, as the delicate balance of caring sympathy and knowing empathy, affirms both the indispensable divine grounding and the integrity of the gounded creation. Does this mean that divine altruism is not constituted by *agape* alone, but by the combination of *agape* and *eros*? If so, does this extend to recognizing that the overflowing divine *agape* is qualified by a real need in God? This consideration has emerged in recent years in the contention that, in contrast to the divine aseity that is implied in *agape* taken on its own, God is to be seen to be characterized by vulnerability that is indicative of the need of *eros*.

THE REVOLUTION IN THEOLOGY

Christian theology has experienced a 180-degree turn over the course of the past century. Traditionally, nothing was more assured and assumed than the imperviousness of God to suffering; in contemporary mainline theology nothing is more assured and assumed than the suffering of God. So dramatic is the reversal that someone unfamiliar with Christian thought, reading patristic or medieval classics, on the one hand, and recent treatises, on the other, would hardly think they were dealing with literature from the same movement. For centuries, the one given was that God was beyond the vulnerabilities known to mortals, especially any hint of suffering; the claim that has grown to the level of obviousness is that if God did not suffer, there would be no gospel.

In the controversies through which Christian orthodoxy was fashioned, nothing was so assured as the assumption that God was characterized fundamentally by self-sufficient imperviousness. Whatever the differences between the two sides in the major controversies, Trinitarian and Christological, the protagonists on both sides tended to be equally convinced about the divine aseity. Thus the leading combatants in the first round of the Trinitarian Controversy promoted their divergent conceptions of the Son within the context of a primary agreement on the basic nature of God. Arius, the soon-to-be heretic, assures Alexander: "We know one God . . . immutable unchangeable."[1] Athanasius, the soon-to-be pillar of orthodoxy, differs from this affirmation only because he insisted that these qualities must also be attributed to the Son: "But the Son being from the Father and peculiar to his substance is unchangeable and immutable as the Father himself."[2]

We might expect that the triumph of the *Homoousios* insistence that the Son was of the same substance as the Father, and the identification of the Son with Jesus, would have occasioned a reconsideration of the divine imperviousness in the Christological Controversy, but, as Athanasius' position indicates, the effect was the reverse. Instead of finding the claim of incarnation indicative of divine sensitivity, the Christological Controversy transposed the assumption of divine immutability into the understanding of the person of Christ, and here again the pervasiveness of the assumption transcends the differences between the two sides in the controversy, the Antiochene and Alexandrian positions. In the shot that launched the Christological Controversy, his sermon against the *theotokos*, Nestorius emphasizes the humanity of him who was born of Mary:

That which was formed in the womb is not in itself God. But since God is within the one who was assumed, the one who was assumed is styled God because of the one who assumed him. That is why the demons shudder at the mention of the crucified flesh; they know that God has been joined to the crucified flesh, even though he has not shared its suffering.[3]

---

[1] "Arius' Letter to Alexander," in *The Trinitarian Controversy*, ed. and tr. William G. Rusch (Philadelphia: Fortress Press, 1980), p. 31.

[2] "Athanasius' Orations against the Arians," in *The Trinitarian Controversy*, p. 99.

[3] "Nestorius' First Sermon Against the *Theotokos*," in *The Christological Controversy*, ed. and tr. Richard A. Norris, Jr. (Philadelphia: Fortress Press, 1980), p. 130.

This Antiochene insistence on the distinction between the divine and human natures in Christ is countered by the Alexandrian emphasis on the unity of the person of Christ as the Word made flesh. Yet this insistence on the genuineness of incarnation does not prevent the champions of the Alexandrian position from invoking a distinction between the natures that would rival anything in the Antiochene corpus, in the interest of preserving the divine Logos from human vulnerability. Thus Cyril of Alexandria writes to Nestorius:

We assert that this is the way in which he suffered and rose from the dead. It is not that the Logos of God suffered in his own nature, being overcome by stripes or nail piercing or any of the other injuries; for the divine, since it is incorporeal, is impassible. Since, however, the body that had become his own underwent suffering, he is – once again – said to have suffered these things for our sakes, for the impassible One was within the suffering body.[4]

The conviction regarding the immutability and the impassibility of God was so fundamental that it was assumed rather than argued. The debates centered on the question of how the impassible God could be associated with passible humanity. Those who deviated from this view were very much in the minority, and readily fell victim to the emerging consensus. Hippolytus records the heresy of one Noetus, who held that God is both invisible and visible, unbegotten and begotten, immortal and mortal. This led him to say the following things: "When indeed, then, the Father had not been born, He [yet] was justly styled Father; and yet it pleased him to undergo generation, having been begotten, He himself became His own Son, not another's."[5] This allowed Noetus to predicate suffering of God. "That this person suffered by being fastened to the [accursed] tree, and that He commended His Spirit unto [the keeping of] Himself, having died [to all appearance] and not being [in reality] dead. And He raised Himself up the third day, after having been interred in a sepulchre. . ."[6] A more

[4] "Cyril of Alexandria's Second Letter to Nestorius," in *The Christological Controversy*, p. 133.

[5] Hippolytus, *The Refutation of All Heresies*, tr. J. H. MacMahon, Ante-Nicene Christian Library, vol. vi (Edinburgh: T. & T. Clark, 1868), p. 335.

[6] Ibid.

famous exponent of patripassianism was the target of Tertullian's ire, Praxeas. The latter's concession that the Father suffered only with the Son did not impress Tertullian.

[Our heretics] indeed, fearing to incur direct blasphemy against the Father, hope to diminish it by this expedient: they grant us so far that the Father and the Son are two; adding that, since it is the Son indeed who suffers, the Father is only his fellow-sufferer. But how absurd are they even in this conceit! For what is the meaning of "fellow-suffering," but the endurance of suffering along with another? Now if the Father is incapable of suffering, he is incapable of suffering in company with another; otherwise, if He can suffer with another, He is of course capable of suffering.[7]

The classical consensus in theology was concerned with preserving God from the reality of suffering. In retrospect, this can be seen to be a primary motivation in the formation of the classical creeds. So the Trinitarian Controversy distinguished the comprehensive Father from the incarnate Son, and, although it was not the official position, for many this amounted to the assurance that it was the Father who really constituted the godhead, so that the most that had to be conceded in the direction of divine passibility was that it was the Son who was associated with the way of the cross. Tertullian's rebuke of this tendency is prophetic for the ensuing Christological development which provided the means for preserving the Son from such contamination as well by confining the suffering to the human nature of Jesus. People like Noetus and Praxeas, who had the temerity to suggest that God might actually be implicated in the sufferings of Jesus, found themselves very definitely on the wrong side of the emerging consensus.

The pervasiveness of the assumption of divine immutability and impassibility, which underlay the consensus of classical Christian orthodoxy, is matched today by an equally impressive consensus to the opposite effect. Richard Bauckham credits English theologians with the initiation of this development. "For once, English theology can claim to have pioneered a major theological development: from about 1890 onwards, a

---

[7] Tertullian, *Adversus Praxean*, Ante-Nicene Christian Library, ed. Alexander Roberts and James Donaldson, vol. 15 (Edinburgh: T. & T. Clark, 1870), pp. 402f.

steady stream of English theologians, whose theological approaches differ considerably in other respects, have agreed in advocating, with more or less emphasis, a doctrine of divine suffering."[8] But Bauckham acknowledges that the same direction has emerged in different quarters, apparently largely independently. No less a champion of traditional theological themes than Karl Barth endorses the reversal. "What are all the sufferings in the world, even those of Job, compared with this fellow-suffering of God Himself which is the meaning of the event of Gethsemane and Golgotha?"[9] The legacy of this admission is evident in Bonhoeffer's prison musings to the effect that God has allowed himself to be edged out of the world and onto the cross, and that only as the suffering God is God available to help us,[10] as well as in Moltmann's trinitarian theology of the cross, articulated under the telling title, *The Crucified God*.[11] A Lutheran version of this direction has emerged in Japan in Kazoh Kitamori's *Theology of the Pain of God*.[12] In America, the tendency is evident in Geddes Mac-Gregor's *He Who Lets Us Be: A Theology of Love*,[13] and in process theology. Tertullian's dissatisfaction with Praxeas' concession that "the Father is only [the Son's] fellow-sufferer" suggests that he would be no more impressed by the Whiteheadian characterization of God as "the fellow-sufferer who understands."[14] The process version of divine passibility has been developed particularly by Charles Hartshorne.[15] The extent of this development, combined with the fact that it constitutes a reversal of classical orthodoxy, lends credence to Daniel Day

---

[8] Richard Bauckham, "'Only the Suffering God Can Help': Divine Passibility in Modern Theology," *Themelios* 9 (1984): 6.

[9] Karl Barth, *Church Dogmatics*, vol. IV, part 3, ed. G. W. Bromiley and T. F. Torrance (Edinburgh: T. & T. Clark, 1977), p. 414.

[10] Dietrich Bonhoeffer, *Letters and Papers from Prison* (London: Collins, 1953), p. 122.

[11] Jürgen Moltmann, *The Crucified God* (New York: Harper & Row, 1974).

[12] Kazoh Kitamori, *Theology of the Pain of God* (London: SCM Press, 1946, 1966).

[13] Geddes MacGregor, *He Who Lets Us Be: A Theology of Love* (New York: Seabury Press, 1975).

[14] Alfred North Whitehead, *Process and Reality*, corrected edition, ed. David Ray Griffin and Donald W. Sherburne (London: The Free Press, 1978), p. 351.

[15] Charles Hartshorne, *The Divine Relativity* (New Haven and London: Yale University Press, 1948); and *Reality as Social Process* (Glencoe, Ill.: The Free Press, 1953).

Williams' description of it as a "structural shift in the Christian mind."[16]

If there is anything more striking than the magnitude of this transformation, it is the apparent naturalness with which it has unfolded. "What is particularly remarkable about the theopaschite mind-set has been its development as a kind of open secret . . . indeed, this doctrinal revolution occurred without a widespread awareness that it was happening."[17] From the long-standing unquestionableness of the impassibility of God, the perspective of large segments of contemporary theology has changed to the point where a recent book on this subject can begin with the words: "The concept of divine suffering is not only the core of our faith but the uniqueness of Christianity."[18] Noetus and Praxeas would enjoy a very different reception if they lived in the late twentieth century.

A total reversal in something as basic as the understanding of God demands explanation. Because of the magnitude of the change, it might seem that the explanation should be obvious. Such an explanation is also readily available. The shift from the invulnerable to the vulnerable understanding of God may be attributed most obviously to the shift in cultural outlooks represented by the premodern and modern eras. In the premodern world God was understood in complete contrast to humanity. God was characterized in particular by all the features that humanity lacked. Close to the top of the list was the contrast between imperviousness and vulnerability. In the modern era, humanity has moved front and center, so that God either drops off the map entirely, or retains some position because of relevance to humanity. The shift in cultural sensibility cannot be ignored as an explanation for the strange reversal in theological sensibility. To accept it as a total explanation, however, would be to concede too much to the contentions of Feuerbach and Freud that God is only finally of our own

---

[16] Daniel Day Williams, *What Present-Day Theologians Are Thinking* (New York: Harper & Row, 1952), p. 138.
[17] Ronald Goetz, "The Suffering God: The Rise of a New Orthodoxy," *The Christian Century* 101 (1986): 385.
[18] Jung Young Lee, *God Suffers for Us: A Systematic Inquiry into a Concept of Divine Passibility* (The Hague: Martinus Nijhoff, 1974), p. 1.

devising. Taken at face value, this explanation could represent a total vindication of Feuerbach in terms of the premodern era, where God could be seen to be a name for human ideals, and of Freud in the modern era, where God could appear simply as an enlargement of ourselves to cosmic proportions. The shift does lend support to the warnings of Feuerbach and Freud about anthropological and psychological influences on theology. To see these as total explanations, however, is only possible if we are willing to elevate ourselves to theological proportions. Thus, either we are considering ourselves as God, or we are dealing with genuine theological issues.

It is possible that willingness to attribute suffering to God has become feasible because of a basic shift in cultural sensibilities, and that this shift might allow theological insight that was previously obscured. It is also possible that the shift essentially reflects loss of theological sensibility, and so is to be resisted through defence of an endangered appreciation of the divine. What is at stake may be posed as the question of whether individuals like Noetus and Praxeas detected something that was buried under Christian orthodoxy or whether orthodoxy was essentially right and is being threatened by the proliferating spiritual offspring of Noetus and Praxeas.

What is at stake is indicated in a confrontation between a defence of divine imperviousness to suffering by Karl Rahner, and an advocacy of divine suffering by Jürgen Moltmann. Rahner insists: "it does not help me to escape from my mess and mix-up and despair if God is in the same predicament."[19] Predicating suffering of God obscures the difference between God and us that makes God significant. "In Moltmann and others I sense a theology of absolute paradox, of Patripassianism, perhaps even of a Schelling-like projection into God of division, conflict, godlessness and death."[20] In Rahner's protest can be heard the reservation of F. H. Bradley at the hints of identifying vulnerability in God that were known in his day: "it

---

[19] Karl Rahner, *Karl Rahner in Dialogue: Conversations and Interviews 1965–1982*, ed. Paul Imhof and Hubert Biallowons (New York: Crossroad, 1986), in Jürgen Moltmann, *History and the Triune God* (New York: Crossroad, 1991), p. 122.

[20] Ibid.

is an illusion to suppose that imperfection, once admitted into the Deity, can be stopped precisely at that convenient limit which happens to suit our ideas."[21] The specter of anthropomorphism hangs over any vision that depicts God with vulnerabilities known to us mortals. Conversely, denial of divine vulnerability can be accused of representing an anthropomorphism of contrast; God is characterized by attributes that we lack. That might provide a rationale for risking predication of suffering in God, but Moltmann's reasoning is much more positive. His experiences as a prisoner of war in 1945 made the God who was known through the suffering and abandonment of Christ relevant for him. "So I am disturbed by your objection that God is 'in a consoling sense the God who does not suffer,'" he tells Rahner. "I find no connection between consolation and apathy and therefore find no way into your experience of God and self."[22] Moltmann finds it inconceivable that God could be thought of in Christian terms without being associated with suffering. "God is capable of suffering because he is capable of love."[23] If God did not suffer, could God really be characterized by love? This is the direction of thought that typifies the recent willingness to predicate suffering of God.

It reflects what we have seen to be the dissatisfaction with equating divine love with *agape*. In contrast to the one-sided dispensation that such love is seen to entail, real love, it is claimed, is above all relational. It receives as well as gives, and it receives because it needs to. The claim is stated forcefully by Arthur C. McGill. "Active love occurs within the fellowship of neediness, within the neediness of the one who serves and leads, of the one who serves in neediness."[24] The usual reading of the parable of the Good Samaritan "imposes the absurd illusion of selfless love,"[25] McGill insists. But that is precisely what *agape* is supposed to be. Has the Christian ideal of helping those in need been essentially misguided? It has been in so far as Christians

---

[21] F. H. Bradley, *Essays on Truth and Reality* (Oxford: Clarendon Press, 1914), p. 430.
[22] Moltmann, *History and the Triune God*, p. 123.   [23] Ibid.
[24] Arthur C. McGill, *Death and Life: An American Theology* (Philadelphia: Fortress Press, 1987), p. 89,
[25] Ibid.

have failed to perceive their own neediness, McGill would insist. Love is a relation, and relations always run two ways. The standard Christian tendency to neglect the importance and necessity of receiving, in its promotion of a willingness to give, must come to recognize our hesitancy to receive, and our readiness to think of ourselves as self-sufficient givers. Yet even if we take this challenge seriously on the ethical level, can we take it seriously theologically? Is God to be thought of as receiving in some fundamental sense?

SUSPICIONS OF DIVINE EGOISM

The distance from a theistic outlook permitted by modern anthropocentrism has provided scope for speculating on the assumptions that seem to underlie traditional theism. Some of this speculation suggests that the concern to insist on the distinctiveness and otherness of God can be seen to carry implications that are the exact opposite of those that are intended. Far from rendering God more worthy of worship, for example, such insistence might have the effect of rendering God particularly suspect. What makes God different from us is not infinite love and grace, that we do not begin to emulate, but a condition with which we are all too familiar, self-centeredness elevated to cosmic proportions. "God is a perfect individual meditating for eternity upon his own perfections," Douglas Meeks suggests, and goes on to explain this *God the Economist* vision in the following terms: "This God is a model for the individual who, according to the logic of the market household, lives privately and narcissistically."[26] Such a vision is far removed from the ultra-altruistic understanding that is usually intended by this insistence on the sufficiency of God. Far from overflowing love, the ultimate implication would seem to be the one proposed by Carter Heyward: "His first and only love is Himself."[27] It would be supremely ironic if the identification of God in the absolutely altruistic terms of *agape* ultimately

[26] M. Douglas Meeks, *God the Economist* (Minneapolis: Fortress Press, 1989), p. 163.
[27] Carter Heyward, *The Redemption of God: A Theology of Mutual Relation* (Lanham, Md.: University Press of America, 1982), p. 156.

reflected an assumption of God characterized by narcissistic egoism.

There is not much room for doubt that traditional accounts of God are subject to such an ironic reading. Saint Augustine and Saint Thomas, for example, not only insist on the self-sufficiency of God, but also maintain that the joy that God takes in creatures and in creation is really a joy in God's self. Augustine sees God to be involved in a state of changeless self-enjoyment. "For what is called life in God is itself His essence and nature. God, then, does not live except by the life which He Himself is to Himself."[28] For Aquinas, God is really rejoicing in himself in rejoicing in other things. "Again, joy and delight are a certain resting of the will in its object. But God, Who is His own principle object willed, is supremely at rest in Himself, as containing all abundance in Himself. God, therefore, through His will supremely rejoices in Himself."[29] A contemporary reading of such references is inclined to question the point of creation, if it does not add to divine satisfaction. If the pleasure God takes in creation is only a variation on the divine self-satisfaction, is creation really significant for God, or is creation really significant itself? It may well be that the obviousness of this contemporary question is indicative of a dimension in the traditional outlook that we may fail to appreciate. It seems that until the modern anthropocentric era, the sense that creation found its rationale in the divine satisfaction was not seen to pose any threat to the significance of creation. At the same time, however, once the issue has been posed, it is no longer possible to avoid the consideration that creation must represent a possible source of satisfaction for God that goes beyond what is possible for divine self-enjoyment as such. If God is altruistic, there must be an *alter* in terms of which this altruism is exercised. Otherwise, the supposed altruism collapses into comprehensive egoism.

[28] Saint Augustine, *The Trinity*, in *The Fathers of the Church*, tr. Stephen McKenna (Washington, DC: The Catholic University of America Press, 1963), bk. 15, ch. 5, p. 459.

[29] Saint Thomas Aquinas, *Summa Contra Gentiles*, tr. Anton C. Pegis (Notre Dame: University of Notre Dame Press, 1975), bk. 1, ch. 90, sec. 4.

Traditional insistence on the self-sufficiency of God and modern, or postmodern, assumptions of the autonomy and independent integrity of humanity may each represent distortions that stand in the way of a full appreciation of divine altruism. A prominent link between the two may be found in the Greek influence on the articulation of traditional Christianity and the reaction against this constituted by modern anthropocentrism. The epitome of self-sufficiency is not the Christian God per se, but the Prime Mover of Aristotle. This influence changes the theistic understanding of a creator who gives birth to a creation with no reality available other than the divine being itself into an architect who designs a product creation in deistic fashion so that, once made, the creation is able to go its own independent way, and the creator is utterly beyond being affected in any way by its fate. Such thinking encourages attributing a sense of self-sufficiency to God in traditional Christian thought and a sense of human self-sufficiency in the modern era. What is required is a dialectical understanding that avoids emphasizing self-sufficiency in either dimension, while preserving the fundamental distinction between God and humanity.

One possibility for such an alternative is represented by Karl Barth's shift of focus from the being to the freedom of God. For Barth, the aseity of God consists not in an inherent self-sufficiency, but in a freedom to choose how God shall be.[30] What makes God supreme is not ontological independence as such but the sovereignty of the divine will. This is the fundamental implication of the identification of God through Jesus. Eberhard Jüngel reflects what is at stake in such a Christocentric understanding of God. "A doctrine of God oriented to the man Jesus must then develop two avenues of thought: God does indeed come from God and only from God, and he is determined by nobody and nothing other than himself; however, he determines himself to be God not without man."[31]

---

[30] Karl Barth, *Church Dogmatics*, vol. II, part I, ed. G. W. Bromiley and T. F. Torrance (Edinburgh: T. & T. Clark, 1961), pp. 301, 307, 303.

[31] Eberhard Jüngel, *God as the Mystery of the World*, tr. D. L. Guder (Edinburgh: T. & T. Clark, 1983), p. 37.

God remains unique and sovereign as the sole determiner of the
divine character, but the presence of God in Jesus shows that
the determination God makes is not for self-sufficiency, but
rather as one who creates and cares about the creation. "Is not
this understanding of divine relationality less monistic and
narcissistic than the traditional one?" Sallie McFague asks
about a view that takes the creation seriously in its own right, in
contrast to C. S. Lewis' insistence on divine self-sufficiency, by
which God "loves into existence totally superfluous creatures."[32] Narcissistic overtones of the traditional emphasis on
the self-sufficiency of God are alleviated by recognizing that an
independent creation represents a qualification on divine narcissism, which the claim of incarnation heightens. The God
who shares life with creation cannot be accused of narcissism.

In so far as Barth is seen to point to the direction for this
solution, such qualifications provide the required dialectic on
the basis of locating the qualification in the divine will. God
chooses not to be self-sufficient, but rather to share life through
creation and redemption. This implies that God could equally
well choose self-sufficiency. It might even be taken to assume
that this is the default, which God renounces in choosing to
make a place for subordinate life forms. Then God is intrinsically self-sufficient, and qualifications on this basic stance
represent a concession. Is this adequate? Can the altruism of
God finally be grounded in the divine will, or must it be rooted
in the divine character and being? As long as it is seen to
represent a choice, on God's part, there is the possibility for a
different choice. If divine altruism reflects the basic character of
God, by contrast, this carries the assurance of an unchanging
condition. But is this possible without acknowledging that
creation must meet a real need in God? If the qualification on
self-sufficiency is not a divine choice and concession, but a
reflection of the very being and character of God, then God
must be characterized by a need for external relation. Paul
Fiddes takes this step beyond Barth's location of divine altruism

---

[32] Sallie McFague, "Response," in *Readings in Modern Theology: Britain and America*, ed.
Robin Gill (Nashville: Abingdon Press, 1995), p. 88. The C. S. Lewis quotation is
from *The Four Loves* (New York: Harcourt Brace & Co., 1960), p. 176.

in the divine will by contending that this reflects desire on God's part. That God is altruistic, rather than self-sufficient, then, is an expression of divine *eros* as well as of divine *agape*. Besides being an outpouring of divine plenitude, creation and redemption reflect a basic need in God. This assures a stability that cannot be assumed when the basis is located in will, even in the divine will. "Understanding God's will as desire indicates that there can be no 'otherwise' in the love of God for mankind. Because he thirsts and longs for fellowship with his creatures, it makes no sense to say that he need not do so."[33] Creation, in origin and continuance, is an expression of the very being of God.

This grounding of creation in the being of God entails a basic shift from traditional Christian understanding of what such grounding would be seen to involve. The traditional reading assumed not only the primacy, but the totality, of *agape* as the only possible characterization of God. Creation represented the overflowing plenitude of divine love. This view would not have settled for an explanation in terms of divine choice and will. Creation did reflect divine choice, but this amounted to a spilling over of the divine *agape* beyond the divine life. The recent account, represented by Fiddes, sees creation as a reflection of divine *eros* as much as of divine *agape*. Creation is not only an indication of a qualification on divine self-sufficiency, but an indication of the impossibility of divine self-sufficiency. God needs the other that creation represents because the love of God is erotic and needy.

The dilemma is stated succinctly by Fiddes. "The conundrum is this: is it more selfish of God to suffer or not to suffer?"[34] The traditional reading of God in terms of purely giving, agapistic love can be seen to conceal a more fundamental egoistic self-sufficiency. However, if creation and redemption do not reflect such purely overflowing love, but actually meet a basic need in God, does this not imply an even more selfish motivation? If creation and redemption represent

[33] Paul Fiddes, *The Creative Suffering of God* (Oxford: Oxford University Press, 1989), p. 74.
[34] Ibid., p. 170.

self-fulfilment for God, E. L. Mascall contends, "then creation, while it might be an act of love, would certainly not be an act of purely unselfish love."[35] Thus Fiddes' conundrum: "which is more unselfish – a love which does not cost God suffering, or a suffering love which does something for God as well as for us?"[36] A God who creates out of need cannot be entirely lacking in self-interest; a God who creates out of pure generosity would seem to be a God of essential self-sufficiency. The implication of self-sufficiency was not particularly evident so long as the emphasis was on the pure generosity of divine *agape*. As modern social consciousness has highlighted the importance of relation, and particularly the sense that love is above all relational, self-sufficiency has become more suspect, even, and for some especially, in God. But can we predicate the reciprocal view of love of God? Can God be seen to be characterized by need, by the love of *eros* as well as the love of *agape*?

Bradley's warning continues to resound; once such vulnerability is predicated of God, how do we daw the line? What distinguishes God from us vulnerable mortals? Such concern prompts Richard Creel to make a distinction that resembles what we considered as the difference between sympathy and empathy. In these terms, his claim is that God can empathize with human suffering, without actually sympathizing with it: "to know the feeling of another is to know that, if you were that individual, that is how you would feel – but it is not necessarily to feel that way yourself."[37] Thus it is possible for God to know our sufferings and joys, without actually experiencing them directly; God may empathize, without sympathizing. This is possible because of how God differs from us. Creel locates the difference particularly in divine omniscience. "In brief, in his omniscience God always knows all possible circumstances and actions of free agents, and in his love and wisdom can be eternally resolved as to how to respond to each of those

---

[35] E. L. Mascall, *He Who Is: A Study in Traditional Theism* (London: Darton, Longman & Todd, 1966), p. 108.

[36] Fiddes, *The Creative Suffering of God*, p. 170.

[37] Richard E. Creel, *Divine Impassibility: An Essay in Philosophical Theory* (Cambridge: Cambridge University Press, 1986), p. 130.

possibilities."[38] As a result "God's actions never need be chosen because of or in response to creaturely actualities."[39] Such an approach preserves the distinctiveness of God, but it does so at the cost of positing an essential divine remoteness and a corresponding lack of significance for creation. At its starkest, this solution would result in a deistic view of God and a mechanistic view of creation. Why would God create what is ultimately a preprogrammed creation? What significance could such a creation have in itself, as well as for God? Thus, contrary to Creel's intention, the conclusion to be drawn from his defence of divine impassibility might be that the traditional identification of divine love with *agape*, and the distinctiveness of God that this is seen to preserve, may fail to do justice to both God and creation. When God is understood particularly through claims of incarnation in an identification that is seen to be epitomized in the cross, an attribution of such actual unresponsiveness to God borders on the incredible.

Recent questioning of understanding of divine love in terms of *agape* may represent a significant qualification, rather than a direct alternative, to this long-standing depiction of divine love. The possibilities and problems evoked for our understanding of ourselves and our social possibilities by the modern notion of altruism may have their parallel in the traditional understanding of God in terms of *agape*. Just as altruism identifies significant directions for human living, but in so doing creates problems precisely though such direct identification, so equating divine love with *agape* may need to be balanced by a recognition of divine *eros*, although predicating *eros* of God creates particular difficulties. Fiddes finds his conundrum "tightened by a simplistic distinction between *Agape* and *Eros*, but loosened by perceiving their involvement in each other."[40] Concern to preserve God from association with *eros* may reflect the kinds of difficulties endemic in attempts to find a nice balance of self-interest and altruism in human life. "The essence of love would be mistaken if the attempt were made to think of God's self-relatedness and selflessness, of God's inner-divine love and his

[38] Ibid., p. 19.   [39] Ibid.
[40] Fiddes, *The Creative Suffering of God*, p. 171.

love of man, or of the 'immanent' and the 'economic' Trinity as
paradox."[41] There is no conflict, much less contradiction,
between God as unbounded self-sufficient love and God as
overflowing self-giving love, between "the one who always
heightens and expands his own being in such great self-relatedness still more selfless and thus overflowing."[42] God is characterized by *eros*, by growing, experiencing, expanding love, and
by *agape*, by complete, all-sufficient, overflowing love. These are
two sides of the same reality. God's *eros* is sustained by God's
agape, just as God's *agape* is enriched by God's *eros*. *Eros* is the
basis of the unifying and uniting activity of God, Sallie
McFague suggests, just as *agape* is the basis of the impartiality
that extends divine love to all being.[43] Our value to God is
assured by the divine *eros*; the assurance of our value to God is
grounded in the divine *agape*. Love is relational even, or perhaps
rather especially, for God. Rather than representing an overflowing divine self-sufficiency, God's love involves giving and
receiving. This view may be seen as a qualification on the
traditional understanding of God, rather than its abandonment,
as Nygren's absolute contrast between *agape* and *eros* would
contend. Yet if this is to be the case, how *agape* is to be qualified,
rather than abandoned, will have to be clarified.

THE PROCESS GOD AS ALTRUISTIC AND EGOISTIC

What might be involved in understanding God and world in
relational terms has been pursued most directly in process
thought. In contrast to the traditional Christian understanding
of God as impervious and immutable, Alfred North Whitehead
described God as "the fellow sufferer who understands."[44]
Although Whitehead pioneered what has come to be known as
process thought, the development of the theological direction
sketched by him was left for others. The most sustained devel-

---

[41] Jüngel, *God as the Mystery of the World*, p. 369.   [42] Ibid.
[43] Sallie McFague, "God as Mother," in *Weaving the Visions: New Patterns in Feminist
Spirituality*, ed. Judith Plaskow and Carol Christ (San Francisco: Harper & Row,
1989), p. 143.
[44] Alfred North Whitehead, *Process and Reality*, corrected edition, ed. David Ray Griffin
and Donald W. Shelburne (London: The Free Press, 1978), p. 351.

opment is represented by the dipolar theism of Charles Hartshorne. According to this view, God is to be thought of as having two sides, or two poles. One side or pole, called the primordial nature, represents the characteristics traditionally associated with God – eternity, immutability, imperviousness to all external influence – but this side differs radically from traditional understandings because the primordial nature is completely abstract. What God really is is determined by the other side or pole, the consequent nature. In this pole, God is temporal, contingent, vulnerable. This is what not only allows God to suffer, but makes suffering inevitable for God. Rather than being totally independent, as the medieval insistence on the aseity, the self-sufficiency, of God assumed, "God is the cosmic or universal form of independence and dependence."[45] Rather than being sheer Absolute, God is absolutely relative.[46] Where the classical portrait of God emphasizes isolation as the warrant of divine supremacy, dipolar theism insists on relatedness. What makes God superior is not detachment from any and every external reality, but the total relevance and relatedness to each and every other reality. God is totally related, and in this sense totally relative.

Transcendent independence, infinity, unchangeability, and the other negatives are indeed necessary aspects of deity; but so also are transcendent dependence, finitude, and capacity for change. Transcendence applies to both sides of the polar contraries that have been used to distinguish God from other beings, not to one side alone.[47]

God is the supreme instance of dependence and change as well as of independence and changelessness.

Here we have the best of both worlds; traditional concern with the distinctiveness of God and recent acknowledgment of the vulnerability of God are both affirmed. Whether this balance is maintained, however, particularly in uses that have been made of Hartshorne's distinctions, and even possibly in

[45] Charles Hartshorne, "Process and the Nature of God," in *Traces of God in a Secular Culture*, ed. George F. McLean (New York: Alba House, 1973), p. 133.
[46] Charles Hartshorne, *The Divine Relativity* (New Haven and London: Yale University Press, 1948).
[47] Charles Hartshorne, "Metaphysics and Dual Transcendence," *Tulane Studies in Philosophy* 314 (1986): 66.

Hartshorne himself, is a source of concern. One concern is precisely the fact that those features that have served to distinguish God are totally abstract. "The absolute, infinite side is abstract and concerns the divine potentiality or capacity to have values, while the finitude or relativity concerns the divine actuality."[48] The absolute, primordial side of God is potential; the relative, consequent side is what makes God actual. This could be taken to mean that the primordial dimension does not really exist, but this is not what Hartshorne means. He makes an important distinction between existence and actuality, a distinction for which he hopes to be remembered.[49] On the basis of this distinction, God as primordial can be said to exist, but this existence lacks the concreteness of actuality, which depends on the consequent nature. This is not seen to detract from the significance of the primordial nature, however. Although lacking actuality in itself, it constitutes the consistency or character of God that is manifest in the actuality of the consequent nature. As a result, for all its abstractness, the primordial nature "is at once conceptual, volitional, and perceptual."[50] It involves the constant elements of all of these aspects of divine experience. It is this rather "substantial" reality of the primordial nature, despite its abstractness, that affords Hartshorne the assurance that "the social beauty of the cosmic system" will be maintained, that there shall be "metaphysical progress toward ever new and greater richness of contrast and harmony."[51]

The underlying motivation for this process vision is the sense that becoming is more basic than being. Reality, including God, is developing, becoming what it has not been before. This is one of the principal motivations behind Hartshorne's insistence on the abstract quality of the primordial nature. As the inclusive

---

[48] Charles Hartshorne, *Existence and Actuality: Conversations with Charles Hartshorne*, ed. John B. Cobb, Jr. and Franklin I. Gamwell (Chicago: University of Chicago Press, 1984), p. 45.

[49] Ibid., p. 75.

[50] Charles Hartshorne, "Whitehead's Idea of God," in *The Philosophy of Alfred North Whitehead*, ed. Paul Arthur Schlipp (Evanston and Chicago: Northwestern University Press, 1941), p. 530.

[51] Ibid., p. 554.

reality, supreme in independence and supreme in dependence, God must be characterized more fundamentally by becoming than by being. "God is neither being as contrasted to becoming nor becoming as contrasted to being; but categorically supreme becoming in which there is a factor of categorically supreme being, as contrasted to inferior becoming, in which there is inferior being."[52] Hesitation over Hartshorne's insistence on the totally abstract character of the primordial nature thus reaches back to the issue of the scope he allows for the "factor of categorically supreme being." His distinction between existence and actuality is intended to allow for this, but in the wider context of being and becoming, the implication is that not only is becoming accorded primacy over the traditional primacy of being, but this raises the question of whether there is sufficient basis to assure the divine consistency and character that Hartshorne takes for granted. Without the constancy of being, what is there to distinguish becoming from sheer chaos?

The concern can also be understood in terms of the issue of the nature and role of becoming itself. In terms of God, the primacy of becoming means for Hartshorne that God is understood primarily in terms of the consequent nature. This is the positive side of the contention that the primordial nature must be seen as an abstraction. For Hartshorne, it is an abstraction from the consequent nature. The consequent nature is the actuality of God. While it is clear that existence and actuality are themselves abstractions, and that both dimensions must be seen to require each other, so that it would not be intelligible to think of existence without actuality or actuality without existence, Hartshorne's treatment does not provide ready assurance that the existence qualifies the actuality nearly as significantly as the actuality qualifies the existence. This is a particularly significant issue because the actuality of God's consequent nature derives from the world. "The world as an integrated individual is not a 'world' as this term is normally and properly used, but 'God.' God, the World Soul, is the *individual integrity* of 'the world,' which

[52] Charles Hartshorne, *Philosophers Speak of God* (Chicago: University of Chicago Press, 1953), p. 24.

otherwise is just the myriad creatures."[53] The position being advanced here is more commonly articulated from the other side, where the world is identified as God's body: "the entire cosmos is the body of God."[54] God as soul of the world; the world as God's body – this suggests that God is to be thought of essentially in terms of soul or spirit. But that is contrary to everything we have seen about Hartshorne's direction. It is the consequent, not the primordial, nature that is primary. The primordial, or soul, dimension of God is an abstraction from the actuality, and perhaps even the reality, of the consequent nature. This does not leave much scope for any "soul" of the world. It comes close to equating God and the world so that the consequent nature does not so much derive from the world as represent the world. But in a scheme that identifies the actuality of God with the consequent nature, this is tantamount to saying that the world is God. This hint of pantheism almost certainly does not do justice to the subtlety of Hartshorne's panentheistic position. It would not do to attempt to assess a thinker of Hartshorne's stature in such a cursory treatment. For our present purposes, the point is that the direction Hartshorne has sketched is often taken in these terms. When the world is presented as God's body, the result may be a means of articulating the reality of divine altruism that goes so far in recognizing the alterity of the world that it compromises the divine alterity.

Fuller scope for maintaining a sense of the distinctiveness of God may be offered by the inspirer of this process approach, Alfred North Whitehead. While it is a cardinal rule of Whitehead's philosophy that God exemplifies basic metaphysical principles, rather than being an exception to them,[55] he is also consistent in maintaining that in God the priority of the physical and mental poles is reversed. Where the processes that constitute the world emerge from the physical pole from the

[53] Charles Hartshorne, *Omnipotence and Other Theological Mistakes* (Albany: SUNY Press, 1984), p. 59.
[54] Charles Hartshorne, *Insights and Oversights of Great Thinkers* (Albany: SUNY Press, 1983), p. 333.
[55] Whitehead, *Process and Reality*, p. 343.

past and new possibilities from the mental pole constituted by God, the processes that constitute God are different in that the mental rather than the physical is primary. This is what led Whitehead to speak of primordial actuality. "God is to be conceived as originated by conceptual experience with his process of completion motivated by consequent, physical experience, initially derived from the temporal world."[56] For Hartshorne, primordial actuality is a contradiction in terms, because actuality is equated with the temporal. For Whitehead, primordial actuality is a necessity because temporality not only does not exhaust actuality, but remains unintelligible without the primordial actuality that gives it order and shape.

This difference between Hartshorne and Whitehead over the nature of actuality can also be seen, from the other side, as a difference over the nature of possibility. One of the principal reasons why Hartshorne confines actuality to the temporal is in order to allow for the reality of possibility. For him, possibilities must be completely open and uncharted. This is required in the interest of true process. For Whitehead, pure possibility would be indistinguishable from pure chaos. God emerged in his system initially as the principle of limitation, required to assure relevant possibilities for the processes that make up the world.[57] Whitehead soon came to see that a principle was not sufficient to perform this function. From that point he went on to speak of God as an actuality. It is consistent with his system in general, and with what he calls the ontological principle in particular, that the distinctive primordial character of God must be thought of as actual. For Hartshorne, the ontological principle means that the primordial nature can only be actual through the consequent nature. This is the case because, for him, actuality is equated with temporality. For Whitehead, actuality is much more comprehensive, encompassing even the realm of possibility. There is a sense in which the possible must be actual, for Whitehead. This is the distinctive character of God. It is what makes God necessary for the world; it is what makes it

---

[56] Ibid., p. 345.
[57] Alfred North Whitehead, *Science and the Modern World* (New York: Macmillan, 1925), p. 250.

necessary to acknowledge the primacy of the primordial dimension in God; it is what allows for and assures the distinctive and inclusive reality of God.

This apparently greater sensitivity to the difference between God and the world in Whitehead may also extend to some dissatisfaction with a basic twofold approach, and an approximation to something like the threefold approach reflected in the Christian doctrine of the trinity. Besides the indefinite dialectic of the primordial and consequent natures, Whitehead makes a single direct,[58] and another oblique,[59] reference to a third nature, which he calls superjective. The suggestion is that this represents divine satisfaction with the past and a basis for providing relevant possibilities for the future. As Whitehead puts it, following the more oblique reference to the function of the superjective nature: "What is done in the world is transformed into a reality in heaven, and the reality in heaven passes back into the world."[60] Perhaps John Lansing's summation of the superjective nature is as good as any. "We conclude, then, that the superjective nature is the objective immortality of God *as a whole.*"[61] This comprehensive reality of God is what seems to be lacking in the dipolar view. No matter how much it is insisted that the two natures qualify one another, in the end they tend to fall apart because there is no overarching unity. With duality, it seems inevitable that the emphasis will fall either on the consequent nature, as with Hartshorne, or on the primordial nature, as with Whitehead. These sparse references to a superjective nature suggest that Whitehead found himself moving toward an affirmation of a comprehensive divine reality that embraced and related the other natures.

The ambiguity in the sparse reference to the superjective nature leaves many uncertainties about how it relates to the other natures, as well as about its own distinctiveness and function. It is possible to see Whitehead approaching a trinitarian type of theology that would express the intimate connection between God and world, while maintaining the distinctiveness of each. The primordial nature can be seen as

[58] Whitehead, *Process and Reality,* p. 88.   [59] Ibid., p. 351.   [60] Ibid.
[61] John W. Lansing, "The 'Natures' of Whitehead's God," *Process Studies* 3 (1973): 150.

the inexhaustible reservoir of divine potentiality out of which all new possibilities emerge. The consequent nature is the way in which God is affected by what the world makes of those possibilities. The superjective nature is the comprehensive, relating nature, that allows for divine satisfaction with the experiences of the consequent nature and the selection of relevant possibilities from the primordial nature for the next step in the process. Such an interpretation of Whitehead has been proposed by Joseph A. Bracken. "Translated into a White-headian frame of reference, this would mean that the Father is to be associated in a special way with the Primordial nature of God; the Son, with the consequent nature; and the Spirit, with the superjective nature."[62] He does concede, in relation to another trinitarian reading of Whitehead, that it is extravagant to attribute a trinitarian understanding to Whitehead himself.[63] However, as he sees it, this does not diminish the legitimacy of interpreting Whitehead in these terms.

Even Hartshorne, for all his commitment to dipolarity, approaches such a relational trinity in suggesting "that we distinguish between the abstract natures or principles of divine independence (the Father?) and divine dependence (the Son?) and the defacto state of the actually dependent God (the Spirit?)."[64] Unfortunately, Hartshorne's trinity reinforces the concern already identified. Even in numerical terms, independence is outflanked by dependence in two of the three persons. A more balanced treatment would require more parity between dependence and independence, between emphasizing the difference between God and world as well as the intimate interconnection. If the Father is seen to reflect divine independence and the Son divine dependence, the Spirit might be more adequately characterized as the mediating dimension that involves dependence and independence. Because this does not happen, it appears that Hartshorne's passing reference to a trinitarian reading remains dualistic in articulation, but ulti-

---

[62] Joseph A. Bracken, "Process Philosophy and Trinitarian Theology – II," *Process Studies* 11 (1981): 84f.

[63] Ibid., p. 95, n. 5.

[64] Hartshorne, "Process and the Nature of God," p. 133.

mately monistic at its base through the primacy accorded dependence. His more primary contrast is between abstractions of dependence and independence and the actuality of dependence. According to his own dipolar view, God should be really independent and really dependent. That independence comes to be equated with abstraction and dependence identified with actuality may be indicative of the inevitability of one side of a dualism being dominant. In order to avoid this, a third dimension may have to be acknowledged, one that relates, and perhaps even incorporates to some extent the other two. This may be what Whitehead is moving toward with the sparse references to the superjective nature, and it may also reflect one of the most distinctive aspects of the traditional Christian understanding of God in trinitarian terms. A trinitarian balance may thus avoid the tendency of a dual perspective to allow one or the other of the two sides to dominate, if not to obliterate, the other, as can be seen to be the danger in the main explanations of both Hartshorne and Whitehead. If the consequent side is allowed to dominate, as in Hartshorne, then it becomes difficult to see what significance is to be found in God at all. For God to perform the unifying function required by Hartshorne himself would seem to demand recognition of the distinctiveness of divine becoming, which in turn implies a consistency of divine being to assure what Hartshorne refers to as the character of God. On the other hand, if the primordial nature is allowed to dominate, as implied at times by Whitehead, this could fall back into the danger of absolute egoism of which traditional theology has become suspect.

If Whitehead's sparse references to a superjective nature are not dismissed as peripheral aberrations, but rather are seen as hints of the internal logic of the theology implicit in his system, this offers a vehicle for understanding divine altruism in a way that affirms appropriate divine and human integrity. As the constantly renewed unity of divine experience, the superjective nature gives substance to the distinctively divine dimension represented most clearly by the primordial nature. The reality and significance of the world are assured through the consequent nature which receives that experience and makes it available for the integration of the superjective nature. In fact, without the integration represented by the superjective nature, it is difficult to see how the possibilities of the primordial nature and the actualities of the consequent nature can really be coordinated. If this happens through the consequent nature itself, as Hartshorne contends, the distinctiveness of God is compromised, and divine alterity threatens to proceed to dissolution. At the same time, Whitehead cannot allow the primordial nature to perform this function without endangering the process vision itself and issuing in a relapse into the egoistic absolute. As the integration of primordial and consequent natures, the superjective nature allows for divine integrity that precludes dissolution, while at the same time affirming the importance of the world as the object of divine altruism. The processes that make up the world receive their possibilities from the primordial nature of God, through the integrations effected in the superjective nature with results from past possibilities received through the consequent nature. In this way, the superjective nature constitutes an indispensable integrative dimension in a Whiteheadian theology, and in so doing, assures an understanding of God in terms of enduring and dependable altruism that elicits a corresponding altruism from the world, and implies a certain degree of self-realization in both God and world.

In traditional Christian thought, the sense was that divine integrity would be compromised by any hint of dependence in God. Recent recognition of the passibility of God challenges this understanding, affirming instead a two-way interdependence between God and the world. For this to involve appropriate dependence on each side, a corresponding degree of independence on the opposite side is presupposed. For the world to be dependent on God assumes a certain independence of God from the world, and vice versa. Without this degree of independence, there would not be interdependence but identity or irrelevance. The independence of God, and corresponding dependence of the world on God, is the standard view of traditional theology. Acknowledgment of independence of the world, and corresponding dependence of God upon the world, is the implication of the recognition of the passibility of God and the affirmation of process thought. In themselves, each of these positions seems untenable. If God is independent and the world dependent, then the reality of the world is illusory. On the other hand, if the world is independent and God dependent, then God is dispensable. Genuine interdependence requires that each be characterized by independence and dependence. However, to possess the relevance to one another that would make this interdependence vital and meaningful, the forms of dependence and independence must be different. If each was independent in the same way, and dependent in the same way, this would again seem tantamount to irrelevance. This is where Whitehead's insistence on the difference between God and the world becomes important. God's independence is primordial, and God's dependence consequent. The world's independence is consequent, and its dependence primordial. Without God, the world would be at most diffuse multiplicity. Without the world, God would lack all the riches of experience that inform the consequent nature of God.

For Whitehead scholars, talk of Whiteheadian trinitarianism may signal complete failure to understand the distinctiveness of Whitehead. For Christians, a trinitarianism that not only permits, but requires, recognition of divine vulnerability, may be a clear indication of heresy. Yet it is striking that the metaphysical reflections of process thought and the normalization of divine suffering in mainline theology should have occurred side by side. It is not insignificant that this has occurred also in conjunction with the suspicion of altruism as being reflective of a more basic egoism. The direction that has emerged in these reflections on these recent developments suggests that they may provide not only a way toward a richer understanding of God, but also toward a fuller understanding of the subtlety of altruism. If *eros* can be recognized in God in a way that allows the connotations of egoism usually associated with *eros* to be qualified by the altruism of *agape*, rather than *eros* being permitted to displace *agape*, this may not only provide a richer sense of God but also point to a way of addressing the paradoxes that we have seen to be endemic to altruism. As God may both give and receive, in ways appropriate to God, so self-fulfilment and other-regard may both find expression in a wider, less deliberate and less self-conscious sense of altruism.

CHAPTER 9

Actual altruism

While altruism has come to be treated with suspicion in some academic circles, either because it is taken to be basically contrary to human nature for some or because it is seen to be detrimental to human prospects as an ideal for others, the general perception of altruism seems not only to regard it as good, but as so obviously good that it is inconceivable that there could ever be too much of it. The significance of these academic and popular perceptions will be considered, in conclusion, by relating what we have seen about the nature of altruism to central issues at stake in it: the "truism" of altruism, the question of how far the assumption of the obvious goodness of altruism is justified; the "ism" of altruism, the question of the merits and liabilities of the prominent ways in which altruism has been assessed; and the "alter" of altruism, the question of the significance of otherness that is most characteristic of the focus of altruism.

THE TRUISM OF ALTRUISM

In spite of the high moral tone the term tends to evoke, "altruism" is not without its difficulties, as we have seen. Looked at in theoretical terms, there are the paradoxes, if not outright contradictions, that we identified: the psychological dilemma that any pleasure, including pleasure in the good of others, is our own pleasure; the moral dilemma, by which the more altruism is seen to be a reality, the less urgency it has as an ideal, and the more it is seen in ideal terms, the less base it is seen to have in reality; and the religious dilemma that deliberate altruism invites the suspicion of self-righteousness, which is directly contrary to an altruistic orientation. As a result, identification of altruism presents intrinsic problems. Careful identification of actual altruism will not be able to avoid the suspicion that any putative instance may not be what it seems. Altruists may be dupes of skillful manipulators, as Herbert A. Simon contends,[1] or they may be skillful manipulators themselves, feigning altruism for its beneficial effects. What is more, the more deliberate the altruism is, the more this suspicion is apt to arise. To defer to this danger entirely, however, would be to endorse a thoroughly self-interested reading of humanity, one that would exclude altruism in any serious form. From the other perspective, it is equally true that without a contrasting self-interest, altruism itself does not really make sense. Altruism requires recipients who are ready to benefit from what altruists are prepared to give. From this point of view, the more thorough the case that is made for altruism, the more it approaches complete contradition. In theory, a society of total altruists is inconceivable. "In a society of such completely unselfish people who would be prepared to accept and benefit from the sacrifice?"[2] Logically, as well as historically and socially, altruism presupposes selves who are the others. Recipients are as essential as practioners of altruistic concern.

The theoretical need for receivers raises the further complication that in practice altruism may really be a refined form of self-interest. Simon's warning about altruism being manipulative need not entail a recognition of this on the part of the would-be altruist. The most intense focus on the other may be an expression of self-interest, if the other is focused on in terms of what I perceive to be their interests. As we have noticed in connection with Thoreau's famous jibe about fleeing the person intent on doing him good, there is an immediate problem precisely in the threat of turning the target of altruistic intent into an object. This threat has been elaborated by C. Dyke as "The Vices of Altruism."[3] In the first place, this may involve a

---

[1] See John Horgan, "In the Beginning . . .," *Scientific American* 264 (March 1991): 20.
[2] A. C. Ewing, *Ethics* (New York: Collier Books, 1962), p. 34.
[3] C. Dyke, "The Vices of Altruism," *Ethics* 81 (1970–1): 249.

basic ignorance of the other person. To make a person an object of our own good intentions is, by definition, to hold that person at a certain distance. This means that we do not get to know that person, inviting the shortcomings of the sympathy–empathy continuum. The danger of this presumption is highlighted in George Bernard Shaw's quip about the liability inherent in the Golden Rule: "Do not do unto others as you would they should do unto you. Their tastes may not be the same."[4] Implicit in this ignorance of the other is the more serious vice of altruism, the paternalism that conceals the ignorance. That there might be some gap between what is best for someone else and what we think is best for them does not occur to us because we simply take it for granted that what we think is best is best. In this way, ironically, concern for others can represent a very self-centered demeanor. Rather than being the straightforward concern for others that it appears to be, even to its practioner, it can represent an attempt to dominate and control the other.

These reservations about altruism could be shared by advocates of both constructive and collegial forms. The reasons for these reservations, and their responses to them, however, will be different. Those for whom altruism is an alternative to the more basic assumption of self-interest will be inclined to focus on the intrusion that altruism can represent into the realm of personal integrity. Nagel observes that "people who are painting, or writing poetry, or making love will usually be ungrateful for assistance."[5] Some activities are best performed singly or in pairs. Pushed to its extreme, this sentiment unfolds to reveal the rugged individualism that informed the architects of the modern outlook and inspired the self-interest reading of human nature. For this outlook, not only certain creative or intimate activities are inherently personal and resistant to external interference; life itself bears this characteristic. This may refer not only to the way life is seen to be by nature, as in socio-

---

[4] George Bernard Shaw, *Maxims for Revolutionists*, in *The Oxford Dictionary of Quotations* (London: Oxford University Press, 1966), p. 490.
[5] Thomas Nagel, *The Possibility of Altruism* (Princeton: Princeton University Press, 1979), p. 129.

biology, but also to the way life should be ideally. Far from being something that must be overcome through altruistic expansion or transformation, self-interest is indicative of the autonomy and independence that should be the goal of every rational individual. According to this view, the ignorance of the other that can be involved in altruism is finally incorrigible. Nobody can really know anybody else. This is why altruism must be impersonal; it is seen fundamentally as the assurance of space for each individual to determine his or her own ends. It is not a matter of sacrificing self-interest to the interests of others. "Instead it involves respect for the psychological boundaries of both, and a disposition to restore the inner integrity of the other that is altruistic without being – literally – self-sacrificial."[6] Constructive altruism thus avoids the extremes of isolated self-interest and interfering paternalism. Its intent is to preserve the integrity of the other.

If constructive altruism were to succeed in its goal, the result would be far too austere for advocates of collegial altruism. From this point of view, constructive altruism remains a formal and artificial construction for reinforcing an individualistic vision of humanity. It is precisely this isolationism that advocates of collegial altruism deplore. As they see it, this altruism that makes space for the other is really a denial of the immediate presence of the real others with whom we are involved every day. Actual altruism is a matter of connection, rather than of separation, of involvement, rather than of withdrawal. However, the collegial altruism that issues from such pursuit of relationships also comes with prescribed limits. Indeed, it can even be seen to intensify the restrictions on altruism imposed by the constructive form. For the focus in collegial altruism tends to fall directly on the self, rather than on the other, abstract or concrete. Reservations about altruism have to do not so much with dangers of imposition on the other, but with demands on the putative altruist. Feminists in particular are wary of expectations of self-sacrifice. The collegial altruism they are apt to advocate is one of mutuality where the

---

[6] Adrian M. S. Piper, "Impartiality, Compassion and Modal Imagination," *Ethics* 101 (1991): 745.

focus is on exchange rather than self-sacrifice. What tends to emerge from this perspective is closer to what sociobiologists call "reciprocal altruism" than to a more distinctive version. It is altruism that seeks the welfare of the self as well as of the other, aiming at a mutuality rather than concern for the other as such. It demands self-sacrifice on the part of neither self nor other. Part of what sustains the expectation that altruism can be so collegial is the recognition that it involves this mutual fulfilment, rather than being identified with self-sacrificing heroism.

Theoretical obstacles and dilution of altruism by those who might be expected to be its most prominent advocates are aggravated further by consideration of social contexts that would encourage or expect serious altruism. Alan Fiske identifies four basic possibilities for social arrangements, all of which tend to exclude altruism, for different reasons.[7] The form most conducive to altruism is the one that Fiske calls "communal sharing." This is the most personal form of society, in which individuals interact directly to a large extent, and even know one another, or at least know who others are. Such a social configuration encourages altruism in practice, but by that very token, renders the altruism identification itself virtually redundant. So natural is sharing in such a society that lines between self and others are vague at best. Self-interest, other-interest, and collective-interest are linked together in ways that preclude their identification, much less the promotion of one aspect such as other-interest in particular. This configuration is represented most directly in these present reflections in terms of what we have been calling collegial altruism. And this is precisely the difficulty with this approach. It takes altruism to be so natural and expected that it does not deal with altruism at its most distinctive, and even resists recognizing it as a moral or social ideal.

Altruism is no less precluded by the social arrangement that would be the prime target for promoters of communal sharing, what Fisk calls "authority ranking." Any hint of hierarchy is

---

[7] Alan P. Fiske, "The Four Elementary Forms of Sociality: Framework for a Unified Theory of Social Relations," *Psychological Review* 99 (1992): 689–723.

anathema to the ideology of community sharing. The antithesis represented by these two forms of social structure reflects corresponding exclusions of serious altruism. As community sharing excludes altruism by its tendency to render it automatic, so authority ranking renders it redundant because responsibilities to others are so clearly established by the levels within the structure. What each person can expect, and what is expected of him or her, is established and enforced by the social system itself.

The third possibility for social arrangement identified by Fiske is what he calls "equity matching." This suggests what we have been referring to as a constructive approach. While Fiske does cite Rawls as an example of this form, he distinguishes his position as one that involves trust rather than contract. This is intelligible if we take contract in a strict Hobbesian form, such as might be involved in a version derived from a sociobiological base. For Hobbes and sociobiologists life is seen in essentially individualistic terms. Contract represents a reaction against the natural aggressive individuality that is seen to typify humanity. In contrast to this strong contractualism, Rawls reflects an outlook that assumes morality as an intrinsic dimension of human life. To characterize this in terms of trust, however, may be to move Rawls closer to the community sharing alternative than he would or could accept. The focus on equity, however, does seem fair to Rawls and could be used to identify the position that we identified in terms of constructive altruism. Fiske's claim is that altruism is precluded here because for the equality focus what is of benefit to others is also beneficial to the self. This confirms the conclusion reached here that this position maintains a fundamental independence of the self. Thus, once again, altruism is not a serious option.

The final position named by Fiske excludes altruism by definition. The "market pricing system," or modern capitalist society, is constituted so directly on a vision of self-interest that insofar as altruism is not totally precluded, it is rendered suspect. The strength of the self-interest assumption carries the implication that what appears to be altruism must really have some ulterior motive that can ultimately be traced back to self-interest. The impersonal nature of the social system constituted in market terms also minimized opportunity for the development of altruism. In this way, it can be seen to represent the antithesis of community sharing as fully as does authority ranking.

It is highly unlikely that any society will reflect one of these options directly and exclusively. Actual societies are more apt to reflect some combinations of these, although it is also likely that any given society will be shaped prominently in one of these directions, with some or all of the others playing subordinate roles. For our purposes, what is salutary is that all of these most fundamental options for social organization virtually exclude altruism. If a society involves genuine community sharing, altruism will be irrelevant because something of its ideal will be realized directly. In the other models, altruism is precluded by impersonal structures and visions. When this reflection on social options is added to the theoretical difficulties inherent in the very notion of altruism, the prospects for its being a serious issue would seem to be very faint. And yet such theoretical considerations run into one stubborn fact. Altruism happens! People do act in the interests of other people, without regard for their own benefit, and even at times without regard for their own welfare. The actuality of altruism has to be reckoned with.

The Batson experiments kept confirming a readiness to assist others that persisted against experiments designed to test alternative explanations. The laboratory evidence of Batson and his colleagues regarding a natural altruism receives further confirmation in demonstrations of how external rewards seem actually to deter altruism. For instance, one study found that blood donors who were reminded of altruistic reasons for donating were more inclined to donate in future than were those whose attention was drawn to benefits to themselves.[8] Another study found that young school children whose mothers had motivated them with rewards were less cooperative than other children who were not thus rewarded.[9] Perhaps the best-known instance

---

[8] Delroy L. Paulhus, David R. Shaffer, and Leslie L. Downing, "Effects of Making Blood Donor Motives Salient upon Donor Retention: A Field Experiment," *Personality and Social Psychology Bulletin* 3 (1977): 99–102.

[9] Richard A. Fabes, Jim Futz, Nancy Eisenberg, Traci May-Plumlee, and F. Scott

of this type of evidence is the conclusion reached by Richard M. Titmuss in his comparison of blood donors in England where giving blood is a voluntary activity and in American where it is a commercial transaction. The expectation of donation is a stronger inducement to attend a blood clinic than is the promise of direct compensation.[10] Scientists and journalists, as well as the public at large, routinely underestimate the generosity of organ donors. Those who do donate kidneys, for example, are expected to have second thoughts and consequent depression, but a leading researcher in the field, Roberta G. Simmons, finds the evidence pointing in the other direction. "Empirically, tests presented above show that the average kidney donor post-donation feels increased happiness rather than increased depression (although a few do show depression, mostly transient)."[11] The most dramatic evidence of native altruism may be the heroic exploits of rescuers of Jews in Europe during the Second World War. Individuals risked themselves, and in some cases their families, by hiding Jews from the Nazi regime that was determined to exterminate them. Interviews with some of those responsible for this activity[12] present unavoidable evidence of behavior that can hardly be classified as anything other than altruistic, although, as we shall see, this is not how rescuers are inclined to classify it. Ironically, their reluctance to accept such labeling is itself some of the most convincing evidence of the actuality of altruism.

THE "ISM" OF ALTRUISM

In spite of the predominant assumption that human beings are characterized fundamentally by self-interest, regnant in aca-

Christopher, "Effects of Rewards on Children's Prosocial Motivation: A Socialization Study," *Developmental Psychology* 25 (1989): 509–15.

[10] Richard M. Titmuss, *The Gift Relationship: From Human Blood to Social Policy* (New York: Pantheon, 1971), p. 245.

[11] Roberta G. Simmons, "Presidential Address on Altruism and Sociology," *The Sociological Quarterly* 32/1 (1991): 14.

[12] Samuel P. Oliner and Pearl M. Oliner, *The Altruistic Personality: Rescuers of Jews in Nazi Europe* (New York: Free Press, 1988); Kristen R. Monroe, Michael C. Barton, and Ute Klingeman, "Altruism and the Theory of Rational Action: Rescuers of Jews in Nazi Europe," *Ethics* 101 (1990).

demia and trumpeted in popular culture, the evidence shows that people do act with concern for others. That such behavior persists against such massive insistence that it is folly indicates that something like what we call altruism is present in human life at a profound level. Calling it altruism, however, invites the difficulties we have identified. The difficulties have a lot to do with the fact that altruism is defined against the background of self-interest. This is how the term originated with Comte, and it does not make sense apart from that context. This is why the term tends to disappear in a context where a more relational social view of life is assumed. The more the distinction between self and other is blurred, the more dispensable, and indeed unintelligible, altruism becomes. While such an alternative may be taken to render altruism superfluous, to see this as total gain is to be prepared to lose the contrast that the spectrum between self-interest and altruism identifies. Thus while altruism has no meaning apart from its contrast with self-interest, and in that sense represents something of an endorsement of self-interest, it does have meaning in terms of that contrast. Altruism points to a way of living, or a particular activity, that is at the polar extreme from taking only ourselves into account. How far we appreciate this, and how meaningful altruism can be for us, would seem to depend on our basic vision of life.

As the notion of altruism originated against the background of the self-interest vision that has dominated the modern west, so all our understanding reflects some basic vision. Among proposals for identifying the broad contours of the most basic approaches to reality, one of the most suggestive is the fundamental categories proposed by the Scottish philosopher, John Macmurray. As he saw it, there are three basic ways of approaching life: as material, organic, and personal.[13] Macmurray's categories will be taken here much more as suggestive than as definitive; he certainly can bear no responsibility for the use I shall make of them.

When life is approached in material, or as I would prefer to say, mechanical, terms, it is seen in terms of its smallest

[13] John Macmurray, *Freedom in the Modern World* (London: Faber, 1932), pp. 175ff., and *Interpreting the Universe* (London: Faber, 1938), pp. 206ff.

components. A classical instance of the mechanical outlook is the strictly inductivist ideal of knowledge that was made central in the early stages of the modern era. The assumption is that knowledge consists in the amassing of items of evidence, piece by piece, gradually building up a firm structure of factual information. Far from representing the modest accumulation of facts that it professes, the mechanical approach involves a total vision that is as comprehensive and categorical as any metaphysical or theological perspective. Beyond the material sphere, where its application is most apparent, it entails a vision of ourselves, its articulators and practitioners. For the mechanical outlook, we are machinists, manipulators of the bits and pieces that we accumulate and structure. Beneath this immediate implication, however, lies the more sinister realization that, in the end, we are ourselves further bits and pieces. That reality is composed of bits and pieces, for the mechanical outlook, carries implications for ourselves. We can hardly escape the fundamental atomism that defines the basic outlook. We too are essentially isolated selves, human atoms, relating to one another in external ways, just like the independent cogs in a machine. This anthropology finds direct expression in the behaviorism of B. F. Skinner, whose social engineering assumes just such malleability on the part of its mechanistic subjects. Ironically, although it should more naturally belong to the next category, the organic, the anthropology of sociobiology also reflects this mechanical outlook. For in spite of the relational, organic connotations of its language, its primary vision centers on individual units, as the concept of the selfish gene clearly illustrates. In its fundamental orientation, sociobiology represents a biological version of early modern physics. Its aim is to explain life in terms of the primitive units called genes, just as physics attempted to explain reality in terms of atoms until smaller units that acted as much like waves as like particles came into view.

This is the outlook that provided the background for the modern concept of altruism. Because we, like every other component of the cosmic machine, are isolated bits, there is a question of how we relate to other isolated bits. Since we are also endowed with consciousness and volition, this means that we have some say in determining these relations. We have the possibility of being concerned primarily, if not exclusively, with ourselves, or of showing some interest in and concern for others. This is the essential context in which the issue of self-interest and altruism gets posed. This most direct background of the altruism concept also poses the initial paradox of altruism. The primary assumption of isolated selves provokes the unavoidable suspicion that anything approaching altruism really derives from some form of self-interest, the direct expression of which is the psychological paradox that all pleasure, after all, is our own pleasure. Thus a mechanistic outlook on life, such as has been prominent from the early stages of the modern era in the west, can account for both the origin of and suspicion about altruism. The situation appears quite different from the perspective of the second major possibility, a fundamentally organic outlook.

In some ways, the organic outlook is almost the exact opposite of the mechanistic. Where the mechanistic perspective focuses on individual units and the structures through which these impinge on each other, the organic outlook takes relation to be definitive of reality. For the organic vision, nothing exists in isolation. All reality is constituted by relationship. The primacy of relation means that an organic outlook sees life from the inside. Life is known through the living of it. It is as active participants, rather than as external observers or spectators, that we gain understanding of reality. We come to know each other through actual encounter, and not through examination of each other's behavior. And what is known ultimately resists reduction to the external language of behavior. It has to do with dreams and ideals and hopes that both inspire and exceed actual behavior. The language of articulation is that of art more than science, as science has generally been understood, but the truth may be that we are becoming more and more aware of the inadequacy of the artificial boundaries of the disciplines we have erected, as both the challenges of ecology and the speculations of postmodernism suggest.

In its own terms, an organic outlook renders altruism as

precarious as a mechanistic outlook serves to identify it. The atomistic shape of a mechanistic outlook invites consideration of connections, such as altruism represents, even though the altruistic direction itself is problematic because of the self-interested bias of atomistic isolation. An organic outlook makes altruism even more precarious because it is unnecessary. Natural relatedness displaces the gap between self and other that is so vital for a mechanistic outlook, with the result that it is virtually impossible to avoid altruism. Mechanistic cynicism that would see this as disguised self-interest would be countered by the insistence on the reality of the relation. We really are connected with others, so that it is illusory to think that we could benefit ourselves without benefiting others or harm others without harming ourselves. In rendering altruism essentially unavoidable, however, this organic outlook also diminishes the distinctiveness of altruism. The altruism that is recognized is essentially an altruism of mutuality, a natural reciprocal altruism. Heroic altruism, the kind that would involve self-sacrifice, is denigrated from the organic perspective. In this way, this outlook raises the moral paradox of altruism, the issue of how altruism as fact relates to altruism as ideal, just as the mechanistic outlook directly poses the psychological paradox. Because altruism is taken to be so natural, it does not stand out particularly as an ideal. Advocates of an organic outlook face the challenge of explaining why life is not much more harmonious than it is, if there is such intrinsic relatedness, as well as being exposed to the charge that they are reducing the standards to which humanity might aspire. The naturalness of an organic outlook can mean a leveling down of moral aspiration.

An organic outlook can make altruism even more problematic than a mechanistic one, precisely because of this combination of assumed inevitability and restricted expectation. The result is not only a domestication of altruism, but also a reversion to the self-interest priority. This dimension is especially noticeable in feminist versions, where reaction against a legacy of expectations of sacrifice for women results in attempts to preclude the whole notion of sacrifice, on the one hand, and to insist on the primacy of self-integrity on the other. Expectations of sacrifice have prevented women from attaining a significant sense of self, the argument goes, so that there was no self to sacrifice. The sacrifice was imposed culturally, and generally accepted by women prior to feminist enlightenment. The advocated alternative is that women must be permitted to develop in their own terms, before sacrifice can have any real meaning. However, this is not the direction that is usually advocated on the feminist agenda. The point is not that a secure sense of self would allow for genuine self-sacrifice, but that sacrifice as such is negative and to be opposed. The genuine mutuality of a truly organic situation should dispense with the need for sacrifice. Presumably this would also permit and encourage the development of selves that are as independent and self-assured as any self could be according to the essentially individualistic, mechanistic outlook.

In this way, contrary to initial impressions, the organic outlook does not so much succeed the mechanistic, as expand it. Besides taking relation very seriously, an organic outlook, particularly as this is developed in feminist theory, places a significant premium on the independent self. Consequently, an organic outlook is not simply an alternative to a mechanistic one; it is more accurately seen as a hybrid that both challenges and incorporates mechanistic concerns. This makes an organic outlook more comprehensive than a mechanistic one, but it leaves it rebounding between an emphasis on the fundamental relatedness of human life and an insistence on the independent integrity of individuals. This result is particularly ironic for an organic perspective, because the insistence on the integrity of the individual, while not incompatible with such a perspective in principle, does represent a clash with this outlook in practice. A self that must be protected against sacrifice not only limits the range of mutuality, but also sets that self apart from the organic relatedness of life in a way that suggests two fundamental foci, rather than one. The organic relational view needs to be supplemented by an emphasis on the importance of the individual. A more adequate perspective would be one in which individuality and relatedness both had their place, so that each is significant as well as being significantly qualified by the other. This brings us to the third basic option, a personal outlook.

Where the mechanical vision sees life in terms of independent particulars impinging on one another, and the organic vision sees life in terms of ongoing relational processes that involve a jarring insistence on the integrity of individuals, the personal perspective understands life in terms of what Macmurray has referred to as persons in relation. We do not exist as isolated units, reacting to the forces exerted upon us; or, at least, that is not the whole story. Neither do we exist in binding communitarian connectedness. As persons, we have scope to determine our own destinies, through consultation with one another and with as much sensitivity to the constraints and novelties available to us as we can manage. The personal involves recognizing both identity and difference. The great irony in the mechanistic perspective is that the distinctiveness of the self, that is supposedly so foundational, really disappears. All cogs are interchangeable. It is possible to see reality in terms of isolated particulars only because of a foundational assumption of sameness. Each unit is complete in its own right, and is implicated with other similarly complete units through systems of exchange, whether an exchange of energy as in machines or of respective advantages as in organizational structures. For such exchanges to be effective, there must be differences, and indeed perceived differences, among the units. However, the differences are secondary to the assumption of a constitutive sameness that assures each unit its own independent integrity. The differences only become significant in their own right when life begins to be seen in the relational terms of the organic perspective.

Reality is rhythmic, from the organic point of view. Real relation is made possible by the alternating rhythms of self and other, for instance. This is why advocates of the realism of altruism insist that it must involve mutuality. Self and other not only offer mutual assistance, but grow together through the give and take of real-life relationships. Altruism is possible because of the similarity and difference that affords a common connection along with the incentive of novelty that promotes and permits growth. The primary sense of an organic outlook, however, is one of harmony. Thus, once again, difference tends to dissolve in sameness, but because the outlook gives more scope to difference, the collapse is that much more acute. The leveling of mutuality evokes an insistence on the integrity of the individual. This could be seen as a more inclusive level of organicism, were it not for the fact that this independence is not permitted to qualify the mutuality. The relations of mutuality operate within prescribed limits, of which the exclusion of self-sacrifice is a prominent example. This is what renders the independent self and the assumption of a pervasive mutuality incongruent. A personal perspective would allow for reciprocal influence between the importance of individual integrity and the inescapable involvements with others.

The advantages of a personal approach are that it allows for a combination of individual initiative that we associate with persons and the relatedness that has come to be recognized as so indispensable through the emergence of social consciousness. Selves are not isolated, as in the mechanistic outlook, where the relation with others is effected essentially within the self, through imaginatively seeing the self as an other. Nor are selves torn between establishing their own security and responding to a limited claim of others, as in the organic outlook, where the other is encountered in restricted ways circumscribed by a concern to affirm the integrity of the self. From a personal perspective, self and other are affirmed in their integrity and relatedness.

To affirm the primacy of the personal is to claim that this is the most comprehensive vision of all. The mechanistic vision of individualism can only account for a limited range of reality, and then only in superficial terms. The most material of the sciences, physics, has moved light years beyond Newtonian mechanism. Yet Newtonian physics remains relevant for understanding many everyday activities. That mechanistic outlook has been carried over in very formative ways into the social sciences. The increasing development of social consciousness has resulted in a qualification of this in the organic direction. Yet if this results in society taking over as some kind of comprehensive organic context, it finds the reality of persons erupting in ways that challenge the organic outlook itself. A personal outlook can recognize the mechanistic and organic approaches, as they cannot accommodate the personal. In a mechanistic outlook, persons can finally only be manipulators or manipulated. Behaviorism is the most conspicuous, but by no means the only, instance of this. In an organic outlook, persons are torn between a quest for identity and involvement in a web of life that can neither finally challenge nor confirm that identity. In a personal outlook, persons are individuals who live in formative and transformative relationships with others. We can treat each other, as well as other forms of life, any aspect of the world, or even God, in mechanistic ways. We can treat each other, other forms of life, any aspect of the world, or even God, in organic ways. This approach takes these others more seriously than a mechanistic approach because we ourselves are at stake in the relation in ways that we are not for a mechanistic outlook. The relation of self and other is most challenging, however, when it is understood in personal terms. Who we are is constituted by the relations we have, just as the other in these relations is affected by who we are in process of becoming.

In providing the most comprehensive perspective, the personal also represents the most challenging. The tension of the organic outlook, between integrity of self and the indispensability of relations with others, is intensified for a personal outlook because here limits are removed between self and other. As persons, we make ourselves in some ways, and bear considerable responsibility for that making; but we do this in inescapable ongoing connections with others, who are similarly disposed, and similarly disposed precisely in their otherness. From a personal perspective, the integrity of the self and the claim of the other are inseparable. This means that no limits can be prescribed for altruism, for a personal outlook. My very life may be claimed by the other. It also means that I cannot possibly meet the claims of others upon me. A personal outlook gives full scope to radical altruism and carries the inevitable corollary that it is virtually certain that I will not measure up.

The rationality of mechanism will protest that we cannot possibly be responsible for what is beyond our capability to do. The sociality of an organic outlook will protest that the standard is hopelessly ideal; we need a more realistic and realizable goal. An advocate of the personal cannot deny that these are legitimate reservations. The counterchallenge that would be posed from the perspective of the personal, however, is whether the mechanical and organic outlooks are really open to the challenge of the other. Altruism is finally a matter of the reality and claim of alterity.

THE ALTER OF ALTRUISM

In itself, altruism is at best paradoxical, if not completely contradictory. If an action is truly altruistic, the last person to call it that is the actor. "Altruism is necessarily self-sacrificial only for purely self-regarding agents."[14] Deliberate altruism is impossible. At the same time, if our welfare is intrinsically interconnected with the welfare of others, altruism is unavoidable. However, since the extent of our interconnection is a subject of considerable debate, and a matter of varied perception, very real scope for altruism remains in the practical business of living. While pure altruism is so focused on the other that self-interest does not enter the picture, and actual interrelation implies that we cannot avoid benefiting others, much of life is lived in greater ambiguity, where altruism and self-interest overlap. We act with mixed motives, indicating some concern for others, with one eye on how we will be affected ourselves. In this real world of compromise, altruism does occur, and sometimes in very conspicuous ways.

Although identification of altruism is a modern phenomenon, the reality to which it points is hardly a modern development. The language of altruism allows us to be more explicit and self-conscious about something that can only be as significant as it appears to be because it is an integral dimension of human life.

[14] David Schmidtz, "Reasons for Altruism," in *Altruism*, ed. Ellen Frankel Paul, Fred D. Miller, Jr., and Jeffrey Paul (Cambridge: Cambridge University Press, 1993), p. 65.

Beneath the psychological, social, moral, and religious variations on this theme there lies the reality of alterity. Life resists our attempts to control it either through intellectual definitions or practical programs. From whatever direction our grasp extends, there waiting for us is the reality of alterity. This may be the most basic paradox in this very paradoxical subject. The self-consciousness that has led us to think and talk about altruism also tends to obscure the very reality it helps to identify. The reason that altruism evaporates when it is made the focus may be more an indication of its pervasive presence than of its absence. By its very nature, life involves alterity. Although altruism has become thematic against the background of self-interest, the connection is easily overlooked, even, and sometimes especially, by those who most insist on it. This is what leads to the rebounding between recognition of the significance, and indeed indispensability, of altruism, and the competing concern that the self must be established in its own right. If life is seen to be characterized by a fundamental alterity, these concerns have to be intimately related.

The elusiveness of altruism implies that what is at stake in life is experienced and appreciated much more indirectly than assumed in the modern pursuit of direct self-realization. One of the most basic implications of recognition of pervasive altruism is that life defies our attempts to take possession of it at any level. This means that, contrary to the strong tendency to seek to take control today, pervasive alterity precludes direct self-fulfilment in psychological, social, moral, or religious terms. Thus the reality of alterity defies the current preoccupation with self-esteem as a goal and vision. An alterity that can be established on the basis of self-esteem is not alterity. This is not to say that the concern with self-esteem is not a legitimate one. The point is that the reality of alterity means that it can only be realized by indirection. Security in the self depends on transcending the self. In this way, self-fulfilment represents a broader version of the hedonic paradox, as it is usually understood. In this form, the point of the hedonic paradox is that the surest way to fail to achieve happiness is to seek it out directly. Happiness remains elusive to attempts to possess it as such. The same thing could be said of self-fulfilment. Concern to cultivate self-esteem provides a lucrative market for psychological and spiritual gurus, but if there is merit in the proposals and programs offered, this will depend on how far they respect the reality of alterity. Like happiness, self-esteem defies direct appropriation. Also like happiness, it has a way of happening when we are least intent on achieving it. Finding ourselves claimed by some activity, another person, a cause, or out of the depths that we designate as religious, our significance is established by this grounding alterity.

The pervasiveness of alterity is especially frustrating to attempts such as this to understand it. The indirection that it entails makes it as resistant to the theoretical perspective of understanding as it is to the practical focus of living. However, recognizing this, we may be able to gain some further appreciation of its significance precisely through reflecting on its indirectness. What our examination of the various approaches to the issue of altruism suggests is that, despite its resistence to direct approach, the presence of altruism is very dependent on vision. For a self-interest vision, as reflected in sociobiological or market stances, altruism must always arouse suspicion. It can only finally be a cloak for self-interest or a manipulation of the putative altruist by others or by the biological legacy. Altruism takes on positive significance for those who take morality seriously in its own right, so much so that morality and altruism can be taken as synonymous for some prominent modern ethical positions. From the self-interest perspective, such moral vision raises the question – why be moral? However that question is answered, it seems that a satisfactory answer must be at least on the moral level. Any attempt to give an answer to this question on the basis of self-interest overlooks the distinctiveness that the moral dimension adds. For altruism to become a serious subject, then, seems to entail a matter of vision. Whether or not we see ourselves claimed by others depends on whether or not moral vision is real for us.

Although moral vision puts altruism on the agenda, it also serves to complicate the issue because of its deliberateness. Morality could deal with altruism, if altruism were susceptible to moral earnestness. Because of its indirection, altruism provides a clear indication of the limits of moral vision. A moral approach cannot finally take alterity seriously because morality is centered on our own activity; morality is essentially a matter of what we do, of how we live. As a result, the more we succeed in realizing the claim of alterity, the more the alterity becomes subject to us. This intensification of the paradoxes of altruism points to the level of religious vision. On this level, the elusiveness of altruism is resolved because we are confronted by supreme alterity. Recognizing that our lives are grounded not only in others like ourselves, but in the Other, involves confronting alterity in its fullest form. This by no means dispenses with the other dimensions. The issues of self-interest and morality are still very much present and still need to be addressed. However, as the most comprehensive sense of alterity, religious vision provides perspective on altruism that is not possible on the levels of morality or self-interest. It is that perspective that is threatened by modern secular mechanistic and organic horizons. How this is so is illustrated in contemporary attitudes to the saint.

While saintliness appears to enjoy widespread popular endorsement, among scholars the saint has evoked a suspicion parallel to that directed to altruism. One of the sources of concern about saintliness is that saints are remote and unreal. They represent impossible ideals and fanciful visions of what life might be like. William James likened saints to utopian social visions. Saints perform the function for individuals that utopian visions do for society as a whole.[15] But while James understood such functions in positive terms, ironically this great advocate of pragmatism would be seen by many today as hopelessly idealistic in outlook. More typical of contemporary sensibilities is the comment of Jeffrey Stout, that "when you unpack the utopia, the batteries are not included."[16] As Stout sees it, utopian vision indulges in the luxury of "wistful alienation,"

---

[15] William James, *The Varieties of Religious Experience* (Garden City, NY: Doubleday Dolphin Books, n.d.), p. 367.
[16] Jeffrey Stout, *Ethics after Babel: The Languages of Morals and Their Discontents* (Boston: Beacon Press, 1988), p. 229.

secure in the remoteness "of its own rage."[17] Saints are the individual version of this social dreaming, stained-glass paragons of impossibility.

Yet the illusory nature of sainthood is not the main reason for suspicion of saints today. As with altruism, the notion of the saint is seen to be even more dangerous when it is taken seriously. This involves the two-sided liability of diminishing our own moral potential by identifying altruistic consideration with the saintly extreme and, conversely, in so doing, absolving us of responsibility for improving our own conduct and relations with others.[18] A prominent example of this complaint of moral displacement is found in the feminist castigation of the ideal of self-denial, which would generally be seen to typify the saint. As a result, feminists may disown this traditional mark of sainthood completely, and without reservation, complaining that "self-denial is taken as a virtue rather than the defect it is."[19] Self-denial is a defect because it is destructive of self, not only of the self who is denied but even of the recipient of this supposed beneficence. "Sacrifice and altruism . . . do not adequately empower another because the 'liberated' one is still dependent and thus without power."[20] Self-denial thus takes on the appearance of the consummate ego trip, the attempt to dominate others through subservience. Susan Wolf speaks for many when she challenges the ideal of a world peopled by moral saints, or even by would-be moral saints. "A world in which everyone, or even a large number of people, achieved moral sainthood – even a world in which they *strove* to achieve it – would probably contain less happiness than a world in which people realized a diversity of ideals involving a variety of personal and perfectionist values."[21] Sainthood thus falls subject to the same suspicions as altruism.

---

17 Ibid., p. 232.
18 Alfie Kohn, *The Brighter Side of Human Nature: Altruism and Empathy in Everyday Life* (New York: Basic Books, 1990), pp. 197f.
19 Sara Ruddick, "Remarks on the Sexual Politics of Reason," in *Women and Moral Theory*, ed. Eva Feder Kittay and Diana T. Meyers (Totowa, NJ: Rowan & Littlefield, 1987), p. 246.
20 Susan Dunfee, *Beyond Servanthood: Christianity and the Liberation of Women* (Lanham, Md.: University Press of America, 1989), p. 138.
21 Susan Wolf, "Moral Saints," *Journal of Philosophy* 79/8 (1982): 427.

The problematic nature of sainthood does not mean that its critics are bereft of moral models and motivators. On the contrary, they would contend that they are pursuing a more promising way. For saintly heroes, they substitute the ideal and practice of practical helpers. "Heroes show us who we are *not*. Helpers show us who we *are*."[22] For the distant and often disillusioning visions of idealists, they substitute the available connections with real people like ourselves, whereby we can offer each other mutual assistance and encouragement. "As our liberators and leaders, popes and presidents, bishops and priests, shrinks and teachers, mentors and gurus, heroes have brought us pipedreams and smokescreens and everything but salvation. And this, I am persuaded, is because we tend to search everywhere except among ourselves-in-relation for peace."[23] Saints represent a mystification that diverts us from our own real possibilities, especially the possibilities that arise through our relations with one another.

This communal focus may be presented as an alternative to the whole notion of saintliness, but it may also be seen as the form that saintliness must take today. Thus Edith Wyschogrod notes that although saints have traditionally been understood against a theistic background, she believes the essential meaning can be retained in more immediate, social terms. The result is a definition of a saint as *"one whose adult life in its entirety is devoted to the alleviation of sorrow (the psychological suffering) and pain (the physical suffering) that afflicts other persons without distinction of rank or group or, alternatively, that afflicts sentient beings, whatever the cost to the saint in pain or sorrow."*[24] The saint can be understood directly in moral terms, according to Wyschogrod. "Saints are 'native speakers' of the language of alterity, poets of the imperative."[25] Where for most of us, consideration of others is elicited grudgingly, if at all, for the saint such duty is natural. Nor is this simply a contemporary ("postmodern" is Wyschogrod's

[22] Carter Heyward, *Touching Our Strength: The Erotic as Power and the Love of God* (New York: Harper & Row, 1989), p. 11.
[23] Ibid.
[24] Edith Wyschogrod, *Saints and Postmodernism: Revisioning Moral Philosophy* (Chicago: University of Chicago Press, 1990), p. 34.
[25] Ibid., p. 183.

preferred term) interpretation of sainthood. It identifies what has always characterized the saint: "the imperative is the grammatical mood that dominates hagiographic narrative."[26] In the translation from theistic to humanistic framework, nothing essential is lost. While Wyschogrod's saints might be too self-sacrificial for some of the critics of sainthood, they operate in the same kind of socially defined context.

Although this rehabilitation of saints might appear far more promising than their outright dismissal, the net result may be precisely the reverse. As with altruism, sainthood may be damned with faint praise, for it is questionable whether the saint can breathe in the confining atmosphere of social and moral horizons, any more than altruism can. Thus Robert Adams takes issue with Susan Wolf's characterization of the saint in moral terms. "The substance of sainthood is not sheer will power striving like Sisyphus (or like Wolf's Rational Saint) to accomplish a boundless task, but goodness overflowing from a boundless source. Or so, at least, the saints perceive it."[27] To categorize the saint in moral terms is to caricature sainthood. The depiction of the saint as one who lives out of the imperative is a modern, Kantian type of reading of sainthood that would not accord with the testimony of the saints generally. "The saint does what he does because he wants to, not because he thinks he ought to do what he thinks is his duty."[28] The saint is not so much a poet of the imperative as of alterity. What characterizes the saint is not fastidious moralism. That would undermine saintliness completely through the fatal preoccupation with self that quickly reduces righteousness to self-righteousness. The saint is spared that fate that so readily awaits us lesser mortals because the saint is so blissfully unself-conscious. There is wisdom in Robert Adams' suggestion that Susan Wolf created her own dilemma in portraying the saint as one devoted to moral purity. "There are other, less voluntary virtues that are

---

[26] Ibid., p. 178.

[27] Robert Merrihew Adams, "Saints," in *The Virtue of Faith and Other Essays in Philosophical Theology* (New York: Oxford University Press, 1987), p. 168.

[28] Philip Mercer, *Sympathy and Ethics: A Study of the Relationship between Sympathy and Morality with Special Reference to Hume's Treatise* (Oxford: Clarendon Press, 1972), p. 117.

essential equipment for a saint, humility, for instance, and perceptiveness, courage, and a mind unswayed by the voices of the crowd."[29] A saint is one who marches to a different drummer. This is why a moral portrayal is far too prosaic to capture what is most distinctive about the saint.

If the saint were identifiable in terms of moral perfection, and this were to be the goal of the saint, sainthood would be the dull, confining phenomenon Wolf takes it to be. At best, it would amount to a more spiritual form of moralism. Saints would be those who pursued what Richard W. Kropf characterizes as a Freudian version of moral perfection, in which one takes delight in the pleasure of one's own righteousness, or an Adlerian version involving a determination to achieve self-mastery or self-realization.[30] In contrast to these directions implanted in the modern western psyche by people like Sigmund Freud and Alfred Adler, saints are more accurately characterized by the third form of Viennese psychiatry, that of Viktor Frankl, and his notion of self-transcendence. Here the meaning of life is understood to be finally religious in that it summons us from beyond ourselves. Frankl applies this basic insight to the saint directly. "I think that even the saints did not care for anything other than simply to serve God, and I doubt that they ever had it in mind to become saints. If that were the case, they would have become only perfectionists rather than saints."[31] Saints may not be morally perfect, but that does not really detract from their sainthood. What makes them saints is not their moral perfection, but the larger vision out of which they live.

Because saints transcend moral categories, reflecting something much larger than the detailed performance of their own lives, it is doubly tragic that they should be reduced to social categories. The social perspective has an inherent tendency to level down, a tendency that is particularly evident in the most deliberately egalitarian form of social approach, social exchange theory. "Exchange theorists are effective levelers of

[29] Adams, "Saints," p. 165.
[30] Richard W. Kropf, *Faith: Security and Risk* (New York: Paulist Press, 1990), p. 142.
[31] Viktor E. Frankl, *Man's Search for Meaning*, tr. Ilse Lasch (New York: Washington Square Press, 1968), p. 158.

human character, formulating notions of equality in the absence of high virtues."[32] This suspicion of high virtues is, as we have seen, one of the main sources of the displacement of the saints by the transference of expectations to processes of socialization. But where are the high virtues to come from in the socialization process? The implication seems to be that all that is needed, or practical, will automatically bubble up through the ongoing interactions of ordinary mortals. However, the experience of history is on the side of respecters of the saints like William James.

They are the impregnators of the world, vivifiers and animators of potentialities of goodness which but for them would lie forever dormant. It is not possible to be quite as mean as we naturally are, when they have passed before us. One fire kindles another; and without that over-trust in human worth, they show, the rest of us would be in spiritual stagnancy . . . If things are ever to move upward, someone must be ready to take the first step, and assume the risk of it.[33]

In the social self-consciousness of the present, James' expectations are bound to appear naive.[34] Yet, his point is that much more important for precisely that reason. "The very cultural 'uselessness' of saints would serve as a judgment on the one-sided technical and utilitarian ethos of the wider society. More than ever, their virtues need to point beyond ordinary morality to virtue's source and ground."[35] Saints sense an alterity that is neither tolerable nor identifiable to the restricted vision of a social horizon that finds heroic altruism dispensable and even threatening to more immediate possibilities for mutuality.

TRUE ALTRUISM IS RELIGIOUS

The lives of the saints and the reality of alterity both suggest that virtue's source and ground is not in morality but in religion.

---

[32] Jonathan B. Imber, "Social Exchange: A Sociological Theory of Satisfaction," in *Sociology and Human Destiny*, ed. Gregory Baum (New York: Seabury Press, 1980), p. 141.

[33] James, *Varieties of Religious Experience*, p. 358.

[34] Imber, "Social Exchange," p. 141.

[35] John A. Coleman, "Conclusion: After Sainthood?" in *Saints and Virtues*, ed. John Stratton Hawley (Berkeley: University of California Press, 1987), p. 223.

Yet this too would be contested by many scholars today, along with the questioning of saints. For instance, Daniel Batson not only challenged conventional wisdom in claiming to discover empirical evidence of altruistic behavior; he also proceeded to demonstrate that altruism owed no particular debt to religion. He and his colleagues cite surveys that indicate that religious people are more concerned about others than are those who have no religious affiliation, but they go on to contend that behavioral studies indicate that this does not translate into action. "Although the highly religious have more stringent moral standards, they are no more likely than the less religious to help someone in need."[36] In fact, it seems that among the religious, it is those who hold more loosely to the authority of doctrine and institution who are most likely to demonstrate concern for others, those whom Batson and his colleagues see occupying the "quest" end of the religious spectrum, as opposed to the more institutionally committed, whose stance is labeled "intrinsic." Yet these researchers also admit that their conclusions are subject to certain limitations. Their concern is with individuals and their religion. This favors the "quest" end. Those on the "intrinsic" end demonstrate their caring through the means provided by religious institutions themselves.[37] When this qualification is taken into account, religion may hold more significance for altruism, including altruistic behavior, than the studies cited would suggest.

A more social approach, considering social involvement, rather than individual initiative, suggests that there might be a significant link between religion and altruism. Robin Gill cites figures from surveys by the European Value Systems Study Group and the British Household Panel Survey which indicate that churchgoers are some three times more likely to be involved in voluntary service than are non-churchgoers.[38] British Social Attitudes data indicate that "a middle-aged

---

[36] C. D. Batson, Patricia Schoenrade, and W. Larry Ventis, *Religion and the Individual: A Social-Psychological Perspective* (Oxford: Oxford University Press, 1993), p. 342.

[37] Ibid., p. 364.

[38] Robin Gill, *Churchgoing and Christian Ethics* (Cambridge: Cambridge University Press, 1999), p. 173.

weekly churchgoer here was four times more likely to be a member of a community or voluntary group than a middle-aged nonchurchgoer and almost seven times more likely than someone in the no-religion category."[39] The most obvious place to look for resolution of conflicting evidence over the significance of religion for altruistic behavior is in the most conspicuous instances of such behavior. Among such candidates, none is more impressive than the heroic performance of rescuers of Jews in Nazi Europe. A study of rescuers led Kristen R. Monroe and her colleagues to conclude that the motivation for their actions did not lie in particular beliefs. "We believe the fact that none of our rescuers mentioned a specific moral, political, or philosophical credo suggests that identity was primary."[40] Religious beliefs in particular do not seem to have been particularly significant, if one includes the major study of rescuers of Jews in Nazi Europe conducted by Samuel P. and Pearl M. Oliner. Their general conclusion is that "overall, rescuers did not differ significantly from bystanders or the nonrescuers with respect to their religious identification, religious education, and their own religiosity or that of their parents."[41] The lack of differentiation is illustrated by the following figures: 49% of rescuers saw their mothers as very religious, but so did 43% of non-rescuers; less than 5% in both groups regarded their mothers as "not at all" religious; 33% of rescuers saw their fathers as very religious, compared to 22% of non-rescuers; in both cases slightly more than 10% saw their fathers as "not at all" religious. Their perceptions of their own religiosity while growing up, and especially in the immediate prewar years, were also similar, with little difference between rescuers and non-rescuers in regarding themselves as very religious, somewhat religious, not very religious, or not at all religious before embarking on their heroic exploits.[42]

The conclusion suggested by these comparisons is that religion is largely irrelevant when it comes to altruistic behavior, at least the dramatic variety represented by those who risked their

[39] Ibid., pp. 174–5.
[40] Monroe et al., "Altruism and the Theory of Rational Action," p. 122.
[41] Oliner and Oliner, *The Altruistic Personality*, p. 156.   [42] Ibid.

lives and endangered their families protecting Jews in Nazi Europe. However, a closer examination of the figures, and more careful consideration of what they might represent, could require some qualification of this obvious generalization. Notice, for example, that more rescuers than non-rescuers regarded their parents as very religious. If religion was irrelevant, there might have been some tendency in the other direction. The difference is particularly striking in terms of perceptions of fathers' religiosity. The significance of this is enhanced when we add the Oliners' own observation that "bystanders . . . were significantly less religious than rescuers in their early years, though not immediately before the war."[43] What this suggests is not that religion is irrelevant, but that its significance is subtle. It is generally held that early influences are the most important in shaping a person's basic direction in life. When to this is added the fact that religion as a cultural influence exerts an impact on non-believers as well as on believers, and that the distinction between believers and non-believers was even less clear in the era of the second world war than it is today, this all suggests that the influence of religion might be more significant than we are inclined to conclude from the rough similarities in religious orientation between rescuers and non-rescuers.

What may be indicated by these studies of rescuers is not that religion is unimportant for altruistic behavior, but that it shares with serious altruism the characteristic of indirection. The essence of religion is not what we believe or do, but the transcendent source on which we draw. Religion is inherently altruistic. Seen in these terms, this may carry the corollary that altruism is ultimately religious. That conspicuous altruists were subject to religious influence in their early years may be far more significant than their adult attitude to religion in eliciting altruistic behavior. Articulated vision may be less significant than the continuing influence of the formative vision in which one's identity was shaped. British Social Attitudes figures indicate that, faced with the dilemma of whether or not to keep

---

[43] Ibid.

excessive change given by mistake by a cashier in a department store, "amongst those who had never been to church as children 51% said that they might do this, whereas only 21% did of those who had been regularly as children."[44] Batson and his colleagues would point out that talk is cheap. The implication, they would conclude, is not that the 21% with early church background would not keep the money, but that they are more inclined to think they should not do it. Whether this would prevent them from keeping the money, however, they would point out, is a behavioral, and not an attitudinal matter. Yet attitude and vision are surely not entirely irrelevant to behavior. That we so readily betray our visions does not necessarily entail the irrelevance of those visions. Further, the most worrisome and formative visions may be ones that are least apparent. People may live out of a religious vision that is not deliberate or owned, and, conversely, people who practice religion faithfully may be more involved with their own beliefs and practices than in the depth of the vision to which these point.

If altruism and religion ultimately coalesce in this depth of indirection, far from representing an advance in honesty and communitarian sensitivity, the contemporary inclination to replace religious with moral vision may harbor threatening consequences for years to come. A popular notion, particularly among academics and even including theologians, is that a humanistic, social horizon is not only viable apart from any theistic background; it is seen to be decidedly superior because it eliminates these superfluous complications. The advantages are taken to be evident in the ways in which the distractions of sainthood are replaced by practical involvement with one another in relations and arrangements that hold the potential for improving life as it is actually lived. Yet, even in its own terms, the moral horizon appears inadequate, as Wolf recognizes: "From the moral point of view, we have reasons to want people to live lives that seem good from outside that point of view. If, as I have argued, this means that we have reason to want people to live lives that are not morally perfect, the only

---

[44] Gill, *Churchgoing and Christian Ethics*, pp. 180–1.

plausible moral theory must make use of some conception of supererogation."[45]

Here Wolf would appear to be approaching the realization that saints are characterized not by the moral perfection of their own performance, but by the depth of their dedication which transcends moral categorization. The problem is that supererogation is itself an extrapolation from the moral point of view. The dilemma faced by the moral point of view, at this point, is that of accounting for acts of supererogation. They exceed moral categories, by definition. Whereas, from a religious perspective, such as the Christian assurance that life at its deepest is characterized by caring, and that this is meant to be reflected in the way we live, there is no place for a category of supererogation because there are no limits to the expectations for caring. "The Christian ethic of charity necessarily makes obligatory what a follower of 'respect for persons,' can see only as super-erogation."[46] The major moral alternatives today to this metaphysical grounding of caring are a Kantian appeal to duty, which must be taken to be somehow self-evident, at least to those who are sufficiently rational, or the direct morality of care that finds a grounding in the immediate social relations we have with one another, but, by that token, leaves us with the challenge of explaining why there is so much lack of care if it is so natural to us. The religious perspective provides rationale and motivation for caring that remain elusive for, or precluded from, moral perspectives.

We have noticed how Ronald M. Green suggests that religion bridges the gap between moral ideal and reality. "That question, 'How can I ever be morally worthy?' finds its answer, we now see, in the belief that there possibly exists a perfect moral causal agency, supreme over all reality, which is not strictly required always to act or judge morally as we are, and which, in its very supremacy, stands as the final objective ground and

[45] Wolf, "Moral Saints," p. 438.
[46] Stanley Hauerwas and Richard Burrell, "From System to Story . . .," from *Truthfulness and Tragedy*, in Stanley Hauerwas and L. Gregory Jones, *Why Narrative?* (Grand Rapids, Mich.: W. B. Eerdmans, 1989), p. 170, n. 17.

arbiter of moral worth."[47] This theoretical conviction has its practical effect in the renewal that sustains morality. "By means of this belief, the individual's necessary self-condemnation is relieved and he is given the possibility – however slight it may be – of rationally doing what his moral reason commands: renewing at every moment of time his commitment to the strict priority of morality."[48] In this explanation, Green attempts to bridge the morality–religion gap from the morality side. The difficulty we noted in this is evident in at least two aspects of his summary. Although, from the moral point of view, it is natural to refer to God in tentative terms, a serious religious perspective exposes the inadequacy of this. A possible God is of no religious use. This difference is endemic to the gap between these perspectives themselves. For the belief in God that distinguishes religion is not primarily a theoretical matter. It makes possible, and is significant because it makes possible, the renewal to which Green refers. But recognition of this involves a sense of inadequacy on our part which is itself of religious proportions. As Richard Swinburne puts it, "the morally guilty man is not merely one who has acquired certain obligations. He has also acquired a present status something like being unclean."[49] This dimension of unworthiness and forgiveness is the province of religion which morality cannot address. The mutual caring that morality advocates is feasible because it is not simply a moral ideal or an immediate social possibility, but because it is under-written by reality in its deepest dimensions. Our failure to realize this moral ideal in life as we live it is not a reason to abandon its pursuit because our basis is not finally in ourselves, but in God who offers renewal through forgiveness.

Altruism discloses its problematic through the psychological paradox that all pleasure is our own pleasure, the moral paradox that the more we take altruism to be real the less we need to aspire to it and the more we feel the need to aspire to it

---

[47] Ronald M. Green, *Religious Reason: The Rational and Moral Basis of Religious Belief* (New York: Oxford University Press, 1988), p. 106.

[48] Ibid.

[49] Richard Swinburne, *Responsibility and Atonement* (Oxford: Clarendon Press, 1989), p. 74.

the less real it is seen to be, and the religious paradox that deliberate altruism ceases to be altruism. The fact that we notice altruistic behavior and that it does occur removes the possibility of dismissing the whole idea as a series of paradoxes approaching self-contradiction. Insofar as it lends itself to explanation, the key to making sense of altruism lies in distinguishing the level of visions reflected in these paradoxes. Altruism becomes evident, both as possibility and problem, on the level of self-interest. It is the widespread outlook that takes self-interest to be the fundamental fact of human life that identifies altruism as a contrasting ideal and it is also this outlook that arouses suspicion of purported instances of its realization. Altruism begins to be taken seriously when this self-interest vision is transcended by the level of moral vision. When a sense of obligation and claim of the other is taken seriously, altruism may actually become synonymous with what is at stake. This raises the very difficult question of how one moves from one type of vision to the other. "Why be moral?" is not a question that can be answered on the level of self-interest. To be able to give that a positive answer is already to be operating on the level of moral vision. This level also has its problems, however, in that the extent to which altruism is required is a reflection of how far it is absent from life as we know it. Moralists divide over this issue. But if that issue is resolved, a more serious moral dilemma emerges, precisely insofar as altruism is actually realized. The more altruism is realized, the more problematic it becomes precisely because deliberate altruism is self-contradictory. This dilemma finds its resolution on the religious level, where we are delivered from ourselves, so that altruism becomes "natural," however poorly we manage to live that vision. The problem of altruism, then, is ultimately a matter of vision. It is problematic for a self-interested vision, mandatory or diversionary for a moral vision, and assumed for a religious vision.

This vision explanation of altruism does not explain its actual presence. A person who espouses the self-interest vision may live more altruistically than a person guided by moral or religious vision. Explanation does not guarantee compliance.

However, the person of self-interest vision finds it impossible to account for altruism. The moralist has a better perspective for such explanation, but the explanation tends to be too good in that deliberateness is really destructive of altruism. The actuality of altruism finds its true home in the indirection that is involved in religion. The divide between theory and practice is not absolute, however. The level of vision on which one operates has practical implications in that the altruism of self-interest is largely accidental, and of the moral too deliberate, while the religious level allows for altruism to be appreciated in its own subtlety. The reason for this is a variation on the hedonic paradox, in its more common form. According to this paradox, the surest way to miss finding happiness is to pursue it directly. Happiness comes when we are so immersed in something that there is no thought of wanting to be happy. Altruism represents a broadened form of this version of the hedonic paradox. Altruism is achieved best where it is least intended. Unintentional altruism is most natural for the transcendent sponsorship of the religious level, where we are delivered from ourselves. It could be said that altruism is a test of the seriousness of religious vision. The fact that there is not more altruism in the world than there is may be an indication of how superficial much of our religion is.

Select bibliography

Adams, Robert Merrihew. "Pure Love," *Journal of Religious Ethics* 8 (1980): 83–99.
"Saints," in *The Virtue of Faith and Other Essays in Philosophical Theology.* New York: Oxford University Press, 1987.
Alexander, Richard D. "A Biological Interpretation of Moral Systems," *Zygon* 20 (1985): 3–20.
Andolsen, Barbara. "Agape in Feminist Ethics," *Journal of Religious Ethics* 9 (1981): 69–83.
Ann Arbor Science for the People Editorial Collective, ed. *Biology as a Social Weapon.* Minneapolis: Burgers Publishing Co., 1977.
Arendt, Hannah. *The Human Condition.* Chicago: University of Chicago Press, 1958.
Armstrong, A. H. "Platonic Eros and Christian Agape," *Downside Review* (1961): 105–21.
Avis, Paul. *Eros and the Sacred.* London: SPCK, 1989.
Axelrod, Robert and William D. Hamilton, "The Evolution of Cooperation," *Science* 211 (1981): 1390–6.
Baier, Kurt. "The Moral Point of View," in *The Definitions of Morality,* ed. G. Wallace and A. D. M. Walker. London: Methuen, 1970.
Barash, D. D. *Sociobiology and Behaviour.* Amsterdam: Elsevier, 1977.
The Whispering Within. Harmondsworth: Penguin, 1979.
Barlow, George W. and James Silverberg, eds. *Sociobiology: Beyond Nature/Nurture?* Boulder, Col.: Westview Press, 1980.
Barth, Karl. *Church Dogmatics,* vol. II, part I, ed. G. W. Bromiley and T. F. Torrance. Edinburgh: T. & T. Clark, 1961.
Church Dogmatics, vol. IV, part 3, ed. G. W. Bromiley and T. F. Torrance. Edinburgh: T. & T. Clark, 1977.
Batson, C. D. *The Altruism Question: Toward a Social-Psychological Answer.* Hillsdale, NJ: Lawrence Erlbaum Associates, 1991.
"How Social an Animal? The Human Capacity for Caring," *American Psychologist* 20 (1990): 336–46.

Batson, C. D., J. G. Batson, C. A. Griffitt, S. Barrientos, J. R. Brandt, P. Sprengelmeyer, and M. Bayly, "Negative-State Relief and the Empathy-Altruism Hypothesis," *Journal of Personality and Social Psychology* 56 (1989): 922–33.

Batson, C. D., J. S. Coke, and Virginia Pych. "Limits on the Two Stage Model of Empathic Mediation of Helping: A Reply to Archer, Diaz-Loving, Gollwitzer, Davis and Foushee," *Journal of Personality and Social Psychology* 45 (1983): 895–8.

Batson, C. D., B. D. Duncan, P. Ackerman, T. Buckley, and K. Birch, "Is Empathic Emotion a Source of Altruistic Motivation?" *Journal of Personality and Social Psychology* 40 (1981): 290–302.

Batson, C. D., J. Dyck, J. R. Brandt, J. G. Batson, A. L. Powell, M. R. McMaster, and C. Griffitt, "Five Studies Testing Two New Egoistic Alternatives to the Empathy-Altruism Hypothesis," *Journal of Personality and Social Psychology* 55 (1988): 52–77.

Batson, C. D., Patricia Schoenrade, and W. Larry Ventis. *Religion and the Individual: A Social-Psychological Perspective.* Oxford: Oxford University Press, 1993.

Bauckham, Richard. "'Only the Suffering God Can Help': Divine Passibility in Modern Theology," *Themelios* 9 (1984): 6–12.

Baum, Gregory, ed. *Sociology and Human Destiny: Essays on Sociology, Religion and Society.* New York: Seabury Press, 1980.

Baumann, D. J., R. B. Cialdini, and D. T. Kenrick, "Altruism as Hedonism: Helping and Self-Gratification as Equivalent Responses," *Journal of Personality and Social Psychology* 40 (1981): 1039–46.

Beehler, Rodger. *Moral Life.* Oxford: Basil Blackwell, 1978.

Berkowitz, L., ed. *Advances in Experimental Social Psychology.* New York: Academic Press, 1984.

Blum, Lawrence A. *Friendship, Altruism and Morality.* New York: Routledge and Kegan Paul, 1980.

"Gilligan and Kohlberg: Issues for Moral Theory," *Ethics* 98 (1988): 472–91.

Bonhoeffer, Dietrich. *Letters and Papers from Prison.* London: Collins, 1953.

Brachen, Joseph A. "Process Philosophy and Trinitarian Theology – I," *Process Studies* 8 (1978): 217–30.

"Process Philosophy and Trinitarian Theology – II," *Process Studies* 11 (1981): 83–96.

Bradley, F. H. *Essays on Truth and Reality.* Oxford: Clarendon Press, 1914.

Breuer, Georg. *Sociobiology and the Human Dimension.* Cambridge: Cambridge University Press, 1982.

Burhoe, Ralph Wendell. "Religion's Role in Human Evolution: The Missing Link Between Ape-Man's Selfish Genes and Civilized Altruism," *Zygon* 14/2 (1979): 135–62.

Cahill, Lisa Sowle. *Sex, Gender, and Christian Ethics.* Cambridge: Cambridge University Press, 1996.

Caporael, Linda R., Robyn M. Dawes, John M. Orbell, and Alphons J. C. van de Kragt, "Selfishness Examined: Cooperation in the Absence of Egoistic Incentives," *Behavioral and Brain Sciences* 12 (1989): 683–739.

Caputo, John D. *Against Ethics.* Bloomington: Indiana University Press, 1993.

Cialdini, R. B., M. Schaller, D. Houlihan, K. Arps, J. Fultz, and A. L. Beamann. "Empathy-Based Helping: Is It Selflessly or Selfishly Motivated?" *Journal of Personality and Social Psychology* 52 (1987): 749–58.

Comte, Auguste. *System of Positive Polity*, vol. 1. New York: Burt Kranklin, 1875.

Cooper, Neil. *The Diversity of Moral Thinking.* Oxford: Clarendon Press, 1981.

Creel, Richard E. *Divine Impassibility: An Essay in Philosophical Theory.* Cambridge: Cambridge University Press, 1986.

Cupitt, Don. *The New Christian Ethics.* London: SCM Press, 1988.

D'Arcy, Martin Cyril. *The Mind and Heart of Love, Lion and Unicorn: A Study in Eros and Agape.* London: Faber & Faber, 1945.

Darwin, Charles. *The Origin of Species*, 6th edition. London: John Murray, 1888.

Dawkins, Richard. *The Blind Watchmaker.* Harlow: Longman Scientific and Technical, 1986.

The Selfish Gene. London: Granada, 1978.

Donaldson, Thomas. *Corporations and Morality.* Englewood Cliffs, NJ: Prentice-Hall, 1982.

Dunfee, Susan. *Beyond Servanthood: Christianity and the Liberation of Women.* Lanham, Md.: University Press of America, 1989.

Dyke, C. "The Vices of Altruism," *Ethics* 81 (1970–1): 241–52.

Edwards, Peter, ed. *Encyclopaedia of Philosophy.* New York: Macmillan, 1967.

Ewing, A.C. *Ethics.* New York: Collier Books, 1962.

Fabes, Richard A., Jim Futz, Nancy Eisenberg, Traci May-Plumlee, and F. Scott Christopher, "Effects of Rewards on Children's Prosocial Motivation: A Socialization Study," *Developmental Psychology* 25 (1989): 509–15.

Fetzer, James H., ed. *Sociobiology and Epistemology.* Dordrecht: D. Reidel, 1985.

Fiddes, Paul. *The Creative Suffering of God.* Oxford: Oxford University Press, 1989.

Fiske, Alan P. "The Four Elementary Forms of Sociality: Framework for a Unified Theory of Social Relations," *Psychological Review* 99 (1992): 689–723.

Foot, Philippa. *Vices and Virtues and Other Essays in Moral Philosophy.* Berkeley and Los Angeles: University of California Press, 1978.

Fox, Matthew. *Original Blessing.* Santa Fe, New Mexico: Bear & Co., 1983.

ed. *Western Spirituality: Historical Roots, Ecumenical Routes.* Santa Fe, New Mexico: Bear & Co., 1981.

Frank, Robert H. *Passions Within Reason: The Strategic Role of the Emotions.* New York: Norton, 1988.

Frankl, Viktor E. *Man's Search for Meaning,* tr. Ilse Lasch. New York: Washington Square Press, 1968.

Friedland, Roger and Alexander Robertson. *Beyond the Marketplace: Rethinking Economy and Society.* New York: Aldine & de Gruyter, 1989.

Fuller, Robert C. *Ecology of Care: An Interdisciplinary Analysis of the Self and Moral Obligation.* Louisville, Ky: Westminster/John Knox Press, 1992.

Fultz, J., C. D. Batson, V. A. Fortenbach, P. M. McCarthy, and L. L. Varney, "Social Evaluation and the Empathy-Altruism Hypo- thesis," *Journal of Personality and Social Psychology* 50 (1986): 761–9.

Fumerton, Richard A. *Reason and Morality: A Defense of the Egocentric Perspective.* Ithaca and London: Cornell University Press, 1990.

Gauthier, David. *Morals by Agreement.* Oxford: Clarendon Press, 1986.

Moral Dealing: Contract, Ethics, and Reason. Ithaca: Cornell University Press, 1990.

"Thomas Hobbes: Moral Theorist," *Journal of Philosophy* 76 (1979): 547–59.

Ghiselin, M. T. *The Economy of Nature and the Evolution of Sex.* Berkeley: University of California Press, 1974.

Gill, Robin. *Churchgoing and Christian Ethics.* Cambridge: Cambridge University Press, 1999.

ed. *Readings in Modern Theology: Britain and America.* Nashville: Abingdon Press, 1995.

Gilligan, Carol. "In a Different Voice: Women's Conception of the Self and of Morality." *Harvard Educational Review* 47 (1977): 481–517.

Gilligan, Carol, Janie Victoria Ward and Jill McLean Taylor, with Betty Bardige, eds. *Mapping the Moral Domain.* Cambridge, Mass.: Center for the Study of Gender, Education, and Human

Development, Harvard University Graduate School of Education, 1988.

Goetz, Ronald. "The Suffering God: The Rise of a New Orthodoxy," *The Christian Century* 101 (1986): 385–9.

Gould, Stephen J. *Ever Since Darwin*. New York: Norton, 1977.

Green, Ronald M. *Religious Reason: The Rational and Moral Basis of Religious Belief*. New York: Oxford University Press, 1978.

Religion and Moral Reason: A New Method for Comparative Study. New York: Oxford University Press, 1988.

Haan, Norma, Robert N. Bellah, Paul Rabinow, and William M. Sullivan, eds. *Social Science and Moral Inquiry*. New York: Columbia University Press, 1983.

Hallett, Garth L. *Christian Neighbor-Love: An Assessment of Rival Versions*. Washington, DC: Georgetown University Press, 1989.

Priorities and Christian Ethics. Cambridge: Cambridge University Press, 1998.

Hamilton, W. D. "The Genetical Evolution of Social Behaviour," *The Journal of Theoretical Biology* 7 (1964): 1–52.

Hampson, Daphne. *Theology and Feminism*. Oxford: Basil Blackwell, 1990.

Hardin, Garrett. "Discriminating Altruisms," *Zygon* 17 (1977): 163–86.

Hartshorne, Charles. *The Divine Relativity*. New Haven and London: Yale University Press, 1948.

Existence and Actuality: Conversations with Charles Hartshorne, ed. John B. Cobb, Jr. and Franklin I. Gamwell, Chicago: University of Chicago Press, 1984.

Insights and Oversights of Great Thinkers. Albany: SUNY Press, 1983.

"Metaphysics and Dual Transcendence," *Tulane Studies in Philosophy* 314 (1986): 65–72.

Omnipotence and Other Theological Mistakes. Albany: SUNY Press, 1984.

Philosophers Speak of God. Chicago: University of Chicago Press, 1953.

Reality as Social Process. Glencoe, Ill.: The Free Press, 1953.

Hauerwas, Stanley and L. Gregory Jones, *Why Narrative?* Grand Rapids, Mich.: W. B. Eerdmans, 1989.

Hawley, John Stratton, ed. *Saints and Virtues*. Berkeley: University of California Press, 1987.

Hefner, Philip. "Sociobiology, Ethics and Theology," *Zygon* 19/2 (1984): 185–207.

Herman, Barbara. "Agency, Attachment, and Difference," *Ethics* 101 (1991): 775–99.

Heyward, Carter. *The Redemption of God: A Theology of Mutual Relation*. Lanham, Md.: University Press of America, 1982.

Touching our Strength: The Erotic as Power and the Love of God. New York: Harper & Row, 1989.

Hippolytus, *The Refutation of All Heresies*, Ante-Nicene Christian Library, vol. vi. Edinburgh: T & T Clark, 1868.

Hirschman, Albert O. *The Passions and the Interests: Political Arguments for Capitalism before Its Triumph*. Princeton: Princeton University Press, 1977.

Rival Views of Market Society. New York: Viking, 1986.

Hobbes, Thomas. *Leviathan*, in *The English Philosophers from Bacon to Mill*, ed. Edwin A. Burtt. New York: The Modern Library, 1939.

Hoffman, M. L. "Is Altruism Part of Human Nature?" *Journal of Personality and Social Psychology* 40 (1981): 121–37.

Horgan, John. "In the Beginning . . . ," *Scientific American* 264 (March 1991): 20.

Hume, David. *An Enquiry Concerning the Principles of Morals*, in *Enquiries Concerning Human Understanding and Concerning the Principles of Morals*, third edition. Oxford: Clarendon Press, 1986.

A Treatise of Human Nature, ed. L. A. Selby-Bigge. Oxford: Clarendon Press, 1928.

Huxley, Thomas. *Evolution and Ethics and Other Essays*. New York: Appleton, 1894.

James, William. *The Varieties of Religious Experience*. Garden City, NY: Doubleday Dolphin Books, n.d.

Jüngel, Eberhard. *God as the Mystery of the World*, tr. D. L. Guder. Edinburgh: T. & T. Clark, 1983.

Kahn, Charles H. "Aristotle and Altruism," *Mind* 90 (1981): 20–40.

Kant, Immanuel. *Critique of Practical Reason*, tr. Thomas Kingsmill Abbott. London: Longmans, Green & Co., 1927.

The Doctrine of Virtue, tr. Mary J. Gregor, Philadelphia: University of Pennsylvania Press, 1964.

Fundamental Principles of the Metaphysic of Morals, tr. Thomas Kingsmill Abbott. London: Longmans, Green & Co., 1927.

Kearney, Richard, ed. *Dialogues with Contemporary Continental Thinkers*. Manchester: Manchester University Press, 1984.

Keen, Sam. *The Passionate Life: Stages of Loving*. New York: Harper & Row, 1983.

Kegley, Charles W. "Religion and Morality, Relations of," in *A Dictionary of Christian Ethics*, ed. John Macquarrie. London: SCM Press, 1967.

King's College Sociobiology Group, Cambridge, ed. *Current Problems in Sociobiology*. Cambridge: Cambridge University Press, 1982.

Kitamori, Kazoh. *Theology of the Pain of God*. London: SCM Press, 1946, 1966.

Kittay, Eva Feder and Diana T. Meyers, eds. *Women and Moral Theory.* Totowa, NJ: Rowman & Littlefield, 1987.

Koestler, A., ed. *Beyond Reduction.* London: Hutchinson, 1969.

Kohlberg, Lawrence. *Essays on Moral Development,* vol. 2 *The Psychology of Normal Development.* New York: Harper & Row, 1984.

Kohn, Alfie. *The Brighter Side of Human Nature: Altruism and Empathy in Everyday Life.* New York: Basic Books, 1990.

Komter, Aafke E., ed. *The Gift: An Interdisciplinary Perspective.* Amsterdam: Amsterdam University Press, 1996.

Krebs, D. L. "Altruism: An Examination of the Concept and Review of the Literature," *Psychological Bulletin* 73 (1970): 258–303.

"Empathy and Altruism," *Journal of Personality and Social Psychology* 32 (1975): 1134–46.

Kropf, Richard W. *Faith: Security and Risk.* New York: Paulist Press, 1990.

Lansing, John W. "The 'Natures' of Whitehead's God," *Process Studies* 3 (1973): 143–57.

Lee, Jung Young, *God Suffers for Us: A Systematic Inquiry into a Concept of Divine Passibility.* The Hague: Martinus Nijhoff, 1974.

MacGregor, Geddes. *He Who Lets Us Be: A Theology of Love.* New York: Seabury Press, 1975.

MacIntyre, Alasdair. *After Virtue.* South Bend: University of Notre Dame Press, 1981.

Mackie, J. L. "The Law of the Jungle," *Philosophy* 53 (1978): 455–64.

Macmurray, John. *Freedom in the Modern World.* London: Faber, 1932.

Interpreting the Universe. London: Faber, 1938.

Reason and Emotion. London: Faber & Faber, 1966.

Macquarrie, John, ed. *A Dictionary of Christian Ethics.* London: SCM Press, 1967.

Madigan, Arthur, S.J. "EN ix 8: Beyond Egoism and Altruism?" *The Modern Schoolman* 62 (1985): 1–20.

Mansbridge, Jane J., ed. *Beyond Self-Interest.* Chicago: University of Chicago Press, 1990.

Mascall, E. L. *He Who Is: A Study in Traditional Theism.* London: Darton, Longman & Todd, 1966.

McFague, Sallie. *Metaphorical Theology: Models of God in Religious Language.* London: SCM Press, 1983.

McGill, Arthur C. *Death and Life: An American Theology.* Philadelphia: Fortress Press, 1987.

McLean, George F., ed. *Traces of God in a Secular Culture.* New York: Alba House, 1973.

Meeks, M. Douglas. *God the Economist.* Minneapolis: Fortress Press, 1989.

Menzel, Paul T. "Divine Grace and Love: Continuing Trouble for a Logically Norm-Dependent Religious Ethics," *Journal of Religious Ethics* 3/2 (1975): 255–69.

Mercer, Philip. *Sympathy and Ethics: A Study of the Relationship between Sympathy and Morality with Special Reference to Hume's Treatise.* Oxford: Clarendon Press, 1972.

Midgley, Mary. *Evolution as a Religion.* London and New York: Methuen, 1985.

"Gene-Juggling," *Philosophy* 54 (1979): 439–58.

Milo, Ronald D. *Egoism and Altruism.* Belmont, Cal.: Wadsworth, 1973.

Moltmann, Jürgen. *The Crucified God.* New York: Harper & Row, 1974.

History and the Triune God. New York: Crossroad, 1991.

Monroe, Kristen R., "A Fat Lady in a Corset: Altruism and Social Theory," *American Journal of Political Science* 38 (1994): 861–93.

Monroe, Kristen R., Michael C. Barton, and Ute Klingemann. "Altruism and the Theory of Rational Action: Rescuers of Jews in Nazi Europe," *Ethics* 101 (1990): 103–22.

Montagu, Ashley. *Darwin: Competition and Cooperation.* Westport, Conn.: Greenwood Press, 1973 (1952).

Mueller, Dennis. "Rational Egoism vs. Adaptive Egoism," *Public Choice* 5 (1986): 2–23.

Murdoch, Iris. *The Sovereignty of the Good and Other Concepts.* Cambridge: Cambridge University Press, 1967.

Nagel, Thomas. *The Possibility of Altruism.* Princeton: Princeton University Press, 1979.

"Rawls on Justice," *Philosophical Review* 82 (1973): 220–34.

The View from Nowhere. New York: Oxford University Press, 1986.

Nielsen, Kai. *God, Scepticism and Modernity.* Ottawa: University of Ottawa Press, 1989.

Norris, Richard A., Jr., ed. *The Christological Controversy.* Philadelphia: Fortress Press, 1980.

Nygren, Anders. *Agape and Eros: The Christian Idea of Love,* tr. Philip S. Watson. Chicago: University of Chicago Press, 1953.

Oliner, Pearl M. *Toward a Caring Society: Ideas in Action.* Westport, Conn.: Praeger, 1995.

Oliner, Samuel P. and Pearl M. Oliner, *The Altruistic Personality: Rescuers of Jews in Nazi Europe.* New York: Free Press, 1988.

Outka, Gene. *Agape: An Ethical Analysis.* New Haven, Conn.: Yale University Press, 1972.

Outka, Gene and John P. Reeder, ed. *Prospects for a Common Morality.* Princeton: Princeton University Press, 1993.

Paul, Ellen Frankel, Fred D. Miller, Jr., and Jeffrey Paul, eds. *Altruism.* Cambridge: Cambridge University Press, 1993.

Paulhus, Delroy L., David R. Shaffer, and Leslie L. Downing, "Effects of Making Blood Donor Motives Salient upon Donor Retention: A Field Experiment," *Personality and Social Psychology Bulletin* 3 (1977): 99–102.

Peters, Ted. *Sin, Radical Evil in Soul and Society.* Grand Rapids, Mich.: William B. Eerdmans, 1994.

Petrinovich, Lewis. *Human Evolution, Reproduction and Morality.* New York: Plenum Press, 1995.

Piliavin, J. A. and H. W. Charng, "Altruism: A Review of Recent Theory and Research," *Annual Review of Sociology* 16 (1990): 27–65.

Piper, Adrian M. S. "Impartiality, Compassion and Modal Imagination," *Ethics* 101 (1991): 726–57.

Plaskow, Judith. *Sex, Sin and Grace: Women's Experience and the Theologies of Reinhold Niebuhr and Paul Tillich.* Lanham, Md.: University Press of America, 1980.

Plaskow, Judith and Carol Christ, eds. *Weaving the Visions: New Patterns in Feminist Spirituality.* San Francisco: Harper & Row, 1989.

Pope, Stephen J. *The Evolution of Altruism and the Ordering of Love.* Washington, DC: Georgetown University Press, 1994.

"Expressive Individualism and True Self-Love: A Thomistic Perspective," *Journal of Religion* 71 (1991): 384–99.

"Love in Contemporary Christian Ethics," *Journal of Religious Ethics* 23 (1995): 167–97.

"The Order of Love and Recent Catholic Ethics: A Constructive Proposal," *Theological Studies* 52 (1991): 255–88.

Porter, Jean. *Moral Action and Christian Ethics.* Cambridge: Cambridge University Press, 1995.

Post, Stephen G. "Communion and True Self-Love," *Journal of Religious Ethics* 16 (1988): 345–62.

"Conditional and Unconditional Love," *Modern Theology* 7 (1991): 435–46.

"Disinterested Benevolence: An American Debate over the Nature of Christian Love," *Journal of Religious Ethics* 14 (1986): 356–68.

Spheres of Love: Toward a New Ethics of the Family. Dallas: Southern Methodist University Press, 1994.

A Theory of Agape: On the Meaning of Christian Love. Lewisburg, Pa.: Bucknell University Press, 1990.

Rahner, Karl. *Karl Rahner in Dialogue: Conversations and Interviews 1965–1982,* ed. Paul Imhof and Hubert Biallowons. New York: Crossroad, 1986.

Ramos, Alberto Guerreiro. *The New Science of Organizations: A Reconceptualization of the Wealth of Nations.* Toronto: University of Toronto Press, 1981.

Rapport, A. and A. M. Chammah, *Prisoner's Dilemma*. Ann Arbor: University of Michigan Press, 1965.

Rawls, John. "Justice as Fairness: Political not Metaphysical," *Philosophy and Public Affairs* 14 (1985): 223–51.

Political Liberalism. New York: Columbia University Press, 1993.

"The Priority of Right and Ideas of the Good," *Philosophy and Public Affairs* 17 (1988): 251–76.

A Theory of Justice. Cambridge, Mass.: Harvard University Press, 1971.

Rigby, Paul and Paul O'Grady. "Agape and Altruism: Debates in Theology and Social Psychology," *Journal of the American Academy of Religion* 57 (1989): 719–37.

Rusch, William G., ed. *The Trinitarian Controversy*. Philadelphia: Fortress Press, 1980.

Ruse, Michael. "Evolutionary Ethics: A Phoenix Arisen," *Zygon* 21/1 (1986): 95–112.

"The Morality of the Gene," *The Monist* 67 (1984): 167–99.

Sociobiology: Sense or Nonsense? Dordrecht: D. Reidel, 1979.

Ruse, Michael and Edward O. Wilson, "The Evolution of Ethics," *New Scientist* 108 (1985): 50–2.

Sahlins, Marshall. *The Use and Abuse of Biology: An Anthropological Critique of Sociobiology*. Ann Arbor: University of Michigan Press, 1976.

Saint Augustine, *The Trinity*, in *The Fathers of the Church*, tr. Stephen McKenna. Washington, DC: The Catholic University of America Press, 1963.

Saiving, Valerie. "The Human Situation: A Feminine View," *Journal of Religion* 40 (1960): 100–12.

Sandel, Michael J. *Liberalism and the Limits of Justice*. Cambridge: Cambridge University Press, 1982.

Santurri, Edmund N. and William Werpehowski, eds. *The Love Commandments*. Washington, DC: Georgetown University Press, 1992.

Schlipp, Paul Arthur, ed. *The Philosophy of Alfred North Whitehead*. Evanston and Chicago: Northwestern University Press, 1941.

Schroeder, D. A., J. F. Dovido, M. E. Sibicky, L. L. Matthews, and J. L. Allen, "Empathic Concern and Helping Behaviour: Egoism or Altruism?" *Journal of Experimental Social Psychology* 24 (1988): 333–53.

Schwartz, Barry. "Why Altruism is Impossible . . . and Ubiquitous," *Social Service Review* 67 (1993): 314–43.

Schweber, S. "The Origin of the *Origin* Revisited," *Journal of the History of Biology* 10/2 (1977): 229–316.

Shibles, Warren A. *Metaphor: An Annotated Bibliography and History.* Whitewater, Wis.: Language Press, 1971.

Simmons, Roberta G. "Presidential Address on Altruism and Sociology," *The Sociological Quarterly* 32/1 (1991): 1–22.

Singer, Peter. "Ethics and Sociobiology," *Zygon* 19/2 (1984): 141–58.

Practical Ethics. Cambridge: Cambridge University Press, 1979.

Slote, Michael A. "An Empirical Basis for Psychological Egoism," *The Journal of Philosophy* 61 (1964): 530–37.

Smart, Ninian and Steven Konstantine. *Christian Systematic Theology in a World Context.* Minneapolis: Fortress, 1991.

Stent, G., ed. *Morality as a Biological Phenomenon.* Berkeley: University of California Press, 1981.

Stout, Jeffrey. *Ethics after Babel: The Languages of Morals and Their Discontents.* Boston: Beacon Press, 1988.

Swinburne, Richard. *Responsibility and Atonement.* Oxford: Clarendon Press, 1989.

Taylor, Mark. *Alterity.* Chicago: University of Chicago Press, 1987.

Tertullian. *Adversus Praxean*, Ante-Nicene Christian Library, vol. 15, ed. Alexander Roberts and James Donaldson. Edinburgh: T. & T. Clark, 1870.

Thomas Aquinas, *Summa Contra Gentiles.* Notre Dame: University of Notre Dame Press, 1975.

Thoreau, Henry David. *Walden and Other Writings.* New York: Bantam Books, 1962.

Tillich, Paul. *Systematic Theology.* Digswell Place, UK: James Nisbet & Co., 1968.

Titmuss, Richard M. *The Gift Relationship: From Human Blood to Social Policy.* New York: Pantheon, 1971.

Wakefield, Jerome C. "Is Altruism Part of Human Nature?" *Social Service Review* 67/3 (1993): 406–58.

Wallace, G. and A. D. M. Walker, eds. *The Definition of Morality.* London: Methuen, 1970.

Warshay, Leon H. *The Current State of Sociological Theory: A Critical Interpretation* . New York: David McKay Co., 1975.

West, Angela. *Deadly Innocence: Feminism and the Mythology of Sin.* London: Cassell, 1995.

Whitehead, Alfred North. *Process and Reality*, corrected edition, ed. David Ray Griffin and Donald W. Shelburne. London: The Free Press, 1978.

Science and the Modern World. New York: Macmillan, 1925.

Will, James E. *The Universal God: Justice, Love, and Peace in the Global Villiage.* Louisville, Ky.: Westminster John Knox Press, 1994.

Williams, Bernard. *Problems of the Self.* New York: Cambridge University Press, 1976.

Williams, Daniel Day. *What Present-Day Theologians are Thinking.* New York: Harper & Row, 1952.

The Spirit and Forms of Love. New York: Harper & Row, 1968.

Wilson, Edward O. "Altruism," *Harvard Magazine* (Nov–Dec 1978): 23–8

"Biology and the Social Sciences," *Daedalus* 106 (1977): 127–40.

On Human Nature. Cambridge, Mass.: Harvard University Press, 1978.

Sociobiology: The New Synthesis. Cambridge, Mass.: Harvard University Press, 1975.

Wispé, Lauren, ed. *Altruism, Sympathy and Helping.* New York: Academic Press, 1978.

"The Distinction between Sympathy and Empathy," *Journal of Personality and Social Psychology* 50 (1986): 314–21.

Wolf, Susan. "Moral Saints," *Journal of Philosophy* 79/8 (1982): 419–39.

Wuthnow, Robert. "Altruism and Sociological Theory," *Social Service Review* 67 (1993): 344–57.

"Giving and Caring in the 1990s," *Second Opinion* 18 (1993): 69–81.

Wynne-Edwards, V. C. *Evolution through Group Selection.* Oxford: Blackwell Scientific Publications, 1986.

Wyschogrod, Edith. *Saints and Postmodernism: Revisioning Moral Philosophy.* Chicago: University of Chicago Press, 1990.

Young, Robert A. "Darwin's Metaphor: Does Nature Select?" *The Monist* 55 (1971): 442–503.

Index

263